PRISONERS' RIGHTS

PRISONERS' RIGHTS

The Supreme Court and Evolving Standards of Decency

JOHN A. FLITER

Contributions in Legal Studies, Number 96

GREENWOOD PRESS
Westport, Connecticut • London

Library of Congress Cataloging-in-Publication Data

Fliter, John A., 1959–
    Prisoners' rights : the Supreme Court and evolving standards of decency / by John A. Fliter.
        p.   cm.—(Contributions in legal studies, ISSN 0147–1074 ; no. 96)
    Includes bibliographical references and index.
    ISBN 0–313–31475–6 (alk. paper)
    1. Prisoners—Legal status, laws, etc.—United States—Cases.   2. United States. Supreme Court.   I. Title.   II. Series.
    KF9731.A7F58   2001
    344.73'0356—dc21   00–035373

British Library Cataloguing in Publication Data is available.

Library of Congress Catalog Card Number: 00–035373
ISBN: 0–313–31475–6
ISSN: 0147–1074

First published in 2001

Greenwood Press, 88 Post Road West, Westport, CT 06881
An imprint of Greenwood Publishing Group, Inc.
www.greenwood.com

Printed in the United States of America

The paper used in this book complies with the Permanent Paper Standard issued by the National Information Standards Organization (Z39.48–1984).

10 9 8 7 6 5 4 3

For Jim, in loving memory

Contents

Preface

At its most fundamental level, this book is about legal change and Supreme Court decision making. Unlike other books on this subject, which typically examine legal change in the context of such controversial issues as abortion rights, obscenity, free speech, or religious establishment, this book attempts to explain doctrinal change in an area of constitutional law that is often overlooked—the rights of convicted persons.

Writing a book on this subject is a challenge. Many citizens are either indifferent or hostile to the concept of prisoners' rights. Most citizens are unfamiliar with the body of case law involving the rights of prisoners, and many cannot understand why the Constitution should even protect prison inmates. Prisoners, it is often argued, should have few, if any, rights because they have committed crimes against society. I know that some of my students feel this way. In my discussions of prisoners' rights with students, the cliché "Don't do the crime if you can't do the time" usually enters the conversation at some point. This statement implies that if an individual commits a crime and is arrested and convicted, he or she should suffer whatever consequences prison life has to offer, even if "doing time" involves physical and sexual abuse by guards and inmates, squalid living conditions, or being denied medical treatment.

As a philosophy of criminal punishment, the cliché makes little sense. Granted, prisons are not supposed to be comfortable places, but neither should they be isolated institutions where anything goes. Despite what some might believe, the U.S. Supreme Court, in *Wolff v. McDonnell* (1974), has unambiguously ruled that "there is no iron curtain drawn between the Constitution and the prisons of this country." Prisoners do have rights protected by the Constitution and federal laws; understanding the historical development and scope of those rights is the goal of this book.

From a policy perspective, we should care about what happens in prisons, because most prisoners are released at some point. Abusive treatment and harsh living conditions in prison will not help make parolees productive members of the community but will only serve to increase their anger and resentment toward society and will do little to deter them from future criminal acts. And if history is any guide, the mistreatment of inmates and poor living conditions only lead to prison riots, the destruction of property, and loss of life. If we want a system of criminal punishment that serves the goals of the community, whether the aim is rehabilitation, incapacitation, retribution, or deterrence, citizens should have some knowledge of what goes on behind the prison gates and of the laws that govern prison administration.

From a human rights perspective, the treatment of prisoners should be a concern to citizens, because it reflects the level of human decency and civility in society. A punishment that does not fit the crime or an action that goes beyond what is considered by the public to be appropriate and necessary to maintain discipline and order within a prison violates the norms of a civilized society. Those norms include the legal principles of due process and proportionality in punishment. Due process demands that government follow certain procedures in prosecuting individuals charged with a crime and in disciplining prisoners during their incarceration. Proportionality requires that the punishment fit the crime—that it not be overly excessive or harsh. These concepts promote fairness within our criminal justice system and help make it more humane compared to authoritarian or totalitarian regimes.

If viewed from both a policy and a human rights perspective, then, most reasonable persons would agree that the arbitrary and abusive treatment of prisoners is fundamentally wrong. Consequently, we should pay attention to the penalties imposed on convicted persons, the treatment of inmates, and the living conditions in our prisons in order to ensure that prisoners are afforded their constitutional and statutory rights. I hope that this book makes a worthwhile contribution toward that goal.

Many people have contributed in various ways to the completion of this book and deserve recognition. I want to thank Wayne McIntosh for developing my interest in law and for being a mentor during my graduate study at the University of Maryland, College Park. I would also like to thank Lee Epstein, Bill Richter, and several anonymous reviewers for their comments on early drafts of this manuscript. I owe an intellectual debt to Christopher E. Smith for his work on the Rehnquist Court and criminal punishment. And I am grateful for the support of my colleagues in the political science department at Kansas State University, where a small research grant and course reduction were helpful in completing this manuscript.

I want to thank the estate of Justice William Brennan for granting me permission to use his papers, and the staff at the Library of Congress manuscript reading room for their assistance as I spent many hours perusing the Douglas, Brennan, and Marshall papers. I am also grateful to my friend Ed Dalere for his hospitality during my research trips to Washington, D.C. The ACLU (American Civil Liberties Union) National Prison Project also provided valuable material.

It has been a pleasure working with my editor, Heather Ruland Staines, Marcia Goldstein, and the staff at Greenwood Press. John Donohue also deserves credit for his meticulous proofreading and editing of the manuscript.

Finally, my wife Leah and my sons Eric and David deserve special thanks for their love and patience during the completion of this manuscript. Any errors or omissions contained within are my own.

Introduction

American society has changed tremendously since the first jail was built in Philadelphia, Pennsylvania, in the late eighteenth century. Public sentiment toward the treatment of men and women incarcerated in prisons and jails is contingent on historically evolving social values and penal philosophies. What is acceptable punishment to one generation another generation may find abhorrent. For example, the stocks, the pillory, and whipping were all considered appropriate methods of punishment during the colonial period. Today, however, these penalties would shock the conscience of most citizens and would likely violate the Eighth Amendment's ban on cruel and unusual punishments.

We appear to be living in a punitive age. It is politically popular to "get tough" on criminals and prisoners. For over a decade, states have engaged in an "imprisonment binge," and the United States now incarcerates a higher percentage of its population than any other nation.[1] At both the federal and state levels, the rehabilitation of inmates has been deemphasized, replaced with corrections policies that stress retribution and incapacitation. The current penal philosophy is reflected in laws that mandate longer prison sentences, abolish parole, and make prison life more harsh.[2] Even the death penalty has experienced a resurgence, with several states making capital punishment available and others quickening the pace of executions. As public opinion and government policy concerning criminal punishment evolve from one generation to the next, the rights of prisoners change as well.

PRISONERS' RIGHTS AND EVOLVING STANDARDS OF DECENCY

For most of our nation's history, prisoners enjoyed few legal protections. Inmates were considered "slaves of the state," and that status was sufficient for the courts to deny jurisdiction in many cases. Federal courts generally maintained a "hands-off" policy when confronted with lawsuits that challenged the internal operation of prisons. The "hands-off" policy was not mandated by the Supreme Court in any formal doctrinal sense and not all courts followed it, but practical and political considerations at both the state and federal level promoted a policy of nonintervention in prison administration that endured well into the 1960s.

Beyond the prison walls prisoners had few allies who were willing to defend their interests. Elected officials have always been reluctant to argue for prison reform because there are few political benefits. Politicians understandably do not want to be perceived by their constituents as being "soft on crime" or "coddling criminals." Indeed, unless there is a sensational case of abuse or a deadly riot, prisoners' rights rarely makes it onto the public agenda. Public indifference toward inmates, coupled with concerns about crime, also made it difficult for prisoners to win relief in the courts. State judges, many of whom are popularly elected, reflected the prevailing attitudes of their communities and did not welcome prison reform litigation in their courts. At the federal level, judges were sensitive to the concepts of separation of powers and federalism embodied in the Constitution. Prison administration is primarily an executive branch function, and it has traditionally been a responsibility of the states. Many judges felt that intervention would weaken the authority of corrections officials and undermine discipline among inmates. These factors contributed to a general reluctance among federal judges to consider petitions from state inmates that challenged their treatment and conditions of confinement.

All of that has changed. Spurred by the civil rights movement and such tragic events as the 1971 prison riot at Attica, New York, where 43 people died, the prisoners' rights movement began to push for fundamental changes in the American prison system. The emergence of a prisoners' rights bar was essential to the success of this reform movement. The NAACP Legal Defense Fund (LDF), together with the National Prison Project of the American Civil Liberties Union (NPP), which was formed in 1972, became the most active and successful legal advocates for prisoners. The LDF began a legal attack on capital punishment in the late 1960s, and the NPP litigated many cases during the 1970s that challenged prison conditions and the treatment of inmates. These social and political forces converged on our legal system, prompting federal courts to intervene to improve the treatment and living conditions of prisoners.

For over 30 years, the federal judiciary has played a major role in the reform of our nation's prisons and jails. This reform effort has been one of the most controversial aspects of policy making by the courts. Confronted with cases involving prison overcrowding and severely inadequate facilities and services, federal judges have intervened in the administration of state prisons and local jails in order to correct what they determine to be violations of constitutional rights. The courts have expanded the legal protections afforded to inmates and have formulated remedies to secure those rights. Judges have ordered changes in prison staffing and procedures, reductions in inmate populations, and capital improvements, and they have extended significant due process guarantees to inmates. In some states, entire prison systems were declared unconstitutional and placed under court order, while in others one or more facilities were targeted for reforms.

More recently, however, the federal courts have shown greater deference to prison administrators and a reluctance to mandate sweeping changes. Federal judges appointed by Presidents Reagan and Bush have been more restrained in reviewing inmate petitions. Some of the important precedents concerning the rights of prisoners have been narrowed or overturned. The conservative majority on the Supreme Court is now openly hostile to inmate appeals that question the legality of their conviction or the conditions of their confinement. In addition, Congress has entered the arena with legislation designed to curtail prisoner lawsuits and limit the power of the courts to review prisoner claims and mandate reforms. These developments do not bode well for the rights of prisoners.

In reviewing the history of prisoners' rights in the United States, an almost cyclical pattern emerges. We have moved from a period when prisoners had essentially no rights under the Constitution to an era of expanded rights protection and back to a period of diminished rights for convicted persons. While it is true that we have not come full circle, because prisoners today still enjoy many more rights than those of the nineteenth century, over the past decade there has been a restriction in rights protection and a diminished role for the courts. How can we account for such fundamental changes in the legal status of prisoners? What role has the Supreme Court played in the development of prisoners' rights? Why did the Warren Court not expand the rights of prisoners as vigorously as it did the rights of criminal defendants? This book attempts to answer those questions.

The title of this book is drawn from the Supreme Court's decision in *Trop v. Dulles* (1958), where the Court stated that the "cruel and unusual punishment" clause of the Eighth Amendment must draw its meaning from "the evolving standards of decency that mark the progress of a maturing society."[3] Like many provisions in the Bill of Rights, the meaning of the Eighth Amendment and the scope of prisoners' rights have been influenced by prevailing public opinion, interest group advocacy, changes in penal philosophy, and the ideological values of the nine individuals who sit on the Supreme Court. These variables need to be incorporated into a model of judicial decision making in order to understand the constitutional development of prisoners' rights.

APPROACH OF THE BOOK

Though much has been written about prisons, penal philosophy, and the impact of prison reform litigation on state budgets and prison management, few authors have attempted to examine the doctrinal development of prisoners' rights from a historical and political perspective. A historical view allows the reader to trace the evolution of prisoners' rights in the federal courts. This approach promotes our understanding of how the constitutional rights of prisoners have been influenced by public attitudes toward crime and punishment, interest group advocacy, case-by-case decision making, and the changing political composition of the Supreme Court. More than any other variable, the policy preferences of the nine individuals sitting on the Court have shaped the development of prisoners' rights.

In order to comprehend the politics of Supreme Court decision making systematically, we need to look at how the justices vote, the internal dynamics of the decision-making environment, and the extralegal factors that influence voting alignments. The best model of decision making in this regard is the strategic model.[4] The strategic model is an extension of the attitudinal model of judicial decision making. Widely accepted among political scientists as an explanation for Supreme Court decision making, the attitudinal model emphasizes the influence of ideological values on voting behavior on the Court. The model has its roots in sociological and Realist jurisprudence of the 1920s and 1930s because of its focus on the law-politics nexus in judicial decision making. Responding to the notion that law was distinct from morals on the one hand, and from social and political forces on the other hand, sociological jurisprudence argued that law was not just a collection of abstract legal principles found in dusty law books but was a social institution that reflected the needs and desires of society. The law embodied socially defined rules to resolve conflicts among competing interests. Specifically, sociological jurisprudence recognized that there was a great deal of discretion in the judicial decision-making process.

Building upon the insights of sociological jurisprudence, legal realists emphasized the uncertainty in law and the relationship between law and policy. Realists argued that legal doctrines are ambiguous and do not lend themselves to neutral, objective interpretation. Each judicial decision involves some discretion as to the relevance of facts and the meaning of past rulings. Legal realists concluded that judges were in fact making policy through their interpretation of the law.[5]

Consistent with the sociological and Realist positions, the attitudinal model rejects many of the assumptions of what is known as the legal model of judicial decision making.[6] The legal model holds that the justices on the Supreme Court decide cases using one or more legally relevant criteria: plain meaning of the statute or Constitution, the intent of the framers, precedent, and balancing of interests. Though justices will not admit that their decisions are based on anything but these legal sources, conflict on the Court with respect to prisoners' rights suggests that political ideologies and values form the foundation for how the individual justices view cases involving prisoners. For the attitudinal model, the votes of the justices are the only relevant subject of inquiry, since votes reflect judicial policy preferences in light of the specific facts of a case.

The difference between the strategic and attitudinal models is that the former does not begin and end with voting. Strategic models assume that individual justices attempt to maximize their policy preferences, but they do so within certain internal and external constraints. Internal constraints are a product of institutional norms and the small group environment of the Court. Because it takes five votes for a majority opinion, justices may have to lobby, bargain, and compromise in order to advance their policy preferences. This strategic interaction takes place under formal rules of procedure and informal norms of behavior. Externally, Supreme Court decisions may be influenced by how other actors, such as Congress or the public, will respond. Therein lies the strength of the strategic approach. It allows a researcher to study not only votes but also legal doctrine and the influence of external forces such as interest groups and public opinion.

Literally thousands of cases involving prison conditions and the treatment of inmates have been litigated since the courts became active in reviewing prisoner claims. I make no attempt to categorize and analyze all of those cases. This book is not intended as a comprehensive analysis of federal court involvement in prison reform; nor is it designed to serve as a reference manual for prison administrators or as a guide for jailhouse lawyers. Rather the focus is on how the Supreme Court has interpreted the rights of prisoners and the sociopolitical forces that have shaped those decisions. As Malcolm Feeley and Edward Rubin have argued, the Supreme Court did not take the lead in prison reform, but it has been the catalyst in the movement to reduce the number of inmate petitions in the federal courts and limit the scope of judicial intervention in state prison administration.[7] This book uses prisoners' rights cases as a window to understand the dynamics of Supreme Court decision making and to perhaps offer an explanation about why the Court played a more restrained role in this area of the Constitution.

The Supreme Court grants review in only a handful of cases affecting prisoners each term, but as the nation's highest court it sends important doctrinal signals to the lower federal courts. It is in the federal district and circuit courts where prisoners' rights are given concrete meaning. A few significant decisions of the lower federal courts are discussed throughout the text where appropriate, but the focus is on the Supreme Court under Chief Justices Warren, Burger, and Rehnquist. The analysis goes beyond death penalty cases and includes noncapital cases arising under the Eighth Amendment, habeas corpus petitions, conditions of confinement cases, and due process claims.

PLAN OF THE BOOK

In Chapter 1, the Prison Litigation Reform Act (PLRA) is used as a springboard for a discussion of some of the issues surrounding prisoner litigation and the role of the federal courts. Passed by Congress in 1996, the PLRA narrows the authority of the federal courts to review prisoner litigation and makes it more difficult for inmates to file claims. The chapter also describes the constitutional and statutory foundations for prisoners' rights and reviews the remedies available to inmates to secure those rights. In addition, the normative debate surrounding court-mandated prison reform is reviewed. Judicial intervention in prison administration has been criticized on separation of powers, federalism, and institutional capacity grounds. It is essential to understand the debate over the propriety and capacity of judicial policy making in prisoners' rights cases because the arguments are closely linked to how individual justices approach prisoner lawsuits.

Chapter 2 describes three models of judicial decision making—the legal, attitudinal, and strategic—that offer different explanations for why the Supreme Court decides cases the way it does. For a variety of reasons, both the legal and attitudinal models are rejected in favor of a strategic model which is used to analyze judicial decision making in prisoners' rights cases in the Warren, Burger, and Rehnquist Courts. Legal criteria are important, but for various reasons they do not effectively constrain the discretion that justices have. By focusing only on the votes of individual justices, the attitudinal model fails to consider both internal and external influences on voting behavior. The strategic model emphasizes the politics of judicial decision making by holding that justices' votes are determined not only by the facts of a case, along with personal values and ideologies, but also by small group dynamics and external forces. Chapter 2 also includes a discussion of three variables that form the external political environment of Supreme Court decision making:

public opinion, political institutions, and interest groups. In cases involving the Eighth Amendment, the courts have looked to prevailing public attitudes on crime and punishment for guidance. The impact of political institutions includes presidential appointments to the Supreme Court and congressional statutes that affect prisoners' rights. Interest groups also influence decision making by litigating cases and framing legal issues before the courts.

The next four chapters are organized around the four periods in the doctrinal development of prisoners' rights. Chapter 3 covers a lot of ground. It traces the development of prisons in America and early efforts at penal reform. It also discusses the legal status of prisoners before the federal courts became actively involved in reviewing prison conditions and articulating rights for those incarcerated. Although there were a number of Supreme Court decisions involving the Eighth Amendment during this period, through the nineteenth century and most of the twentieth century, the federal courts generally assumed a "hands-off" approach when confronted with lawsuits that challenged prison conditions and the treatment of inmates. There were efforts to reform prisons during the nineteenth century but they were based on utilitarian and religious arguments rather than the law, and most of the reforms were initiated by state legislatures.

The Supreme Court gradually weakened the "hands-off" policy with a series of decisions in the 1960s. Chapter 4 examines this reform period under the Warren Court (1953–1969). Famous for its activism in criminal defendants' rights, the most important contribution of the Warren Court to prisoners' rights was the expansion of access to the courts for rights violations. Beyond that, however, the Warren Court did little to expand the substance of prisoners' rights. Chapter 5 focuses on the 1970s and 1980s, a period when the federal courts began to actively intervene in the administration of prisons. President Nixon had the opportunity to appoint four new justices to the Court, including Chief Justice Warren Burger. These new justices were expected to promote tough law and order policies, and it was widely believed that the Burger Court (1969–1986) would narrow or overturn Warren Court precedents that favored prisoners and criminal defendants. To the surprise of many conservatives, however, the Burger Court issued several decisions during its first few terms that expanded the rights of prisoners. Prison administrators and state legislators reacted strongly to these decisions, and the Court seemed to respond to the criticism. By the late 1970s, the Burger Court and lower federal courts began to show more deference toward state legislatures and administrators. Chapter 6 looks at the decisions of the Rehnquist Court and describes how the Supreme Court has scaled back prisoners' rights in many areas. The Reagan–Bush appointments to the Court created a conservative majority that has been clearly more restrained in its treatment of prisoners' religious freedom, due process, habeas corpus, and prison conditions cases.

Chapter 7 reviews the amount of strategic interaction on the Warren, Burger, and Rehnquist Courts in prisoners' rights cases from 1953 to 1991. Though justices often hold strong policy preferences on criminal punishment issues, strategic interaction in the form of vote changes, opinion revisions, and dissents from denial of certiorari were commonplace in prisoners' rights cases decided by the Warren Court and to a lesser extent on the Burger and Rehnquist Courts.

This chapter also evaluates the role that the respective Courts played in the development of prisoners' rights, and it discusses recent developments in Congress and in state legislatures that affect prison conditions and the rights of inmates. As mentioned earlier, Congress passed the Prison Litigation Reform Act, which limited the authority of federal courts to hear prison inmate suits, and enacted the Anti-Terrorism and Effective Death Penalty Act, which imposed restrictions on habeas corpus petitions in order to hasten the execution of inmates on death row. In 1994 crime legislation, Congress expanded the federal death penalty statute to apply to over 50 crimes and enacted a federal "three strikes" law. In addition to these developments at the federal level, many states have passed laws making incarceration more punitive. For example, states have abolished parole, eliminated weight rooms and other programs for prisoners, passed mandatory minimum sentencing statutes, and enacted "three strikes" laws, which usually mandate life in prison without parole for three felony convictions. The impact of these developments on prisoners is discussed and evaluated.

NOTES

1. See John Irwin and James Austin, *It's About Time: America's Imprisonment Binge* (Belmont, Calif.: Wadsworth, 1994), 1.

2. Representative of this trend are the practices of Sheriff Joe Arpaio in Maricopa County, Arizona. "Sheriff Joe" houses 1,400 of his 7,000 inmates in a "tent city," where temperatures sometimes reach 120 degrees, serves them green bologna, makes them wear pink underwear, and forces them to work on chain gangs. Public opinion polls have given him approval ratings as high as 93 percent. See Sue Anne Pressley, "The Meanest Sheriff—and Proud of It," *Washington Post National Weekly Edition*, September 1, 1997, 31–32.

3. *Trop v. Dulles*, 356 U.S. 86 (1958), 99–101.

4. For the most current and complete discussion of the strategic model, see Lee Epstein and Jack Knight, *The Choices Justices Make* (Washington, D.C.: Congressional Quarterly, 1998).

5. For a collection of Realist thought, see William W. Fisher III, Morton J. Horowitz, and Thomas Reed, eds., *American Legal Realism* (New York: Oxford

University Press, 1993). See also Jerome Frank, *Courts on Trial: Myth and Reality in American Justice* (Princeton, N.J.: Princeton University Press, 1949).

6. See Jeffrey A. Segal and Harold Spaeth, *The Supreme Court and the Attitudinal Model* (New York: Cambridge University Press, 1993).

7. Malcolm M. Feeley and Edward L. Rubin, *Judicial Policy Making and the Modern State: How the Courts Reformed America's Prisons* (New York: Cambridge University Press, 1998), 47.

Chapter 1

Federal Courts, Politics, and Prisoners' Rights

On April 26, 1996, President Bill Clinton signed into law an unprecedented piece of legislation that would affect the rights of those incarcerated in state and federal prisons by limiting the power of the federal courts to review prisoner litigation. Known as the Prison Litigation Reform Act (PLRA), the law was part of a massive budget reconciliation bill and was barely noticed by the press and most citizens.[1] For the lawyers, prison administrators, judges, and politicians who handle the thousands of inmate lawsuits filed each year, however, the new law was a watershed event in the history of prisoners' rights. After decades of court decisions expanding the rights of prisoners, the PLRA was an attempt by Congress to curb the courts and reduce the number of lawsuits filed by inmates in state and federal prisons.

CONGRESS TARGETS PRISONER LITIGATION

Criticism of prisoner litigation had been building in Congress and in the states for many years. Conservatives, who generally argue that judges should refrain from making policy, had long opposed federal judicial intervention in state prison administration. Proposals to restrict prisoner lawsuits were part of the "Contract with America" that many Republicans signed during the campaign for the 1994 midterm congressional elections. When the Republicans gained control of both the House and the Senate in the 1994 elections, they set out to reform prisoner lawsuits. Reformers argued that states had been forced to spend millions of dollars defending prisoner lawsuits, many of which they believed were frivolous.

Critics of prisoner litigation did not waste any time. In July 1995, the Senate Judiciary Committee conducted hearings on the topic "Prison Reform: Enhancing the Effectiveness of Incarceration." In his opening statement, Senator Orrin Hatch (R) of Utah identified what he felt were a number of interrelated problems facing our prison system. Acknowledging that prison conditions that actually violate the Constitution should be eliminated, Senator Hatch nevertheless felt that the federal courts had gone too far in exercising their remedial powers. He complained of "the inappropriate utilization by the federal courts of population caps and intrusive micromanagement on state and local prisons, the costly effects of frivolous inmate lawsuits filed in the federal courts, and a lack of sufficient capacity."[2] He cited two examples of frivolous prisoner lawsuits in his state. In one case, "an inmate deliberately flooded his cell, and then sued the officials who cleaned up the mess because they got his Pinochle cards wet," while in another case "a prisoner sued officers after a cell search, claiming that they failed to put his cell back in a 'fashionable' condition, and mixed his clean and dirty clothing."[3] Senator Hatch concluded that it was "time to restore sanity to this system by imposing legislative limits on the ability of inmates to tie the courts and prisons in knots through frivolous lawsuits."[4]

Another Republican on the Judiciary Committee, Senator Spencer Abraham of Michigan, was concerned about excessive prisoner lawsuits and prisoners who serve only a portion of their sentences because they are either paroled or released under court-imposed population limits. As examples, Senator Abraham cited lawsuits over "how warm the food is, how bright the lights are, whether there are electrical outlets in each cell, whether windows have [been] inspected and certified up to code, whether prisoners' hair is cut only by licensed barbers, and whether air and water temperatures are comfortable."[5] Abraham argued that "through these lawsuits in many States, prisoners, their lawyers, and unelected judges have replaced the people and their legislature in controlling the character of prison life."[6] During the hearings, Republican reformers such as Senators Hatch and Abraham argued that there were too many unnecessary prisoner lawsuits and that excessive intervention by the federal courts violated principles of federalism and separation of powers. Now in control of Congress, reformers drafted legislation to address these concerns. The PLRA was designed to curtail prisoner lawsuits and return more power and responsibility to the states for prison management.

The PLRA attacks prisoner litigation on three fronts by targeting prisoners, legal advocates for inmates, and the power of the federal courts. Inmates must now exhaust all administrative remedies before filing suit under federal civil rights laws. Additionally, no prisoner may file suit if on three or more prior occasions the action or appeal was dismissed on the grounds that it was frivolous, malicious, or failed to state a claim upon which relief may be granted, unless the prisoner is in immediate physical danger. The law also imposes restrictions on the ability of inmates to proceed *in forma pauperis*, which literally means in the manner of a pauper. In these cases, petitioners do not have to pay a filing fee. Since many prisoners are indigent and do not have the funds to pay filing fees, this restriction has discouraged some inmates from filing suits. Another provision of the law penalizes inmates who file "frivolous" suits or give false testimony with the loss of good time credits. The PLRA targets the prisoners' rights bar by imposing numerous restrictions on attorneys' fees. By making it difficult for groups such as the National Prison Project of the American Civil Liberties Union to collect fees, the law denies nonprofit groups the funds to sponsor prisoner litigation.

The law also makes it easier for state and local governments to terminate or modify consent decrees and court orders that govern conditions in federal and state prisons and local jails. Prior to the PLRA, many meritorious prisoner lawsuits were settled by a consent decree in which prison officials agreed to rectify unconstitutional prison conditions before trial and without acknowledging any guilt. In such cases, federal judges retained jurisdiction over prison administration in order to ensure compliance with the consent agreement. Often a special master or human rights committee would be appointed by the judge to monitor the state's progress in meeting the conditions of the consent agreement or court order. Court supervision could extend indefinitely, and in some cases judicial oversight lasted more than fifteen years.

With two-thirds of the state prison systems under consent decree or court order in late 1996 to reduce inmate populations or improve prison conditions in one or more facilities, the PLRA would have a significant impact on prison litigation.[7] In fact, within six months of its passage, attorneys general in ten states and in the District of Columbia filed motions under the PLRA seeking to end consent decrees and court-ordered prison reforms.[8] The law is not without its critics, however, and several constitutional challenges have been filed in the federal courts against various provisions in the PLRA.

While it may seem odd to begin a book on the Supreme Court and prisoners' rights with a description of a law passed by Congress, in many ways the PLRA is a good starting point for the discussion that follows, because the law is a response to over 30 years of court-mandated prison reform, and its provisions address the most contentious issues surrounding prisoner litigation. The act also supports and broadens efforts by the Rehnquist Court to scale back judicial intervention in prisons and to limit the number of prisoner suits.

A lawsuit filed in the federal courts by a state prison inmate raises fundamental questions of constitutional rights, federalism, and separation of powers. What are the statutory and constitutional foundations for prisoners' rights, and what are the limits to those rights? Does court-mandated prison reform violate the principle of separation of powers between the judicial, legislative, and executive branches? Do courts have the institutional capacity to make policy for public institutions that have traditionally been administered by the executive branch? Does federal court intervention in state prison administration violate principles of federalism? How much deference should the courts show to state authority in the administration of prisons when constitutional rights are possibly being violated? These are difficult questions, and the issues they raise require closer scrutiny before we turn our attention to the four periods in the evolution of prisoners' rights.

PRISONERS' RIGHTS AND REMEDIES: CONSTITUTIONAL AND STATUTORY FOUNDATIONS

Forty years ago, inmates had few "rights" and prisoner lawsuits were practically unheard of. While imprisonment necessarily entails the loss of some civil rights enjoyed by free citizens, the courts have declared that prisoners do not forfeit all constitutional protections when they enter the prison gates. The "residual rights" retained by those incarcerated in state and federal prisons are often measured against the need to maintain prison discipline and security. These rights are derived from a variety of sources, including the U.S. Constitution, state constitutions, federal statutes, and state laws. Substantive rights, such as protection from cruel and unusual punishment, religious freedom, and adequate medical care, are only one side of the coin, however. It is necessary for prisoners to have remedies when rights are being violated by federal or state officials, because without them, substantive rights would, as James Madison feared, become "mere parchment barriers." The chapters that follow will examine more closely how the courts, specifically the Supreme Court, have used constitutional provisions and statutes to define the rights of convicted persons; for present purposes, it is useful to identify the mechanisms for judicial review and the sources of substantive rights.

CATEGORIES OF PRISONER LITIGATION

Thousands of lawsuits are filed by prisoners in the federal courts every year. Few of these are successful. Because the authority of the federal courts is limited to cases arising under the Constitution or federal law, a federal court cannot render a decision unless a prisoner can demonstrate that he or she is being denied a right secured by either the Constitution or a federal statute. Many complaints of improper prison practices or conditions by inmates, however, are found meritless and are dismissed by the courts.

Prisoner lawsuits can be divided into two basic categories: *U.S. cases* and *State cases*. United States cases are lawsuits where the federal government is the defendant, usually because a federal prisoner files a claim against a federal correctional institution and federal officers. State cases are often filed against state prison officials for violations of prisoners' constitutional rights.[9] The key difference between the categories is the status of the party being sued—U.S. cases involve the federal government, and state cases are directed at state prisons and administrators. Because the states incarcerate over 90 percent of prisoners, the bulk of prisoner litigation consists of state inmates who file claims in the federal courts alleging some violation of constitutional rights by state officials (see Table 1.1). Within these broad categories of litigation, there are two basic mechanisms for review: habeas corpus petitions and civil rights. A third, less common type of review includes tort claims under the Federal Tort Claims Act and motions to vacate sentences.

Writ of Habeas Corpus

The U.S. Constitution and most state constitutions provide for a writ of habeas corpus. Described by Alexander Hamilton as "the greatest liberty of all," the "Great Writ" of habeas corpus allows convicted persons to challenge the *fact* of their confinement in reference to decisions made during their trial and sentencing. Translated from Latin as "you have the body," the writ orders the person responsible for the detention—the prison warden or local jailer—to produce the petitioner (the *corpus*) in court so that a judge can determine the constitutionality of the detention.[10] The historic function and modern rationale for the writ is to control the use of public power to unlawfully detain an individual.

The historical roots of habeas corpus date back to the Magna Carta (1215) and English common law. In the American colonies, the writ was available as part of common law and could be found in most state constitutions after the Revolutionary War. Though not mentioned in the Articles of Confederation, Article I, Section 9, of the U.S. Constitution states, "The Privilege of the Writ of Habeas Corpus shall not be suspended, unless when in Cases of Rebellion or Invasion the public safety may require it." In the Judiciary Act of 1789, Congress authorized all federal courts "to grant writs of habeas corpus for purpose of an inquiry into the cause of commitment."[11] Under this law, however, the scope of review was limited to the actions of federal executive officers. For example, a habeas petition could be used to either protest an unlawful detention by federal law enforcement officials or challenge military au-

Table 1.1
State Prisoner Litigation by Filing Category, 1968–1995

Year	Habeas Corpus	Civil Rights	Other	Totals	State Prison Population*	Total per 100 prisoners
1968	6,488	1,072	741	8,301	167,571	4.95
1969	7,359	1,269	684	9,312	177,513	5.25
1970	9,063	2,030	719	11,812	176,403	6.69
1971	8,372	2,915	858	12,145	177,113	6.86
1972	7,949	3,348	791	12,088	174,379	6.93
1973	7,784	4,174	725	12,683	181,396	6.99
1974	7,626	5,236	561	13,423	196,105	6.84
1975	7,843	6,128	289	14,260	216,462	6.59
1976	7,833	6,958	238	15,029	235,853	6.37
1977	6,866	7,752	228	14,846	247,507	5.99
1978	7,033	9,730	206	16,969	260,176	6.52
1979	7,123	11,195	184	18,502	271,295	6.82
1980	7,031	12,397	146	19,574	285,667	6.85
1981	7,790	15,639	178	23,607	322,972	7.30
1982	8,059	16,741	175	24,975	363,713	6.86
1983	8,532	17,687	202	26,421	381,665	6.92
1984	8,349	18,034	198	26,581	404,245	6.57
1985	8,534	18,491	181	27,206	436,021	6.24
1986	9,045	20,072	216	29,333	470,659	6.23
1987	9,542	22,972	283	32,797	536,135	6.11
1988	9,880	23,559	270	33,709	577,660	5.84
1989	10,554	25,039	367	35,959	653,386	5.50
1990	10,763	25,072	301	36,136	705,717	5.12
1991	10,511	25,920	291	36,722	711,643	5.16
1992	na	na			803,397	
1993	11,394	31,725	483	43,602	879,714	4.96
1994	11,636	34,748	393	46,777	959,668	4.87
1995	12,706	39,972	412	53,090	1,026,037	5.17

Notes: Case statistics represent the number of private cases commenced during a calendar
   year.
*Total state population figures exclude inmates housed in local jails, except in those states
   where prisons and jails form an integrated system.
Sources: *Federal Judicial Workload Statistics*, Annual Publication, 1979–1995, Table 3-C (Washington, D.C.: Administrative Office of the U.S. Courts, Statistical Analysis and Reports
   Division) (no statistics for the year 1992 were reported for this series); *Historical Statistics on Prisoners in State and Federal Institutions. Yearend 1925–1986* (Washington, D.C.:
   U.S. Department of Justice, Bureau of Justice Statistics, 1988).

thorities who arrest and hold civilians when civil courts are in operation.[12]

Throughout the first half of the nineteenth century, the Supreme Court interpreted the writ of habeas corpus narrowly, often following the common law principle that the writ was not available to those convicted of a crime by a court of competent jurisdiction.[13] The Court was reluctant to review the actions of prison wardens and jailers unless there was clear evidence of constitutional violations.

Modern habeas corpus suits are based on post–Civil War legislation and federal court decisions. Congress passed the Habeas Corpus Act in 1867, which authorized federal courts and judges to grant writs whenever any person is restrained or deprived of liberty in violation of the U.S. Constitution or law. In 1944, a federal court ruled that habeas corpus could be applied to the conditions of one's confinement as well.[14] Subsequent Supreme Court decisions have affirmed this interpretation of federal habeas corpus, although most prisoners prefer to challenge prison conditions under federal civil rights statutes, because the federal habeas statute requires state inmates to exhaust state judicial and administrative remedies before they pursue a federal habeas petition.[15]

Death row inmates would typically file several successive writ of habeas corpus petitions, raising different constitutional claims each time in an attempt to overturn their convictions and sentences. Because of this opportunity to file successive petitions, death row inmates often could delay their execution by eight to ten years after being sentenced. These delays have long been criticized by death penalty advocates, who believe that prisoners on death row should be executed in a timely fashion if the goals of retribution and deterrence are to be served. In response to the perceived abuse of habeas corpus filings, the Supreme Court and Republican members of Congress have worked to limit the number and duration of filings. Since his early years as an associate justice, current Chief Justice William Rehnquist has advocated curtailing the number of habeas corpus appeals in death penalty cases, and he has led a conservative majority on the Court in restricting what are deemed excessive appeals from inmates on death row.

A series of decisions since the late 1980s have drastically limited the scope of federal district court review of habeas corpus petitions. In *Teague v. Lane* (1989), the Rehnquist Court began its assault on the "Great Writ." In *Teague*, the Court announced a "no new rule" rule, stating that habeas corpus will not be available in the federal courts to state prisoners who seek to establish new constitutional rules of criminal procedure or attempt to benefit from rules announced since their conviction became final. In *McCleskey v. Zant* (1991), the Supreme Court adopted a tough standard when a petitioner files successive habeas corpus petitions. By a six-justice majority, the Court said that death row prisoners, following exhaustion of state court appeals, should be allowed only one round of federal court review through petitions for habeas corpus, unless there are extraordinary circumstances. Apparently not satisfied with these court-imposed restrictions on habeas corpus petitions, or perhaps worried that the Court might reverse its policy if new justices are appointed, Congress enacted the Anti-terrorism and Effective Death Penalty Act in 1996. The law heightens the standards for federal court habeas review of state criminal proceedings. Under the statute, federal judges cannot grant a writ of habeas corpus unless a state court decision upholding a prisoner's conviction is "unreasonably wrong" or flatly contradicts clearly established Supreme Court rulings.[16] In addition to the more stringent standards, the law for the first time imposes a statute of limitations on the filing of habeas corpus petitions. Inmates have one year from the time their conviction becomes final to file, but if the state provides counsel in a post–conviction proceeding, the state prisoner has only six months to file a habeas corpus petition. These developments are discussed in Chapters 6 and 7.

Civil Rights Cases

Once a small percentage of prisoner litigation, civil rights cases are now the most popular method of challenging prison conditions. Civil rights complaints are based on post–Civil War legislation, particularly on the Fourteenth Amendment, and various civil rights statutes, the most important of which is Title 42 U.S.C. Section 1983. In these cases, prisoners allege that state officials have violated Bill of Rights protections found in the First Amendment (freedom of speech, free exercise of religion, freedom of association); the Fourth Amendment (unreasonable search and seizure); the Eighth Amendment (no cruel and unusual punishment); and the Fifth and Fourteenth Amendments (due process). Civil rights lawsuits have been used to dramatically reform prison policies and conditions.

These cases are often called Section 1983 suits because they are filed under Section 1983 of the Civil Rights Act of 1871. Passed by Congress during the period of Reconstruction, the law enabled black Americans to sue on constitutional issues in federal courts, thus bypassing prejudiced state courts. The post–Civil War statute provides:

Every person who under color of any statute, ordinance, regulation, custom, or usage of any state or territory, subjects, or causes to be subjected, any citizen of the United States or other person within the jurisdiction thereof to the deprivation of any rights, privileges, or immunities secured by the Constitution and laws, should be liable to the party injured in an action at law, suit in equity, or other proper proceeding for redress.[17]

The act only protects clearly established rights found in the U.S. Constitution and federal laws. Only state inmates can file a Section 1983 claim, because federal prison officials are not acting "under color of any statute, ordinance, regulation, custom, or usage" of a state. In a landmark decision, the U.S. Supreme Court, in *Cooper v. Pate* (1964), held that state prisoners could bring suit against prison officials under Section 1983. By the end of the decade, federal courts found themselves inundated with Section 1983 prisoner suits. In *Preiser v. Rodriguez* (1973), the Supreme Court clarified questions surrounding the use of Section 1983 suits, holding that they were a proper remedy for a state prisoner to challenge the conditions of confinement but not the fact or length of incarceration.[18] Constitutional challenges to the fact or length of confinement must be made under habeas corpus.

U.S. Constitution

No other clause in the Constitution has generated as much prisoner litigation as the Eighth Amendment. In addition to prohibiting excessive bail and fines, the amendment protects those convicted of a crime from "cruel and unusual" punishment. This provision of the Eighth Amendment has been applied to methods of capital punishment, noncapital punishment, and prison conditions. Originally intended to restrict forms of barbaric punishment, such as burning at the stake, torture, and dismemberment, the protections of the Eighth Amendment were virtually meaningless during the nineteenth century, because those types of punishments were no longer imposed. Other forms of punishment authorized by statute—hanging, shooting, and electrocution—were eventually upheld by the Supreme Court. Over the years, the courts have also applied many of the civil rights enumerated in the First, Fourth, and Sixth Amendments to prisoners. Prisoners have, within limits, a right to expression, which includes mail privileges, freedom of religion, a right to marry, protection from unreasonable searches and seizures, and a right to counsel. Due process and equal protection claims under the Fourteenth Amendment have been used to challenge racial segregation of inmates, capital sentencing procedures, disciplinary actions resulting in a loss of liberty, and differences in educational and recreational opportunities between men's and women's prisons.

Other Prisoner Cases

A small number of prisoner claims are filed under the Federal Tort Claims Act (FTCA), or are based on state constitutions and laws. Under the doctrine of sovereign immunity, the federal government was immune from lawsuits, and until Congress adopted the FTCA in 1946, tort suits against the federal government got nowhere in court. The FTCA allows government to be sued in certain situations; the Supreme Court ruled in *United States v. Muniz* (1963) that federal inmates could file a legal claim under the FTCA, but federal prisoners may sue only for injuries inflicted on them by prison personnel's nondiscretionary actions (actions required by law). When federal personnel act within their discretionary authority, they are not actionable for damages. Nearly all administrative acts involve some degree of discretion, so it is difficult to prove in court that prison personnel were not acting within their discretionary authority.

A number of state constitutions and statutes also provide protections specifying particular rights. In a Tennessee prison reform case, *Grubbs v. Bradley* (1982), the prisoners' claims were based not only on the Eighth Amendment's prohibition of cruel and unusual punishment but also on Tennessee's unique state constitutional guarantee of "safe and comfortable" prisons and the "humane treatment" of prisoners.[19] Prison reform litigation in Indiana, *French v. Owens* (1982), was based in part on a state code that required the Indiana Department of Corrections to provide recreational and cultural activities, medical care, and vocational education to inmates. In Arizona, a state criminal statute provides that "A public officer who is guilty of willful inhumanity or oppression toward a prisoner under his care or in his custody shall be punished by a fine not exceeding one thousand dollars, by imprisonment in the county jail for not to exceed six months, or both."[20]

Together, these federal and state constitutional and statutory rights allow a wide variety of prison practices and conditions to come under judicial scrutiny. Judges can now examine alleged constitutional violations in the areas of religious freedom, communication, legal access, searches, due process, and equal protection.[21] The central question surrounding prisoner litigation is no longer whether inmates have rights under the Constitution; instead, the current debate is over the scope of those rights and the appropriate limits of judicially mandated remedies.

THE DEBATE OVER COURT-MANDATED PRISON REFORMS

Prison reform cases represent just one dimension of a general pattern of expanded judicial authority in state and local government administration that has occurred over the past 40 years. In addition to prisons and jails, federal judges have mandated changes in the operation of school systems, mental health facilities, public housing agencies, and other public institutions.[22] As with these other areas of judicial intervention, court-mandated prison reform has been controversial since the federal courts began reviewing prison conditions in the 1960s. Even though the scope of federal court intervention into prison administration peaked during the 1970s, federal judges still review thousands of prisoners' rights cases each year.[23] As the comments by Senators Hatch and Abraham in the hearings on prison litigation reform suggest, many conservative politicians, scholars, and citizens believe that there are still too many prisoner suits and that the courts have abused their power by expanding rights and ordering reforms in nearly every area of prison administration. Critics of court-mandated prison reform argue that it is inappropriate for the courts to be making policy in this area, and they question the capacity of federal judges to make wise decisions concerning prison administration.

Federalism and Separation of Powers Concerns

Arguments about the propriety of judicial policy making deal with the proper role of the courts in a political system based on federalism and separation of powers between the legislative, executive, and judicial branches. Traditionally, the management of public institutions has been the concern of legislators and administrators. The management of correctional institutions in particular has been the responsibility of the states. Critics such as Raul Berger, Nathan Glazer, and Donald Horowitz claim that the involvement of the courts in prison reform places the judge in an administrative and a legislative role that not only violates the separation of powers between the branches of government but also encroaches upon states' rights. Judicial remedies are often criticized as being arbitrary, unilateral impositions from liberal judges who neither comprehend nor consider problems of cost and the need for administrative flexibility.[24]

Critics of judicial policy making are concerned, moreover, about what they see as a lack of judicial deference to democratic processes. They believe that the courts should show more restraint in reviewing the actions of representative political institutions. After all, federal judges are not elected but are appointed for life terms. How do we hold judges accountable for decisions that may, de facto, alter state spending on prisons and disrupt administrative policies? Judicial critics argue that courts may undermine their institutional legitimacy if their constitutional interpretations are perceived as violating state powers and democratic processes. Recall that these were some of the concerns voiced by Senator Hatch during the Senate Committee hearings on prison reform.

The second type of criticism of court-ordered reform questions the capacity of courts to make policy and spend money wisely. According to Lon Fuller, there are a number of structural limitations on the judiciary defined by the "attributes of adjudication" that lead many observers to doubt the capacity of courts to decide the "polycentric" issues brought before them.[25] The courts are criticized as being passive policy makers.

They cannot initiate policy on their own but have to wait for litigants to bring cases before them. This usually means that the policy problem that prompted the litigation is already well developed. Any judicial remedy at this point may be both belated and insufficient to effectively address the problem. In other words, judicial reforms may be a day late and a dollar short.

Another limitation of judicial policy making results from the nature of adjudication. Since litigants and their lawyers shape the issues by their presentation of the case, judges have to direct their decision to the particular circumstances raised in each case. This gives judicial policy making an ad hoc character. Instead of dealing with a problem in its entirety, courts often address issues in an incremental fashion. This usually is not the most efficient way to make policy. Critics such as Horowitz also assert that judges, because of their position, are policy generalists; hence, they may lack the experience and skill to understand and interpret the complex issues involved in prison administration.

Finally, opponents argue that an interventionist judiciary hinders effective state administration because their decisions frequently fail to achieve objectives and often produce negative consequences.[26] This problem extends to prison litigation where judicial decisions may undermine administrative authority and lead to increased violence among inmates and between inmates and corrections officials.[27] Others complain that court-imposed population limits force states to release prisoners, even some violent ones, well before they have served their entire sentence. Critics maintain that judges fail to comprehend the need for certain correctional policies and the implications of mandated changes upon the prison environment and society.

The Case for Judicial Intervention

While some of the criticisms of court-mandated prison reform are valid, they are at best expressions of political values and preferences. The Constitution does not spell out in detail the proper relationship between the three branches of government or the relationship between the federal government and the states. There is no compelling reason why concerns about propriety and capacity should dominate the judicial function, especially if constitutional rights are being violated. It is a mistake to view each governmental branch as a separate actor with easily defined, narrowly focused functions. The powers and responsibilities of each branch overlap in a complex administrative state. In prison reform, the actions and omissions of legislative bodies and executive agencies have created the impetus for judicial intervention. Moreover, appeals to federalism and states' rights are not a sufficient argument against federal judicial intervention. In the words of one federal judge, "Officials who engage in massive, systemic deprivations of prisoners' constitutional rights are entitled to, and can expect, no deference from the federal courts, for the constitution reserves no power to the states to violate constitutional rights of any citizens."[28]

Below the surface, the criticisms of court-mandated prison reform are a reformulation of the activist/restraint debate surrounding the courts' power of judicial review. Advocates of judicial restraint have been more concerned about the substantive results of particular cases than about the proper function of the courts. Many federal judges who presided over prison reform cases intervened only reluctantly, after they were presented with significant evidence of constitutional violations. The comments of one federal judge illustrate the concern for state authority:

As I have stated in my bench ruling, there is, from the beginning of my assignment to this case to the present time, a complete and utter distaste for having to cross the Rubicon which separates the federal government from the state government. . . . Nevertheless, the plaintiffs have presented substantial, often compelling, evidence of long existing and continuing constitutional violations. Except in fashioning the necessary relief, deference is no longer possible.[29]

Stephen Wasby and Abram Chayes have argued that courts possess a greater capacity for adaptation than critics concede.[30] Judges can overcome legislative and bureaucratic intransigence because of their independence from electoral politics and because of the flexibility of the equitable relief remedy. Federal trial judges may be generalists, but they are familiar with the problems within their district and are sensitive to local political issues. They also can consult outside policy experts to provide additional information on difficult issues.

A number of studies have attempted to show that the remedial decree process used in prison reform litigation is more complex than the many criticisms suggest.[31] Because of the scope and complexity of institutional reform cases, the formal limits on judicial power, and budgetary constraints, the changes mandated and implemented are more likely products of compromise and negotiation between the parties than the raw exercise of judicial power.[32] In fact, the threat of a judicially imposed remedy usually brings the parties together to work out a mutually agreeable solution. Negotiated consent decrees are the norm rather than the exception.[33] That is one reason why the PLRA is so significant; by placing limits on consent decrees, the PLRA may generate more litigation because advocates for prisoners will have little incentive to negotiate a consent agreement.

The trial judge also is constrained by a number of political-economic forces at the national level. These include changes in personnel in the executive office and Supreme Court; statutory provisions passed by Congress; rulings of the Supreme Court and Courts of Appeal; and Justice Department policies.[34] A president who does not favor an active judiciary may make appointments to the Supreme Court consistent with his political philosophy. These appointments can shift the political divisions on the Court and head it in a different policy direction. Granted, this process may take time, but it can be effective. In response to institutional reform cases, the Burger Court moved to place limits on district court authority in the remedial decree area.[35] This was accomplished by narrowing the rules of procedure in the areas of standing and class actions.[36] These developments are discussed in Chapter 5. As head of the federal bureaucracy, the president also can order the Department of Justice and other agencies to either moderate or expand efforts to enforce federal statutes. Most important, any remedial order issued by a district judge can be reviewed by the federal Court of Appeals or Supreme Court. In fact, many of them are.

Judicial Review and Prisoners' Rights

It is impossible to separate the debate over court-mandated prison reform from the doctrinal development of prisoners' rights. Judicial conservatives, who are generally more sensitive to federalism and separation of powers concerns, often take a restrained approach when confronted with prisoner claims and are prone to defer to state action. Placed in the context of Herbert Packer's classic models of the criminal justice system, judicial conservatives can be said to favor crime control policies and community interests over the due process rights of individual prisoners.[37] As a result, prisoners' rights are given less protection, while state power is enhanced. Activists, on the other hand, perceive their role differently. Judicial activists often view the courts as a protector of minority rights against the tyranny of the majority. Prisoners, probably more so than any other minority group in society, need to have their rights protected by the courts, because it is not in the political interests of members of Congress or state legislatures to champion the rights of convicted persons. In prisoner litigation, however, the restrained and activist roles do not neatly parallel conservative and liberal ideologies. For example, the more conservative Rehnquist Court has been described as activist in cases involving prisoners because a narrow majority of the justices are quite willing to overturn or weaken precedents of the Warren and Burger Courts, which favored the rights of prisoners.

The restraint/activist role orientations are based primarily on political values and policy preferences, and these values ultimately influence judicial interpretation of prisoners' rights under the Constitution and federal laws. Justices are not unfettered in pursuing their policy goals, however. A variety of internal constraints and external political forces influence the ability of justices to maximize their policy preferences. We turn now to a discussion of models of judicial decision making in the context of prisoners' rights cases.

NOTES

1. Public Law 104-134, U.S. Congressional Code.

2. Committee on the Judiciary, United States Senate, *Prison Reform: Enhancing the Effectiveness of Incarceration*, S. Hrg. 104-573 (Washington, D.C.: U.S. Government Printing Office, 1996), 3.

3. Ibid.

4. Ibid.

5. Ibid., 5.

6. Ibid.

7. National Prison Project, "Quarterly Report: The Courts and Prisons" (Washington D.C.: ACLU Foundation, 1997).

8. Joseph Wharton, "Courts Now Out of Job as Jailers," *ABA Journal* (August 1996): 40–41.

9. Jim Thomas, *Prisoner Litigation: The Paradox of the Jailhouse Lawyer* (Totowa, N.J.: Rowman and Littlefield, 1988), 52.

10. For a brief history of habeas corpus, see Kermit L. Hall, ed., *The Oxford Companion to the Supreme Court of the United States* (New York: Oxford University Press, 1992), 357–358.

11. Judiciary Act, 1 Stat. 73, Section 14 (1789).

12. See Sheldon Goldman and Thomas P. Jahnige, *The Federal Courts as a Political System* (New York: Harper and Row, 1985), 17.

13. Thomas, *Prisoner Litigation*, 76.

14. *Coffin v. Reichard*, 143 F.2d 443 (6th Cir. 1944).

15. See *Johnson v. Avery*, 393 U.S. 483 (1969) and *Preiser v. Rodriguez*, 411 U.S. 475 (1973).

16. American Civil Liberties Union, Special Report: "Court-Stripping: Congress Undermines the Power of the Federal Judiciary," June 1996, 5.

17. 42 U.S.C. Section 1983 (1970).

18. *Preiser v. Rodriguez*, 411 U.S. 475 (1973).

19. Gordon Bonnyman, "Recent Federal Court Orders Spur Tennessee toward Prison Reforms," *National Prison Project Journal* 8 (1985): 1.

20. Ariz. Rev. Stat. Ann. Sect. 31-127 (1956), quoted in John W. Palmer, *Constitutional Rights of Prisoners*, 4th ed. (Cincinnati, Ohio: Anderson, 1991).

21. Bradley S. Chilton, *Prisons under the Gavel: The Federal Takeover of Georgia Prisons* (Columbus: Ohio State University Press, 1991), 13.

22. See Phillip J. Cooper, *Hard Judicial Choices: Federal District Court Judges and State and Local Officials* (New York: Oxford University Press, 1988).

23. For a comparison of 1970s and 1980s prison reform cases, see John Fliter, "Another Look at the Judicial Power of the Purse: Courts, Corrections, and State Budgets in the 1980s," *Law and Society Review* 30 (1996): 399.

24. Raul Berger, *Government by Judiciary: The Transformation of the Fourteenth Amendment* (Boston: Harvard University Press, 1977); Nathan Glazer, "Should

Judges Administer Social Services?" *The Public Interest* 50 (1978): 64; Donald L. Horowitz, *The Courts and Social Policy* (Washington, D.C.: Brookings, 1977).

25. Lon L. Fuller, "The Forms and Limits of Adjudication," *Harvard Law Review* 92 (1978): 353.

26. See Daniel L. Horowitz, *The Courts and Social Policy* (Washington, D.C.: Brookings, 1977); John J. DiIulio, Jr., *Courts, Corrections, and the Constitution* (New York: Oxford University Press, 1990).

27. See Ben M. Crouch and James W. Marquart, *An Appeal to Justice: Litigated Reform of Texas Prisons* (Austin: University of Texas Press, 1989); John J. DiIulio, Jr., *Governing Prisons: A Comparative Study of Correctional Management* (New York: Free Press, 1987); DiIulio, *Courts, Corrections, and the Constitution*.

28. *Palmigiano v. Garrahy*, 443 F.Supp. 956 (1977).

29. *Ramos v. Lamm*, 485 F.Supp. 122 (D. Colo. 1980).

30. Abram Chayes, "The Role of the Judge in Public Law Litigation," *Harvard Law Review* 89 (1976): 1281; Stephen L. Wasby, "Arrogation of Power or Accountability: 'Judicial Imperialism' Revisited," *Judicature* 65 (1981): 209.

31. Bradley S. Chilton, *Prisons under the Gavel: The Federal Takeover of Georgia Prisons* (Columbus: Ohio State University Press, 1991); Phillip J. Cooper, *Hard Judicial Choices: Federal District Court Judges and State and Local Officials* (New York: Oxford University Press, 1988); Tinsley E. Yarbrough, "The Political World of Federal Judges as Managers," *Public Administration Review* 45 (1985): 660.

32. Yarbrough, "The Political World," 664.

33. Colin Diver, "The Judge as Political Power Broker: Superintending Structural Change in Public Institutions," *Virginia Law Review* 65 (1979): 43.

34. Cooper, *Hard Judicial Choices*, 9.

35. Ibid., 5.

36. Abram Chayes, "Foreword: Public Law Litigation and the Burger Court, the Supreme Court 1981 Term," *Harvard Law Review* 96 (1982): 4.

37. Herbert L. Packer, *The Limits of the Criminal Sanction* (Stanford, Calif.: Stanford University Press, 1968), 2–10.

Chapter 2

Law, Politics, and Strategy in Supreme Court Decision Making

Since the objective of this book is to trace the evolution of prisoners' rights in the Supreme Court and to identify the agents of change in the legal status of prisoners, it is worthwhile to examine the complex decision-making environment of the Court. Many explanations exist regarding how judges decide cases and how the law changes over time. Some theories are court centered, while others focus on the political environment in which courts operate. The three most prominent court-centered models of Supreme Court decision making are the legal, attitudinal, and strategic.

MODELS OF SUPREME COURT DECISION MAKING

In a nutshell, the legal model asserts that justices decide cases using only legally relevant criteria, including the text of a statute or constitutional provision, legislative or framers' intent, precedent, and a balancing of interests. In contrast, the attitudinal model claims that Supreme Court decisions are based on the facts of a case in light of the political ideologies and values of the justices. The attitudinal model asserts that justices use precedent or framers' intent as a tool to mask their underlying policy preferences. Legal criteria may be an important starting point in the decision-making process, but they do not effectively constrain judicial discretion. According to Jeffrey Segal and Harold Spaeth, the two leading advocates of the attitudinal model, "Rehnquist votes the way he does because he is extremely conservative; Marshall voted the way he did because he was extremely liberal."[1] The legal and attitudinal models then focus on different factors to explain decision making; the former concentrates on the legal arguments used by justices to support their opinions, while the latter focuses on the actual votes of the justices.

Lee Epstein and Jack Knight, proponents of another court-centered model—the strategic model—argue that justices are rational, goal-oriented decision makers who have certain policy preferences about the outcomes of cases, and that they seek to join opinions that reflect those preferences.[2] Where the attitudinal model focuses on the votes of individual justices, the strategic model emphasizes the interactions among the justices in a small-group environment. Individual justices may want to pursue policy goals, but they do so within certain internal and external constraints. Justices realize that success in advancing policy preferences often depends on the preferences and actions of others—such as their colleagues, Congress, the president, and the American people.[3] This approach seems to have merit because a majority vote is necessary for an opinion, and there may be a certain amount of bargaining and compromise to garner enough votes to reach a decision and establish a precedent. Moreover, since the Court lacks the power to enforce its decisions, the justices may be sensitive to how Congress, the president, and the public might respond to their opinions.

The strategic model of decision making recognizes that political forces from outside the Court may influence voting patterns among the justices. Federal judges may be independent of politics in a formal sense, because they are appointed and essentially serve for life provided they exhibit good behavior, but they do not operate in a political vacuum. Public opinion, political institutions such as the president and Congress, and interest groups converge on the decision-making process and often determine how constitutional issues are framed and ultimately decided.

LIMITATIONS OF THE LEGAL AND ATTITUDINAL MODELS

For reasons that will be fully explored below, a strategic approach is utilized in Chapters 4–6 to examine the doctrinal development of prisoners' rights in the Supreme Court. The "myth" of judicial decision making is that judges decided cases according to the law. Citizens expect that judicial outcomes are the result of an objective interpretation of the law. Although justices claim that they use only legally relevant criteria in deciding cases, the four variants of the legal model—text, intent of the framers, precedent, and balancing interests—do not fully explain Supreme Court decision making, nor do they effectively reduce the discretion judges have in interpreting the Constitution and federal laws. The attitudinal model is parsimonious in that it explains decision making by a single variable—policy preferences. There is strong empirical support that justices are influenced by their personal ideologies, but the attitudinal model also has its limitations. It focuses exclusively on the votes of individual justices while ignoring the small-group environment and external factors that may influence voting. Moreover, a preoccupation with votes tells us nothing about subtle or significant changes in legal doctrine. Given the fundamental changes in the legal status of prisoners over the past 50 years, and the conflict among the justices in interpreting prisoners' rights, it is essential to utilize a model of decision making that examines the opinions of the Court. For these reasons, a strategic approach is best suited for a developmental study of prisoners' rights.

Because the legal model is rejected as an explanation for the doctrinal development of prisoners' rights, it is important first to describe the variations of the model and to examine critically some of the assumptions that are made concerning judicial decision making within the context of prisoner litigation. I then turn to a description of the attitudinal model as it applies to the Supreme Court and prisoners' rights and identify some of its strengths and weaknesses as an explanatory tool. Finally, the elements of the strategic model are discussed, including three important variables comprising the political context of decision making: public opinion, political institutions, and interest groups.

THE LEGAL MODEL AND PRISONERS' RIGHTS

The traditional approach to doctrinal change places emphasis on the law. According to the "legal model" of judicial decision making, the decisions of the Supreme Court are based on the facts of the case with reference to the plain meaning of the text of the Constitution or statutes, the intent of the framers, precedent established in previous cases, and a balancing of societal interests.[4] Change in constitutional doctrine occurs through a case-by-case modification of legal principles using one or more of the four methods mentioned above. Since the limitations of the legal model have been cogently argued by Segal and Spaeth, this section will only highlight some of the general problems with each variant. We will then look more closely at how the different approaches apply to the constitutional rights of prisoners.[5]

In a scientific sense, the legal model is not really much of a model because, until recently, it has not been subject to empirical testing.[6] The justices will not admit to using anything but legally relevant criteria in deciding cases, and indeed their opinions are replete with references to precedent and textual provisions, but there are no hard and fast rules about which legal components to use or how much weight framers' intent or precedent should be assigned in each case.[7] That is why Richard Brisbin suggests that the "legal model" is best viewed as a list of factors that judges use when deciding cases, rather than an explanatory model of decision making.[8] Few political scientists believe that legal criteria alone explain judicial decisions. If the text of the law or precedent primarily determined judicial outcomes, there would be much more agreement among the justices and more unanimous opinions. But disagreement and conflict on the Court is commonplace. Phillip Cooper has described how ideological differences, ego clashes, leadership contests, procedural differences, and contrasting role orientations are the causes for many of the conflicts on the Court.[9]

While it is obvious to most scholars that the law alone cannot explain judicial outcomes, it is still necessary to critically evaluate the role that legal components play in decision making, because in the normative debate surrounding judicial review and constitutional interpretation, advocates of judicial restraint argue that justices *should* adhere to the text or intent of the framers in order to avoid reading their own policy preferences into constitutional provisions and federal laws. Critics of an activist federal judiciary, such as Robert Bork and Ed Meese, argue that the courts should return to a "principled" jurisprudence based on legally relevant methods such as the intent of the framers, the text of the Constitution, or other purportedly objective criteria.[10] The following analysis, however, demonstrates that the components of the legal model do not effectively constrain judicial discretion. Even though legal criteria may be important in some cases to some justices, the legal model does not provide a parsimonious explanation for Supreme Court decision making in the area of prisoners' rights.

Plain Meaning

This variant of the legal model holds that judges base their decisions on the plain meaning of a statute or constitution. The plain meaning may refer to the meaning of the text in ordinary usage or the original meaning of the words at the time they were drafted. The plain meaning approach also extends to standards and tests the Court has created to apply various provisions of the Constitution to contemporary problems. The rationale behind the plain meaning approach is clear: by adhering to the ordinary meaning of the text, justices can avoid imposing their own values into constitutional provisions and congressional statutes. It follows then that the Court should refrain from creating any right not explicitly stated in the language of the Constitution or federal law.

Most justices and court scholars agree that the language of a statute or relevant constitutional provision is the obvious starting point for the decision-making process. Segal and Spaeth have noted that the plain meaning variant of the legal model assumes a precision to the English language that is often lacking. Words may be vague or may have more than one meaning. Many provisions in the Constitution are ambiguous, and judges have wide discretion in construing the meaning of the words.

For example, what makes a search under the Fourth Amendment "unreasonable"? What kinds of "speech" are protected by the First Amendment? Similarly, the plain meaning of the Eighth Amendment, which is the only constitutional provision dealing specifically with the rights of prisoners, cannot be discerned by the text alone.[11] Former Justice Hugo Black, known for his strict textual approach and absolutist interpretations, once said that the Eighth Amendment prohibition on cruel and unusual punishment is "one of the less precise provisions" of the Constitution, and that, "The courts are required to determine the meaning of such general terms as 'unusual.' "[12] Numerous questions are raised by the amendment: Which punishments are cruel and unusual? Does the text refer only to the modes of punishment, or does it set limits on the severity of the punishment regarding the seriousness of the crime? Is capital punishment prohibited? Does the prohibition extend to prison conditions? Just how the justices answer these questions determines the scope of protection guaranteed by the Eighth Amendment.

If the meaning of the Eighth Amendment is limited to methods of punishment, then the responsibility of the Supreme Court is restricted to deciding whether torture is cruel and unusual as opposed to hanging or electrocution. On the other hand, if the meaning of the Eighth Amendment is to guarantee proportionality in the imposition of criminal sanctions—in other words, to require that the punishment fit the crime—then the Court must determine, for instance, if the gas chamber is a suitable punishment for the crime of petty theft, or if a life sentence without the possibility of parole is appropriate for a first-time drug conviction.[13] A more expansive but just as plausible interpretation of the Eighth Amendment goes beyond a focus on methods of punishment and proportionality by applying the cruel and unusual provision to the conditions of confinement. Here the question is whether the treatment and living conditions of prisoners is so terrible that it constitutes cruel and unusual punishment. The general language of the amendment could support any one of these interpretations. As we will see, the Supreme Court has construed the meaning of the Eighth Amendment in all three ways described above: with reference to modes of punishment, proportionality, and conditions of confinement.

The problems thus far identified in interpreting the plain meaning of the cruel and unusual punishment clause hold true for another provision of the Constitution that is important for the rights of prisoners—Section One of the Fourteenth Amendment Due Process Clause. The Due Process Clause states, "nor shall any state deprive any person of life, liberty, or property, without due process of law." By referring to the text alone, the plain meaning of this provision is not apparent. What does due process entail? When is it required? Is due process for prisoners different from that accorded free citizens? How much process is due when prisoners are transferred to solitary confinement for disciplinary purposes? Again, these questions cannot be answered by referring only to the plain meaning of the text.

It is important to remember that as part of the Bill of Rights, the Eighth Amendment was originally directed against federal action alone. Whatever the plain meaning of the text may be, only the federal government was prohibited from imposing cruel and unusual punishments. With the passage of the Fourteenth Amendment in 1868, the Supreme Court would eventually incorporate many of the protections of the Bill of Rights to the states through the Due Process Clause. In 1892, however, the Court refused to apply the Eighth Amendment to state action.[14] By the 1940s, the speech, press, assembly, and religion clauses of the First Amendment had been incorporated to the states, but the Eighth Amendment cruel and unusual punishment provision was not formally applied to the states until *Robinson v. California* (1962). For nearly 200 years then, the Eighth Amendment was a protection only against actions by the federal government.

The text of the Eighth Amendment is borrowed almost verbatim from Section 10 of the English Bill of Rights (1689): "That excessive bail ought not to be required, nor excessive fines imposed; nor cruel and unusual punishments inflicted." The prohibition was a response to the severity of English criminal law as it had developed before the Norman conquest. In thirteenth-century England, only a few crimes were punished by loss of life or limb, but by the eighteenth century, over 200 capital offenses were punishable under the common law or by statute. During the reign of Henry VIII, for example, it is estimated that 72,000 executions took place.[15] Probably the most notorious institution was the English Court of the Star Chamber, which sat from the late sixteenth century until it was abolished by Parliament in 1641. Moderate penalties imposed by the Star Chamber included the loss of ears for perjurers, face branding and nose splitting for forgers, and whipping. For more serious crimes, crucifixion, public dissection, and burning alive were some of the punishments inflicted on offenders.[16] The ban on cruel and unusual punishments in the 1689 English Bill of Rights was clearly intended to prevent the recurrence of such inhumane and barbaric punishments.[17]

Because the language of the Eighth Amendment is taken verbatim from the English Bill of Rights, we can assume that, at a minimum, it too was intended to apply to the kinds of barbaric punishments mentioned above. But the terrible punishments imposed under English law, except for whipping, were not used in colonial America. The Eighth Amendment would be meaningless if it was interpreted to prohibit only the punishments meted out under English law. Such a narrow interpretation, therefore, cannot be sustained. If the Cruel and Unusual Punishments Clause is read in conjunction with the prohibitions against excessive bail and fines, it would seem to mean that the amendment guarantees protection from not just barbarous punishments but excessive punishments as well. That is not how the Supreme Court originally interpreted the meaning of the cruel and unusual punishment prohibition, however.

For most of the nineteenth century, the Court viewed the amendment as prohibiting certain *forms* of capital punishment rather than guaranteeing proportionality. The death penalty was in use in all of the states at the time the Constitution was ratified. Death by hanging, which has been around since ancient times, was a form of execution used during the colonial period, and it has not been regarded as a cruel or unusual punishment. In its early decisions on the Eighth Amendment, the Supreme Court confronted new methods of administering the death penalty—shooting squad and electrocution—and had to determine if these new modes of execution were cruel and unusual. The Court has generally taken the position that the novelty of a penalty does not in itself amount to cruelty. This seems to weaken the significance of the term *unusual* in the Eighth Amendment, and in fact the Court upheld both forms of execution in the late nineteenth century.[18]

In *Weems v. United States* (1910), the Supreme Court revived the Eighth Amendment by applying a proportionality standard to a sentence of fifteen years of hard labor for falsifying public records. In its holding, the Court remarked that the amendment's protections were not tied to a particular theory or moment in time but "should be determined by current sensibilities."[19] This interpretation was reaffirmed in 1986 when the Court held that "the Eighth Amendment's proscriptions are not limited to those practices condemned by common law in 1789."[20] In a now-famous description of the Eighth Amendment, Chief Justice Earl Warren stated:

The basic concept underlying the Eighth Amendment is nothing less than the dignity of man. While the state has the power to punish, the Amendment stands to assure that this power be exercised within the limits of civilized standards. . . . The Court [has] recognized . . . that the words of the amendment are not precise, and that their scope is not static. The Amendment must draw its meaning from the evolving standards of decency that mark the progress of a maturing society.[21]

These decisions make it clear that the meaning of the Eighth Amendment is not fixed or static. But even the plain meaning of Chief Justice Warren's judicially created standard is elusive. In determining the "standards of decency" of a maturing society, the Supreme Court has utilized state laws, sentences imposed by juries, and opinions expressed by the public and interested groups in polls.[22] The justices themselves are often divided over how to determine the standards of decency that govern

Eighth Amendment protections. For example, in *Stanford v. Kentucky* (1989), Justice Antonin Scalia asserted that we should look to society as a whole in discerning the evolving standards of decency, and that it is "American conceptions of decency that are dispositive," rejecting any comparison of U.S. sentencing practices to the norm in other countries.[23] Reflecting his preference for judicial restraint, Justice Scalia also emphasized that the Court should use objective factors to the maximum extent possible, rather than the "subjective views of individual Justices," and that it should be guided by both the language of the Amendment and by "the deference we owe to the decisions of state legislatures under a federal system."[24] In dissent, Justice William Brennan, joined by Justices Marshall, Blackmun, and Stevens, warned that "Justice Scalia's approach would largely return the task of defining the contours of the Eighth Amendment protection to political majorities." He insisted that the justices must exercise independent judgment regarding which punishments are cruel and unusual. Justice Brennan obviously viewed the Court's role as protector of individual and minority rights against majoritarian demands. Justice Scalia's arguments won the day, however, and the Court held that the imposition of the death penalty on defendants who were 16 and 17 years old at the time the crime was committed did not amount to cruel and unusual punishment. By contrasting the arguments of Justices Scalia and Brennan, we begin to glimpse how judicial policy preferences shape decision making.

The protections of the Eighth Amendment have been applied to the conditions of confinement and the practices of prison administrators.[25] In *Hutto v. Finney* (1978), the Court said that "confinement in a prison . . . is a form of punishment subject to scrutiny under Eighth Amendment standards."[26] While a precise definition of which prison conditions constitute cruel and unusual punishment remains elusive, the Court has ruled that conditions of confinement "must not involve the wanton and unnecessary infliction of pain, nor may they be grossly disproportionate to the severity of the crime warranting imprisonment."[27] More recently, the Court has said that the Eighth Amendment is violated if prison officials acted intentionally or as the result of "deliberate indifference" to improper prison conditions.[28] Again, the plain meaning of these standards is not readily apparent and thus does not provide an objective reference for violations of the Eighth Amendment.

Whether one looks at the text of the Eighth Amendment or the standards created by the Court to give meaning to that constitutional provision, the plain meaning approach does not solve problems of interpretation with respect to prisoners' rights. A significant amount of discretionary decision making remains. In many Supreme Court decisions over the past century, justices have been divided over the meaning of the Eighth Amendment and Due Process Clause as applied to prison practices and conditions. If the plain meaning fails to provide guidance, the Court will often look at the intent of those who drafted the text.

Legislative or Framers' Intent

Another variant of the legal model uses the legislative or framers' intent to interpret statutes and the Constitution. Advocates of framers' intent argue that by adhering to the preferences of those who originally drafted the Constitution and its amendments, justices can avoid reading their own policy preferences into the law. A search for framers' intent may yield neutral constitutional principles that provide stability to the meaning of the document. But neither legislative nor framers' intent enhances our understanding of Supreme Court decision making. There are several serious limitations with intent as a reference for judicial decision making.

Harold Spaeth argues that, unlike the plain meaning approach, where justices are at least limited by the finite words of a constitutional provision or statute, just about anything in the historical record leading up to the enactment of a provision may be used to discern the intent of the framers.[29] The search for intent faces several problems. First, the historical record is either incomplete or nonexistent and often does not provide definitive answers. The Constitutional Convention proceedings were conducted in secrecy, and no record of the speeches, resolutions, or votes of the delegates occurred until 1819, when the official *Journal* of the Constitution was published. James Madison's notes, widely considered the most detailed, were edited for publication 32 years after the event and were not published until 1840.[30] Some scholars have argued that Madison's notes and those of a few others who attended the convention were manipulated for political purposes following the emergence of political parties during George Washington's second term. The records from the state ratifying conventions are even less reliable. Our information about the state conventions comes from one source: a four-volume work published between 1827 and 1830 by Jonathan Elliot.[31] The debates in the state conventions were open to the public, but those who took notes often did so for financial reasons or for political gain, which raises questions about their accuracy.

A second problem with this approach is deciding who to count as the framers. There were 55 delegates at the Constitutional Convention. Some drifted in and out, and few stayed the entire time. Only 39 signed the final document. Rhode Island did not send delegates, and three of those who did attend the convention—George Mason, Edmund Randolph, and Elbridge Gerry—refused to sign the Constitution. Should we count those elected to the state ratifying conventions as well? If so, the framers would number over 2,000.[32] Should only those who supported the Constitution be considered framers? What about the authors of the Anti-Federalist Papers? For constitutional amendments and federal civil rights laws, should we count among the framers all 535 members of the House and Senate, or only those who voted for a particular law? These questions indicate that simply identifying the "framers" is a complicated, often frustrating endeavor.

Assuming that we could agree on who the framers were, we would still face an impossible task of discerning intent. The intentions that motivate individuals to act are subjective and differ for each person. To assume that an entire group (the framers) intended the same thing because they voted for the Constitution is, in the words of one critic of the legal model, "simply absurd."[33] A review of the historical evidence shows that the framers were divided over many provisions in the Constitution, including the meaning of the Eighth Amendment.

Although the historical record is scant in regard to the framers' intent with the Eighth Amendment, we do know that most citizens of colonial America were familiar with the concept of cruel and unusual punishment, which can be traced back to the English Bill of Rights (1689). As previously mentioned, none of the barbaric punishments of English law, with the exception of whipping, was used in the colonies. The death penalty was a common sanction of colonial law, with hanging the preferred mode of execution. Following independence, most state constitutions had a provision prohibiting cruel and unusual punishment.[34] Of the thirteen original states, only Connecticut and Pennsylvania failed to include protections against cruel and unusual punishment.[35] Under the Articles of Confederation, cruel and unusual punishment was prohibited, but the original Constitution contained no comparable provision.

A defender of the Constitution, responding to some of the criticisms made by George Mason, explained why he felt that a clause prohibiting cruel and unusual punishment was omitted from the original document:

The expressions "unusual and severe" or "cruel and unusual" surely would have been too vague to have been of any consequence, since they admit of no clear and precise signification. . . . If to avoid this difficulty, they [the framers] had determined, not negatively what punishments should not be exercised, but positively what punishments should, this must have led them into a labyrinth of detail which in the original constitution of a government would have appeared perfectly ridiculous, and not left room for such changes, according to circumstances, as must be in the power of every legislature rationally formed.[36]

Interestingly, this statement anticipates some of the problems with a plain-meaning approach to the Eighth Amendment. Constitutions are not supposed to read like legislative codes. To give concrete meaning to the cruel and unusual punishments clause, the framers would have had to

include an extensive list of punishments that would fall under the prohibition. Such detail, however, is not only inappropriate for a constitution but also would make the document so inflexible that it would make
it difficult for Congress to respond to changing circumstances.

Concern was expressed in the state conventions that convened to ratify
the Constitution regarding the lack of any prohibition against cruel and
unusual punishments. Abraham Holmes, a delegate at the Massachusetts
ratifying convention, voiced his fears over the omission of any protections against cruel and unusual punishments:

They [Congress] are nowhere restrained from inventing the most cruel and
unheard-of punishments, and annexing them to crimes; and there is no constitutional check on them, but that racks and gibbets may be amongst the most
mild instruments of their discipline.[37]

In the debates in the Virginia ratifying convention, Patrick Henry, a
prominent critic of the proposed Constitution, was concerned about the
lack of protections for individual rights, and he appealed to the delegates
by invoking the Virginia Bill of Rights:

But when we come to punishments, no latitude ought to be left, nor dependence
put on the virtue of representatives. What says our [Virginia] bill of rights?—
"that excessive bail ought not to be required, nor excessive fines imposed, nor
cruel and unusual punishments inflicted." Are you not, therefore, now calling
on those gentlemen who are to compose Congress, to . . . define punishments
without this control? Will they find sentiments there similar to this bill of rights?[38]

Despite these objections, the Constitution was ratified, but only with
the understanding that amendments to protect individual rights would
be added to the document. Of the various amendments proposed in the
first Congress, only one—the Eighth Amendment—directly addressed
the rights of convicted persons. The Eighth Amendment itself received
little debate in Congress. One member objected to "the import of [the
words] being too indefinite,"[39] which amounts to early criticism of the
plain meaning of the provision. Another congressman was concerned
that the prohibition on cruel and unusual punishment went too far in
restricting the power of Congress:

No cruel and unusual punishment is to be inflicted; it is sometimes necessary to
hang a man, villains often deserve whipping, and perhaps having their ears cut
off; but are we in the future to be prevented from inflicting these punishments
because they are cruel? If a more lenient mode of correcting vice and deterring
others from the commission of it would be invented, it would be very prudent
in the Legislature to adopt it; but until we have some security that this will be

done, we ought not to be restrained from making necessary laws by any declaration of this kind.[40]

Given the paucity of debate surrounding the Eighth Amendment and
the conflicting arguments of those views that were expressed, contemporary scholars have been divided over the original intent of the amendment. For example, Raoul Berger, a conservative constitutional scholar,
argues that the framers never intended that the Eighth Amendment em-
body a proportionality principle. He cites as evidence a law passed by
Congress in 1790 that made murder, forgery, and counterfeiting of public
securities punishable by death.[41] Placing forgery in the same category as
murder, according to Berger, demonstrates that the framers had no concept of proportionality. To a certain extent, Berger may be correct, but
the 1790 law also could mean that the framers considered what we now
call "white-collar" crimes just as serious a threat to society as murder.
In an era of financial instability, forgery and counterfeiting could ruin
the economy of the young United States.

A different reading of the Eighth Amendment has been suggested by
Anthony Granucci. In a carefully researched study of the origins of the
amendment, he argued that the framers misinterpreted the meaning of
the cruel and unusual punishments clause of the English Bill of Rights.[42]
According to Granucci, the clause "was first, an objection to the imposition of punishments which were unauthorized by statute and outside
the jurisdiction of the sentencing court, and second, a reiteration of the
English policy against disproportionate penalties."[43] Under this interpretation, the cruel and unusual punishments clause did not prohibit barbarous punishments as long as they were sanctioned by statute and
proportionate to the crime. A heinous crime might warrant a terrible and
cruel punishment. If we accept Granucci's argument, the framers' intent
with respect to the cruel and unusual punishments clause, which by most
accounts was designed to prohibit torture and barbarous punishments,
was itself historically inaccurate because the original meaning of the
clause did not exclude those kinds of punishments.

From the available evidence, it is difficult if not impossible to determine what the framers intended with respect to the Eighth Amendment.
They were obviously familiar with the concept of cruel and unusual punishments and most understood that it prohibited barbarous punishments,
but it is not clear how many of the framers supported a proportionality
requirement. Even if we include the representatives in the state legislatures that ratified the Bill of Rights into the orbit of the framers, the intent
behind the Eighth Amendment remains just as murky. No published
references to the cruel and unusual punishments clause in the debates
of the state legislatures that ratified the Bill of Rights exist.[44] With the
number of individuals who can be considered framers, and the political

differences that existed among them, those searching for intent can se-
lectively quote one or more framers whose arguments support preferred
policy outcomes while ignoring the words of others.

Suppose that we could determine with some certainty the intent of the
framers of the Eighth Amendment. Should future generations be bound
by that intent? This question represents one of the most enduring con-
troversies of constitutional interpretation. Prisons as we know them did
not emerge until the mid-nineteenth century. Death by electrocution, the
gas chamber, and lethal injection were not forms of capital punishment
that existed at the time the Constitution and Bill of Rights were drafted.
The framers' intent on modern forms of capital punishment or twentieth-
century prison conditions is not available, thus the courts must interpret
the meaning of cruel and unusual punishments for contemporary problems.

For all of the reasons mentioned above, framers' or legislative intent
does little to restrict the discretion of justices in interpreting the rights
of prisoners. In fact, two current members of the Rehnquist Court,
Justices Scalia and Stevens, reject attempts by their colleagues to search
for an intent behind constitutional language. Justice Scalia argues that
only the text is the law, not some subjective intent of those who framed
it. He believes that the search for legislative intent divorced from the text
should be abandoned because "It is simply not compatible with democratic theory that laws mean whatever they ought to mean, and that
unelected judges decide what that is."[45] On constitutional questions,
however, Justice Scalia supports what can be called an original meaning
approach, because he argues that each provision should be interpreted
in light of the original understanding of the framers and ratifiers. His
original meaning approach, though different from original intent because
of its focus on the text, serves the same goals as intent in its desire to
constrain judicial power. But he himself has confessed that he may be
only a faint-hearted originalist because "I cannot imagine myself, any
more than any other federal judge, upholding a statute that imposes the
punishment of flogging."[46]

Precedent

Adherence to precedent, or *stare decisis*, means to decide cases on the
basis of principles established in prior cases. Precedents are previous
cases that are close in fact or that raise similar legal issues to the case
under consideration by a court. Following precedent gives the law an
appearance of stability, continuity, and legitimacy. Although the justices
always use one or more variants of the legal model in rendering a decision, appeal to precedent is "the primary justification justices provide
for the decisions they reach."[47] Indeed, all courts cite precedent in sup-

port of their opinions. As a variant of the legal model of judicial decision making, however, precedent is no more effective than plain meaning or intent in limiting judicial discretion, nor does it provide a useful explanation for why justices decide cases the way they do.[48]

First of all, the Supreme Court has produced so many decisions that it is possible to find precedents to support both sides to a controversy. One need only look at the nonunanimous decisions of the Court to find that both majority and dissenting opinions cite precedents that support the contrary positions of the litigants. Even when there is a clear line of precedent that appears to control a particular dispute, there are ways that judges can avoid adherence to what has been decided.[49] Justices are only legally bound by the holding or *ratio decidendi* of a previous decision. Other comments and arguments made in an opinion that are not central to the holding, known as *obiter dicta*, have no legal weight and are therefore not part of the precedent that the opinion established. The courts are responsible for separating the *ratio decidendi* from *dicta*. This is often difficult, and the process allows justices to ignore or dismiss precedents that are contrary to their policy preferences by declaring portions of a previous decision *dicta*. For example, Chief Justice Warren's "evolving standards of decency" interpretation of the cruel and unusual punishments clause in *Trop v. Dulles* (1958) is sometimes dismissed by judges and scholars as mere *dicta*. That may be true, but the standard has been cited and used in numerous federal court opinions over the years as a guide to deciding when punishments violate the Eighth Amendment. Another way the Court may avoid adherence to previous rulings is to distinguish precedent. If the *ratio decidendi* of a precedent leads to an undesirable outcome, the Court could simply say that the facts of the case before it are decidedly different from those of the precedent case and therefore not bound by the holding. This method does not alter the scope of precedent; it merely says that two cases are dissimilar, and that the precedent does not apply.

Finally, most justices on the Court recognize the limits of adhering to precedent in constitutional interpretation. Though the Court has been cautious with its power to overrule precedents, it did so 115 times between 1946 and 1992. Research conducted by Saul Brenner and Harold Spaeth found that liberal courts, such as the Warren Court, tend to overturn the precedents of conservative courts, and that conservative courts, such as the current Rehnquist Court, tend to alter liberal precedents.[50] Brenner and Spaeth also found that the politics of *stare decisis* follow the same pattern at the individual level—liberal justices tended to overrule conservative precedents, and conservative justices did just the opposite.[51] Moderate justices fell somewhere in between. These results are consistent with the attitudinal model of decision making, because they suggest that respect for precedent is based on the policy preferences of the justices.

There are numerous cases where the Supreme Court has ignored, distinguished, or overturned precedent, but a few examples from prisoners' rights cases will suffice to demonstrate the limitations of *stare decisis* in restricting judicial discretion. In a decision that overturned two recently decided precedents, the Rehnquist Court in *Payne v. Tennessee* (1991) held that the admission of victim impact statements during the sentencing phase of a capital trial was not barred by the Eighth Amendment. The ruling effectively overturned holdings in *Booth v. Maryland* (1987) and in *South Carolina v. Gathers* (1989).[52] In a dissenting opinion, Justice Marshall noted that neither the law nor facts supporting *Booth* and *Gathers* had changed since they were decided; the only difference was the composition of the Court—Justice Brennan, who had voted to exclude victim impact evidence, was replaced by Justice Souter, who voted with the conservative justices in *Payne* to admit such statements.

Balancing of Interests

Of the four variants of the legal model, the balancing of interests is perhaps the least effective in restricting justices from pursuing their policy preferences. Bradley Canon has argued that judicial resort to balancing is evidence of the subjectivity of the interpretive process, because balancing is nothing more than a rank ordering of individual values given the facts of the case.[53] Most cases before the Court involve a variety of interests that are often in conflict. Typical is the clash between individual rights and the interests of society. For instance, the First Amendment free speech right of the media to report on crimes and high-profile trials may conflict with a criminal defendant's Sixth Amendment right to an impartial jury.[54] Prisoners' rights cases pit the interests of the individual (prisoner) against those of the community (state). When rights or interests conflict, the Supreme Court often uses a balancing approach.

There are a variety of approaches to balancing. Sometimes the Court balances interests by resorting to a specific test or standard, such as the "evolving standards of decency" or "legitimate penological test," while other times it uses an ad hoc approach that considers the facts of a case without reference to a rule or standard.[55] But there are no hard and fast rules about which approach to use or when balancing interests is even desirable. Judicial moderates may sincerely attempt to find a middle ground in a case, but justices who are driven more by ideology and policy preferences usually tilt the scale in one direction or the other. As far as balancing the rights of prisoners, liberal justices tend to place greater weight on the Eighth Amendment and due process rights of the individual, whereas conservative justices favor deference to state action in criminal justice administration.

In his study of the criminal punishment decisions of Justices Antonin

Scalia and Clarence Thomas, Christopher E. Smith reports that both Justices Thomas (94.1%) and Scalia (90.0%) almost always vote for the government. Conversely, former Justices William Brennan and Thurgood Marshall, who were known as the most liberal members of the Court, never voted for the government in dozens of prisoners' rights cases over a seven-year period.[56]

Balancing interests, then, is not an effective check on judicial discretion. In fact, rights may be "balanced away" over time, depending on how each justice tips the scale, especially if there is a conservative majority on the Court. Conservative justices are more likely to take a restrained approach by supporting the government's position. With the retirements of Justices Brennan and Marshall, there are no justices on the Rehnquist Court who consistently "balance" in favor of the rights of prisoners. Perhaps this explains why the Rehnquist Court, aside from a few decisions supporting inmate claims, has consistently narrowed the rights of prisoners in many areas. Now that some of the limitations of the legal model as applied to prisoners' rights have been examined, it is time to turn our attention to an alternative explanation for Supreme Court decision making—the attitudinal model. The possible influence of judicial attitudes has already been noted in our discussion of the meaning of the Eighth Amendment and adherence to precedent.

THE ATTITUDINAL MODEL

In contrast to the legal model, a behavioral approach asserts that "law" explains only some aspects of judicial decision making and cannot account for conflict on the Court. If judges used only the plain meaning of the text or the intent of the framers, why did they consistently reach different conclusions on many of the issues before them? Empirical political science has demonstrated that there are a number of extralegal forces that influence judicial outcomes. These include judicial attitudes and values, role orientations, small-group dynamics, public opinion, politics, and interest groups.

The attitudinal model rejects the assumptions of the legal model regarding doctrinal change by emphasizing the importance of the justices' ideologies on voting behavior, usually on a liberal-conservative continuum. Basically, Justice William Brennan voted the way he did because he was a liberal, and Justice Clarence Thomas votes the way he does because he is a conservative. Justices who are less ideological are often characterized as moderates.

There are several ways to measure the ideological preferences of the justices. One method is to analyze the justices' votes in all nonunanimous decisions using independent measures of judicial attitudes.[57] Scholars have had some success in using both prior votes as predictors of voting behavior and content analysis of newspaper editorials at the time of nomination. Other procedures used to analyze judicial attitudes include bloc analysis of voting alignments and doctrinal analysis of decisions in specific areas of constitutional law. This book utilizes these methods to examine the development of prisoners' rights under the Warren, Burger, and Rehnquist Courts.

The attitudinal model is a useful tool for understanding court decisions in this area of constitutional law because the development of corrections policy and prisoners' rights is inseparable from politics, and judicial voting patterns appear consistent with political ideologies. A "liberal" vote in a prisoners' rights case is a vote for the inmate asserting a claim under the Constitution or federal law. A "conservative" vote is a vote to uphold state law and the actions of government officials. Two of the most important provisions of the Constitution with respect to prisoners' rights are the Eighth Amendment, which protects those incarcerated from "cruel and unusual" punishments, and the Fifth and Fourteenth Amendments, which state that "life, liberty, or property shall not be denied without due process of law." Under the attitudinal model, liberal justices favor an expansion of prisoners' rights, while conservative justices prefer a narrow interpretation of Eighth Amendment and due process claims. Conservatives favor judicial restraint and are more willing to defer to state action, while liberals tend to be more suspicious of state power by emphasizing due process guarantees.

As the composition of the Supreme Court has changed, so has the meaning of the Eighth Amendment and the due process rights of prisoners. For example, when President Bush nominated Judge David H. Souter to replace the retiring Justice William Brennan, the new nominee strengthened the conservative majority on the Rehnquist Court. In seven different 5–4 decisions during the 1990–1991 term, Justice Souter provided the pivotal "fifth" vote to establish new precedents that limited the scope of judicial protection for criminal defendants and prisoners. In *Wilson v. Seiter* (1991), Justice Souter joined a majority opinion that revised judicial standards for prisoner litigation. Under the standard announced by the Court, prison conditions do not amount to "cruel and unusual" punishment unless prisoners can demonstrate that prison officials acted with "deliberate indifference" to living conditions. Previously the Court assessed the constitutionality of conditions of confinement by examining whether conditions involve the "unnecessary or wanton infliction of pain" or are "grossly disproportionate to the severity of the crime warranting imprisonment."[58] If Justice Brennan, rather than Justice Souter, had still been on the Court, it is likely that this case and the others would have been decided differently. Justice Brennan had one of the Court's most liberal voting records in criminal procedure and due process cases.[59]

Since his first term, Justice Souter has demonstrated increasing support for the due process rights of prisoners and criminal defendants. His jurisprudential evolution may be a response to the more strident conservatism of Justices Scalia and Thomas. Clarence Thomas, for example, believes that the Eighth Amendment only protects criminal defendants from cruel and unusual punishments or sentences, and that it was never meant to apply to prison conditions and practices. His views not only conflict with his predecessor Thurgood Marshall but run counter to decades of precedents that have applied the Eighth Amendment to prison conditions and the treatment of inmates as well. When a conservative justice such as Clarence Thomas replaces one of the Court's most liberal members, the voting dynamics and policy direction of the Court are affected.

Critics of the attitudinal model argue that it places too much emphasis on ideology while ignoring other factors that are important to the decision-making process. But we need only look at the real world of politics to understand that judicial attitudes are important. Presidents almost always select nominees to the Court who share their ideology, values, and party affiliation. Once nominated, interest groups research the writings and opinions of the nominee for any hint of ideology and policy preferences on key issues. Finally, during confirmation hearings in the Senate, senators probe the nominee for information that might reveal attitudes on important constitutional questions such as abortion, the right to privacy, affirmative action, and federalism. Though there have been a few notable exceptions such as Warren, Brennan, and Souter, for the most part, Supreme Court nominees do not stray too far from the ideology and values of the presidents who appointed them.

STRATEGIC DECISION MAKING IN CONTEXT

The strategic model offers a nice balance between legal and political explanations. While it acknowledges that individual justices have preferences that they would like to see maximized in the opinion of the Court, the strategic model argues that justices must work within the constraints of a small-group setting and an external political environment. Specifically, individual justices must consider three different strategic relationships: (1) among the justices themselves; (2) between the Court and other political institutions; and (3) between the Court and the American people.[60] Strategic decision making is reflected in decisions to grant or deny review of a case, changes in voting between the initial vote on the merits in conference and the final voting alignment, and opinion revisions that accommodate the views of justices who might be uncertain about their vote.

To understand the influence of informal bargaining and coalition building on voting behavior and opinion writing, however, it is necessary to go behind the scenes by researching the private papers of former justices. Personal letters, memos, draft opinions, conference vote forms, and personal anecdotes provide the primary resource material for analyzing judicial strategies within the Court.[61] These materials are not widely available to many researchers, which explains why most strategic studies have been case specific and historically time bound. Despite these limitations, the strategic model is still useful in understanding decision making. For example, Lee Epstein and Joe Kobylka found that in death penalty cases such as *Furman v. Georgia* (1972), arguments made by the NAACP Legal Defense Fund (LDF) did influence the policy preferences of the justices.[62] While evidence of judicial strategy may be evident in some cases, the strategic model, like the legal model, runs the risk of being idiosyncratic by not providing a systematic explanation for decision making. Nonetheless, a strategic approach is best suited for a study of the doctrinal development of prisoners' rights.

Because courts do not operate in a vacuum, it is essential to consider the broader social and political environment in which judicial decisions are made. This is especially true for a study of prisoners' rights, because prison reform has been influenced by the civil rights movement, public attitudes toward crime and punishment, the changing political composition of the Supreme Court, and the emergence of a prisoners' rights bar to litigate on behalf of the rights of convicted persons. A strategic approach considers these factors, whereas the attitudinal model does not. Scholars have identified three important variables that are part of the political context of a case: public opinion, political institutions, and interest groups.

Public Opinion

Scholars and Supreme Court justices are divided over the influence that public opinion has on the Court. At first glance it seems odd that public opinion would play a role in Supreme Court decision making. After all, federal judges are appointed for life and are not subject to retention elections. This structure was designed to make the judiciary independent of political pressure so that justices would decide cases on the basis of the Constitution and federal law and not according to the whims of political majorities. Of course, the Court is not completely insulated from politics, but compared to Congress and the president, it is more independent and certainly less representative. Given the relative independence of the federal judiciary, it is worth asking why the Supreme Court would even consider public opinion in deciding cases.

One explanation why justices might be sensitive to public opinion is that they want to be liked by their fellow citizens and are concerned

about their judicial legacy.[63] This is especially true if the justice has political aspirations once retired from the bench. More important, however,
the justices may be hesitant to stray too far from prevailing opinion on
issues because they are concerned about the legitimacy of the Court and
need the support of the people to implement their decisions. Once the
Court announces a decision, it relies on the executive branch for enforcement and the will of the people for compliance.

Most justices deny being directly influenced by public opinion. Former
Justice William Brennan, when asked what impact public opinion has on
the Court, answered emphatically, "None!"[64] In his highly acclaimed
book on the Supreme Court, David O'Brien describes an interview that
Justice Blackmun gave for ABC News' *Nightline* in 1993. In discussing
his opposition to the death penalty, Justice Blackmun twice mentioned
public opinion and support for capital punishment. But when asked why
public opinion would have any influence on the thinking of a Supreme
Court justice on an issue as important as the death penalty, Justice Blackmun responded, "Well, the reference I have just made, of course, I have
made because I disagree with it. I don't agree with it (public opinion),
and I am not influenced by it."[65] On the other hand, Chief Justice Rehnquist has been more candid about the influence of public opinion on the
Court:

Judges, so long as they are relatively normal human beings, can no more escape
being influenced by public opinion in the long run than can people working at
other jobs. And if a judge on coming to the bench were to decide to hermetically
seal himself off from all manifestations of public opinion, he would accomplish
very little; he would not be influenced by current public opinion, but instead
would be influenced by the state of public opinion at the time he came to the
bench.[66]

Even though some justices deny that public opinion influences their
view of cases, it is clear that the Court occasionally uses public sentiment
as a guide for decisions. This is especially true for standards governing
the Eighth Amendment's prohibition against cruel and unusual punishment. As previously discussed, the Court has referred to public opinion
in defining standards for cruel and unusual punishment. In *Weems v.
United States* (1910), the Court said that the Eighth Amendment's protections should not be restricted to a particular theory or historical period
but "should be determined by current sensibilities." In *Trop v. Dulles*
(1958), the Court said that the Eighth Amendment "must draw its meaning from the evolving standards of decency that mark the progress of a
maturing society." Invoking public sentiment as a guide to deciding
cases is only half the battle, however; the Court must then determine
what sources to use to gauge public opinion. This is not an easy task,

and the Court may have only a general sense of what the public favors on criminal justice issues. Even when the views of the public are well known, as they were in a case involving the death penalty for mentally retarded individuals, the Court may choose to ignore public sentiment.[67]

Political Institutions

Justices are not merely neutral arbiters of law but political animals who arrive at the Court carrying a lot of ideological baggage. Many justices either have served in the legislative or executive branches of government before being appointed to the bench, have been active in state government, or have been affiliated with a particular political party.[68] In general, justices are going to reflect the philosophical preferences of the political party or groups to which they have been associated.

In addition to their own policy preferences, the strategic approach asserts that members of the Supreme Court confront political pressure from the other branches of government. These political pressures emanate from the separation of powers principle built into the Constitution.[69] Each branch of government has power and authority over its respective sphere of policy. This power may be enumerated, implied, delegated, or inherent in the institution and, along with informal rules of procedure, this power has evolved over time. The principle of separation of powers enables each branch to exercise power but it also provides a system of checks and balances. For example, when the Supreme Court exercises the power of judicial review in a prisoners' rights case, Congress and the president have constitutional mechanisms available to reverse or to alter the opinion.

The president has several ways to influence Supreme Court decision making. The policy positions of the U.S. government are represented by the Solicitor General's office. Appointed by the president, the Solicitor General is responsible for representing the U.S. government in federal cases and filing *amicus curiae* briefs in cases where the government has an interest in the outcome. By deciding which cases to appeal and on which to file *amicus curiae* briefs, the Solicitor General helps the Supreme Court shape its docket. In making these decisions, the views of the Solicitor General are almost always consistent with the president's position.

The most important and direct influence the president has with the Supreme Court is appointment power. A president may be able to change the policy direction of the Court by appointing justices who share his party affiliation and political philosophy. For example, between 1969 and 1971, President Richard Nixon had the opportunity to appoint four new justices to the Court, including Chief Justice Warren Burger, Harry Blackmun, William Rehnquist, and Lewis Powell. All four justices had conservative credentials, and the appointments had the potential to alter the voting dynamics and policy direction of the Court. Even though it takes five votes for a majority, the Nixon appointees could, and sometimes did, win the support of the two more moderate Warren Court holdovers: Byron White and Potter Stewart. The impact of the Nixon appointees in cases involving prisoners' rights is discussed in detail in Chapter 5. As it turns out, the four Nixon appointees were just the first in a succession of Republican appointments to the Supreme Court. During his short tenure, President Ford appointed John Paul Stevens. Democratic President Jimmy Carter did not have an opportunity to fill a vacancy on the Court during his four-year term. By the time Presidents Ronald Reagan and George Bush had placed their imprimatur on the Supreme Court with five new justices, many of the decisions of the Warren Court were in jeopardy of being narrowed or overturned by the more conservative Rehnquist Court. If not for the election of Bill Clinton as president in 1992, the Supreme Court would be composed entirely of Republican justices. Of course, a Court composed of nine justices with the same party affiliation, whether Republican or Democratic, would not mean that there would be a consensus on every case, but it would shift the terms of debate to one side of the ideological spectrum.

To a certain extent, the Supreme Court also must be aware of congressional sentiment on issues, because Congress can overturn a decision through constitutional amendment or legislation. Though it is rare for Congress to propose an amendment, or even legislation, to reverse a Supreme Court decision, it does happen. The PLRA, while not a statutory response to a specific Supreme Court decision, can be seen as a reaction to the impact of numerous federal court decisions on state prison administration. In addition to changing a decision through legislation, Congress has other tools at its disposal to place pressure on the federal courts. For instance, Congress may restrict the jurisdiction of the courts, as it did with the PLRA, or increase its scrutiny of judicial nominees during the confirmation process. Because the preferences of Congress and of the president on the issue of prisoners' rights generally favor the government, there is probably less of an institutional influence on Supreme Court decision making than in other civil rights or liberties issues. If members of the Supreme Court seriously considered the preferences of the president and Congress, few if any decisions would favor the prisoner.

Interest Groups

Litigants and interest groups are another source of political influence on judicial decision making. In Congress, lobbyists roam the halls and hearing rooms of the Capitol and meet directly with representatives and senators to press their agendas. In the halls of the Supreme Court building, however, direct lobbying of justices is considered a violation of judicial ethics. Still, there are a variety of ways for interest groups to advance their agendas in the courts. They may sponsor cases, file *amicus curiae* briefs, and initiate class action lawsuits.

In sponsoring cases, groups will supply attorneys and funds to carry a case all the way to the Supreme Court, if necessary. Direct sponsorship can be costly, however, so groups may choose to submit *amicus curiae* briefs. When filing an *amicus curiae* brief, interest groups do not directly participate in cases; instead, they provide legal and policy arguments in support of one of the parties to the case. Judicial scholars have noticed a significant increase in interest group litigation before the Supreme Court. In the 1940s, only 18 percent of the cases before the Court contained an *amicus curiae* brief; between 1986 and 1996, 76 percent of the full opinion cases contained at least one *amicus curiae* brief, and the average *amicus curiae* case contained 4.4 briefs.[70] These statistics illustrate that the Supreme Court has increasingly become another battleground for interest groups to advance their agendas.

The influence of interest groups in the development of prisoners' rights in the federal courts cannot be overstated. Until the emergence of an organized prisoners' rights bar, inmates had few allies who would represent their interests in court. The NAACP LDF had long been active in civil rights litigation; in fact, the NAACP's legal attack on segregation in the federal courts is a classic example of how an interest group can utilize the judiciary when other political forums are either closed off or unresponsive. Many of the leading prisoners' rights lawyers were activists who had honed their skills in the black civil rights movement. People such as William Bennet Turner and Stanley Bass of the LDF brought experience and a national perspective to the prisoners' rights movement.

The LDF achieved initial success with its goal of abolishing capital punishment in *Furman v. Georgia* (1972). The LDF's arguments convinced a majority of the justices that the death penalty, as imposed at the time, was so arbitrary as to amount to a denial of due process and equal protection.[71] But the success was short lived. In *Gregg v. Georgia* (1976), the Court upheld Georgia's revised death penalty statute, and capital punishment was once again constitutional. Though the LDF would continue to argue against the death penalty, public support for capital punishment remained high during the 1980s and 1990s, and there were few victories in capital punishment cases in the Supreme Court during this period.

Another important player in the prisoners' rights movement has been the American Civil Liberties Union (ACLU). The ACLU's involvement in prisoner litigation dates back to the late 1950s. Representing Black Muslims, the ACLU won some important early cases involving the free exercise of religion for Black Muslim prisoners. Since the 1970s, the

ACLU National Prison Project has been actively involved in prisoner litigation. It sponsors numerous cases and actively monitors compliance with court orders. The organization also publishes a quarterly journal that reviews pending cases and discusses emerging issues surrounding the rights of prisoners.

Public opinion, political institutions, and interest groups, along with the policy preferences of individual justices, have influenced the development and scope of prisoners' rights in America. Public opinion is sometimes utilized in developing standards for constitutional rights under the Eighth Amendment. Presidential appointments alter the political composition of the Court, and Congress can play a role by passing legislation that either expands or restricts the statutory rights of inmates. Interest groups have had some success in litigating prisoners' rights in the federal courts, but perhaps their most important role is monitoring prison conditions and compliance with court-ordered reforms. As we trace the evolution of prisoners' rights in the Supreme Court, it is important to examine the role that these political variables have played. A strategic analysis incorporates these variables and enhances our understanding of the dynamics of decision making in cases involving the rights of convicted persons. Before we apply the strategic model to the decisions of the Warren, Burger, and Rehnquist Courts, it is worthwhile to examine the pre-reform period, when federal courts, including the Supreme Court, generally took a hands-off approach in cases involving prisoners' rights.

NOTES

1. Jeffrey A. Segal and Harold J. Spaeth, *The Supreme Court and the Attitudinal Model* (New York: Cambridge University Press, 1993), 65.

2. Lee Epstein and Jack Knight, *The Choices Justices Make* (Washington, D.C.: Congressional Quarterly, 1998), 10–13.

3. Lee Epstein, ed., *Contemplating Courts* (Washington, D.C: Congressional Quarterly, 1995), 6.

4. In his review of Segal's and Spaeth's *The Supreme Court and the Attitudinal Model*, Bradley C. Canon criticized the authors for including the balancing of interests in the legal model. I agree with Professor Canon that the balancing of interests component of the legal model seems misplaced. When judges resort to balancing, they appear to be admitting that legal criteria cannot resolve the questions before the Court. Balancing interests, such as freedom versus equality or individual rights versus the public good, only reinforces the impression that justices engage in subjective decision making. Canon suggests that balancing is "but a justice's own ranking of his or her attitudes toward those values in the factual situation at bar." See Bradley C. Canon, "Review of *The Supreme Court and the Attitudinal Model*," *The Law and Politics Book Reviews* 3 (1993): 98–100.

5. Segal and Spaeth, *The Supreme Court and the Attitudinal Model*, 33–52.

6. See Jeffrey A. Segal and Harold J. Spaeth, "The Influence of *Stare Decisis* on the Votes of United States Supreme Court Justices," *American Journal of Political Science* 40 (1996): 971. The authors found that out of 32 justices, only two—Justices Potter Stewart and Lewis Powell—followed precedent in any systematic fashion.

7. Canon, "Review of *The Supreme Court and the Attitudinal Model*," 98.

8. Richard A. Brisbin, Jr., "Slaying the Dragon: Segal, Spaeth, and the Function of Law in Supreme Court Decision Making," *American Journal of Political Science* 40 (1996): 1004.

9. Phillip J. Cooper, *Battles on the Bench: Conflict inside the Supreme Court* (Lawrence: University Press of Kansas, 1995), 6–8.

10. Robert H. Bork, *The Tempting of America: The Political Seduction of the Law* (New York: Simon and Schuster, 1990), 5.

11. The text of the amendment reads: "Excessive bail shall not be required, nor excessive fines imposed, nor cruel and unusual punishments inflicted." The Supreme Court has never applied the excessive bail and fines provisions to the states, and there are few decisions involving those clauses at the federal level. The Court has had much more to say about the cruel and unusual punishments clause.

12. Hugo Black, "The Bill of Rights," *New York University Law Review* 35 (1960): 865.

13. See *Harmelin v. Michigan*, 501 U.S. 957 (1991), where the Court held (5 to 4) that a state may require life in prison without parole for a first-time nonviolent drug offense without violating the Eighth Amendment ban on cruel and unusual punishment.

14. *O'Neil v. Vermont*, 144 U.S. 323 (1892).

15. Stanley Mosk, "The Eighth Amendment Rediscovered," *Loyola University Law Review* 1 (1968): 5.

16. *Wilkerson v. Utah*, 99 U.S. 130 (1878), 135.

17. Leonard W. Levy, a noted scholar on the Bill of Rights, has argued that the provision against "cruel and unusual" punishments in the English Bill of Rights was primarily a response to the case of Titus Oates. Oates underwent punishment that, even by seventeenth-century standards, seemed excessive. An English cleric, Oates authored the infamous Popish Plot hoax, accusing English Catholics, led by Jesuit priests, of planning to assassinate Charles II. During the hysteria following the allegations, fifteen people, including the leader of the Jesuit order, were disemboweled, quartered, and beheaded for high treason. When it became clear that the accusations were false, Oates was tried for perjury. He was convicted and sentenced to be defrocked, to pay a fine of two thousand marks, to be whipped along a route covering three and a half miles, and then to be imprisoned for life as well as being pilloried four times annually. See Leonard W. Levy, *Origins of the Bill of Rights* (New Haven, Conn.: Yale University Press, 1999), 236–237.

18. See *Wilkerson v. Utah*, 99 U.S. 130 (1878) [upholding the shooting squad] and *In re Kemmler*, 136 U.S. 436 (1890) [upholding death by electrocution].

19. David Rudovsky et al., *The Rights of Prisoners: An American Civil Liberties Union Handbook* (Carbondale: Southern Illinois University Press, 1988), 1.

20. *Ford v. Wainwright*, 477 U.S. 399 (1986).

21. *Trop v. Dulles*, 356 U.S. 86 (1958), 99–101.

22. Jack W. Peltason, *Understanding the Constitution*, 14th ed. (Fort Worth: Harcourt Brace, 1997), 363.

23. *Stanford v. Kentucky*, 492 U.S. 361 (1989), 369.

24. Ibid., 369–370.

25. *Estelle v. Gamble*, 429 U.S. 97 (1976).

26. *Hutto v. Finney*, 437 U.S. 678 (1978), 685.

27. *Rhodes v. Chapman*, 452 U.S. 337 (1981).

28. *Wilson v. Seiter*, 501 U.S. 299 (1991).

29. See Harold Spaeth, "The Attitudinal Model," in *Contemplating Courts*, Lee Epstein, ed. (Washington, D.C.: Congressional Quarterly, 1995), 300–301.

30. Jack N. Rackove, *Original Meanings: Politics and Ideas in the Making of the Constitution* (New York: Alfred A. Knopf, 1996), 3–5.

31. Jonathan Elliot, *The Debates in the Several State Conventions on the Adoption of the Federal Constitution*, 2nd ed. (Washington, D.C.: U.S. Congress, 1836).

32. Rakove, *Original Meanings*, 6.

33. Spaeth, "The Attitudinal Model," 300.

34. The Virginia Declaration of Rights, Sect. 9, 1776, stated "that excessive bail ought not to be required, nor excessive fines imposed, nor cruel and unusual punishments inflicted." The provision was drafted by George Mason and is an exact copy of the statement found in the English Bill of Rights.

35. Pennsylvania corrected the omission in 1790 when it adopted a clause that contained the prohibition. See Larry C. Berkson, *The Concept of Cruel and Unusual Punishment* (Lexington, Mass.: D.C. Heath and Company, 1975), 6.

36. James Iredell, "Marcus Answers to Mr. Mason's Objections to the New Constitution" (1788), quoted in Phillip B. Kurland, *The Founders' Constitution*, Vol. 5 (Chicago: University of Chicago Press, 1987), 376.

37. See Jonathan Elliot, *The Debates in the Several State Conventions on the Adoption of the Federal Constitution*, 2nd ed. (Washington, D.C.: U.S. Congress, 1836), 2:111.

38. Ibid., 3:447–448.

39. 1 *Annals of Congress* 754 (1789).

40. Ibid.

41. Raoul Berger, "The Cruel and Unusual Punishments Clause," in *The Bill of Rights: Original Meaning and Current Understanding*, Eugene W. Hickok, Jr., ed. (Charlottesville: University Press of Virginia, 1991), 305.

42. Anthony F. Granucci, "Nor Cruel and Unusual Punishments Inflicted: The Original Meaning," *California Law Review* 57 (1969): 839.

43. Ibid., 860.

44. Leonard Orland, *Prisons: Houses of Darkness* (New York: Free Press, 1975), 86.

45. Antonin Scalia, *A Matter of Interpretation: Federal Courts and the Law* (Princeton, N.J.: Princeton University Press, 1997), 22.

46. Antonin Scalia, "Originalism: The Lesser Evil," *Cincinnati Law Review* 57 (1989): 849, 864.

47. Segal and Spaeth, "The Influence of *Stare Decisis* on the Votes of United States Supreme Court Justices," 971.

48. Segal and Spaeth, *The Supreme Court, and the Attitudinal Model*, 44.

49. Spaeth, "The Attitudinal Model," 303.

50. Saul Brenner and Harold Spaeth, *Stare Indecisis: The Alteration of Precedent on the Supreme Court, 1946–1992* (New York: Cambridge University Press, 1995).

51. Ibid.

52. In *Booth v. Maryland*, 482 U.S. 496 (1987), the Court said that survivor victim impact statements were irrelevant to the blameworthiness of the defendant, and only evidence relating to the guilt of a defendant is relevant to the capital sentencing decision. In *South Carolina v. Gathers*, 490 U.S. 805 (1989), the Court held that a description of the victim's traits was indistinguishable from an impact statement and therefore contrary to the Eighth Amendment.

53. Canon, "Review of *The Supreme Court and the Attitudinal Model*," 98–99.

54. Segal and Spaeth, *The Supreme Court and the Attitudinal Model*, 52.

55. Spaeth, "The Attitudinal Model," 304.

56. Christopher E. Smith, "The Constitution and Criminal Punishment: The Emerging Visions of Justices Scalia and Thomas," *Drake Law Review* 43 (1995): 593.

57. Jeffrey A. Segal and Albert D. Cover, "Ideological Values and the Votes of U.S. Supreme Court Justices," *American Political Science Review* 83 (1989): 557.

58. *Rhodes v. Chapman*, 452 U.S. 337 (1981).

59. Segal and Spaeth, *The Supreme Court and the Attitudinal Model*, 246.

60. Epstein and Knight, *The Choices Justices Make*, 112.

61. The resources for this manuscript are drawn from the public papers of Justices William O. Douglas, William Brennan, and Thurgood Marshall. The Marshall Papers are the most current, running through the 1990–1991 term.

62. Lee Epstein and Joseph Kobylka, *The Supreme Court and Legal Change: Abortion and the Death Penalty* (Chapel Hill: University of North Carolina Press, 1992), 79–81.

63. Lawrence Baum, *The Supreme Court*, 4th ed. (Washington, D.C.: Congressional Quarterly, 1992), 175.

64. Ibid., 136. The quote was taken from an interview by Carl Stern and broadcast on *NBC Nightly News*, April 21, 1986.

65. David M. O'Brien, *Storm Center: The Supreme Court and American Politics* (New York: W. W. Norton, 1996), 362.

66. Baum, *The Supreme Court*, 137.

67. Segal and Spaeth, *The Supreme Court and the Attitudinal Model*, 240. The authors mention that the Court noted that in Texas, Florida, and Georgia, three states where support for capital punishment is strong, opinion against execution of the mentally retarded was 73 percent, 71 percent, and 66 percent, respectively. Yet in *Penry v. Lynaugh* (1989), the Court concluded that there was insufficient evidence of a national consensus on the issue, and it upheld the death penalty for retarded prisoners.

68. Lee Epstein and Thomas G. Walker, *Constitutional Law for a Changing America: Rights, Liberties, and Justice* (Washington, D.C.: Congressional Quarterly, 1998), 39.

69. Epstein and Knight, *The Choices Justices Make*, 139.

70. Ibid., 41.

71. Epstein and Kobylka, *The Supreme Court and Legal Change*, 78–81.

Chapter 3

Early Court Decisions and Prisoners' Rights

Although efforts to secure federally protected rights for prisoners did not begin until the middle of the twentieth century, it is important to recognize that the prison reform movement dates back to the revolutionary period. The distinction is that, prior to the 1960s, there were few attempts to use the judicial system to alter prison conditions. There are several reasons why courts were not the catalyst for prison reform. First, prisons as we know them today did not develop until the beginning of the nineteenth century. Most of the early reform efforts focused on the physical design of prisons and the methods employed to discipline inmates and correct their behavior. These reforms had more to do with penal philosophy than with the constitutional rights of prisoners. Second, prisoners had few legal guarantees that courts would recognize. The U.S. Supreme Court did not even hear an Eighth Amendment case until 75 years after the Bill of Rights was ratified. Moreover, the Eighth Amendment was not applied to the states until the 1960s, so state courts were not compelled to follow its prohibitions. Most state constitutions contained a ban on cruel and unusual punishments, but state courts usually deferred to the authority of the legislative and executive branches in defining punishments and administering prisons. At the federal level, prison reform advocates knew that judges would not be very receptive to prisoner litigation so they did not look to the courts to initiate reforms. Instead, reformers made religious and utilitarian arguments to change penal philosophy, and they directed their campaign toward state legislatures rather than federal courts. Many of the reforms during this period had a direct influence on the development of prisons, the conditions within penal institutions, and the treatment of inmates, therefore, they are worthy of discussion.

PRISON DEVELOPMENT AND REFORM

Imprisonment as a form of punishment is commonplace today, and the imposition of long prison sentences, even for nonviolent crimes, enjoys broad public support. But prior to the American Revolution, incarceration as a form of punishment was rare.[1] One study found only nineteen cases in New York between 1691 and 1776 in which jail was the basic form of punishment.[2] Jails were used primarily to hold for trial people who could not make bail and for debtors who could not pay off their creditors. These jails were often small, dirty, and crowded, and there usually was no attempt to segregate prisoners by gender or by seriousness of offense.

Community and corporal punishments were the norm during the colonial period. These punishments were designed to bring public humiliation and shame upon the offender. Prisoners often wore distinctive striped clothing and were forced to work on public roads, where they were the target of verbal and physical abuse by passing citizens. Penalties for serious crimes included public hangings, floggings, and mutilations; for minor offenses, the stocks and pillory were common punishments.[3] These kinds of public and corporal punishments were eventually replaced by the penitentiary system. Political and demographic changes prompted the movement toward imprisonment as punishment. Leading up to the American Revolution, numerous citizens complained of the abuses of authority under British colonial rule and rejected many of the extreme punishments that had long been associated with English common law. In the post-revolutionary period, a republican political philosophy that expressed concern for individual rights and fear of unrestrained government power led to calls for reform of criminal laws and penalties. Public executions, whippings, and other forms of corporal punishment became unpopular. In his study of criminal punishment, Lawrence Friedman argues that the growth of American cities and the mobility of the population also contributed to the demise of these punishments. Public shaming punishments, which worked best in small, close-knit communities, seemed less effective in urban environments where people are virtually strangers.[4]

An important influence in the movement toward prisons as punishment was the writings of John Howard, whose monumental study, *The State of Prisons in England and Wales* (1777), led Parliament to pass the Penitentiary Act of 1779. The act provided four principles for reform: secure and sanitary structures, systematic inspection, abolition of fees, and a reformatory regime that resulted in the establishment of the first penitentiary in Norfolk, England.[5] Among its features, the Norfolk prison provided for the separation of sexes and of hardened criminals from petty offenders, separate cells for prisoners at night, and a workshop for the employment of able-bodied prisoners.[6]

The Quakers of Philadelphia were among the first to advocate prison reform in the United States. In 1682, William Penn, the founder of Pennsylvania and leader of the Quakers, argued for a more humanitarian treatment of criminal offenders. Like the other colonies, Pennsylvania had been governed by the British under criminal codes that were similar to those imposed in England. These codes provided for capital and corporal punishments for a wide array of crimes. Pennsylvania's Great Law of 1682 abolished all capital offenses except premeditated murder and established "houses of correction," where most punishment was imposed in the form of hard labor. The Great Law was quite humane for its time, but it was short lived. One day after Penn's death in 1718, the law was repealed and replaced with a much more punitive code. Capital punishment was reinstated for thirteen offenses, and corporal punishments, including branding and mutilation, were restored.[7]

Concern for inmates in local jails can be traced back to the efforts of Richard Wistar, a Philadelphia Quaker. Wistar had heard that several inmates at the local jail had starved to death, so he prepared soup at his house and distributed it among the inmates.[8] Other residents became involved in helping the inmates, and in February 1776, they formed *The Philadelphia Society for Assisting Distressed Prisoners*. With the outbreak of the Revolutionary War and the occupation of Philadelphia by the British, the work of these early reformers was interrupted.

In 1787, a group of Quakers and others, including Benjamin Franklin and Dr. Benjamin Rush, formed *The Philadelphia Society for Alleviating the Miseries of Public Prisoners*. The organization, considered the first modern prison reform society, was formed at a time when modern prisons had not yet been developed. This group was successful in changing the Pennsylvania penal code of 1718 and establishing the first penitentiary. Under a reformist code in 1786, capital punishment had been abolished for all crimes except treason and murder, and punishment was meted out in the form of hard labor. Dressed in striped garb, offenders were forced to work in chain gangs along city streets. The practice often led to public disturbances, because citizens and convicts would taunt each other. Led by the Quakers, a public outcry against this kind of treatment pressured the Pennsylvania legislature in 1790 to declare a wing of the Walnut Street Jail a penitentiary house for convicted felons. Though certainly not the first jail or prison, the Walnut Street Jail was the first true correctional institution in America, because it was built and operated according to a specific penal philosophy.

The Quakers felt that offenders could be "corrected" by subjecting them to solitary confinement or "penitence" for their "sins." Initially, convicts spent the entire day in silence in small dark cells reflecting on their crimes so they could repent and return to the community. But the total isolation of the convicts created physical and psychological problems, and in 1829 the legislature amended the program. Solitary confinement was maintained, but inmates were required to work eight to ten hours a day in larger outside cells. These changes influenced the development of the Eastern Penitentiary in Philadelphia. The correctional methods developed at the Walnut Street Jail and utilized at the Eastern Penitentiary became known as the "Pennsylvania" or "separate" system because inmates were kept separate for most of their imprisonment. After a period of initial success, the Pennsylvania system was soon adopted in at least ten states and in numerous foreign countries.[9] Ultimately, however, the penitentiary system failed to live up to its ideals. According to Lawrence Friedman, in practice, it was impossible to enforce the strict code of silence, and most institutions could not adhere to the system of regimentation. Overcrowding also had made it difficult to segregate prisoners and to maintain discipline. What is true today was true then—incarceration rates outpaced the ability of the states to build new prisons and cellblocks.

In 1819, an alternate system of prison management was developed at Auburn, New York. The Auburn system was almost in complete contrast to the Pennsylvania system used at the Eastern Penitentiary. The architecture of the Auburn prison was based on small inside cells designed only for sleeping, not for labor. This difference in living quarters supported a new style of discipline known as the "Auburn" or "congregate" system. The Auburn system consisted of congregate work in prison shops during the day, congregate meals in the prison cafeteria, the separation of inmates into small cells at night, and strictly enforced silence at all times.[10] Discipline was further enforced by devices such as the lockstep and, under Warden Elam Lynds, the whipping of inmates. The Auburn system became the model for over 30 state prisons built between 1825 and 1869. For years the Pennsylvania and Auburn systems competed with one another for adherents, but economic forces finally decided the matter in favor of the Auburn model. Auburn-style prisons were cheaper to build, provided better vocational training, and the prison industries produced more money for the state.[11] Almost every prison in America adopted the congregate system, including those in Pennsylvania.

In Southern states, where penal philosophy was driven by racial considerations, the Auburn system was not as prevalent. There were few black prisoners in the South prior to the Civil War. Most blacks were slaves, and those who committed offenses were whipped and sent back to the plantations rather than prisons. After the war, Southern prisons were filled with young black men, half of them completely illiterate.[12] Many Southern prisons developed along a plantation model. In a policy that returned these inmates to virtual slave status, prisoners were leased to private contractors and were forced to labor in mines or on the railroads under deplorable conditions. Others were forced to work from sunrise to sundown on prison farms. Inmates slept in large, dormitory-style buildings with little or no segregation of inmates by the seriousness of their offense. Because of these features of the plantation model, Southern prisons would become the target of the most extensive judicial intervention during the reform period of the 1970s.

By the end of the nineteenth century, most large cities had jails, and many states had at least one large prison. The use of prisons and jails as a method of punishment had become central to the American criminal justice system, and thousands of inmates were incarcerated throughout the United States. Conditions in many of these prisons were harsh. Cell blocks were overcrowded, prison guards were corrupt, and the treatment of inmates was often brutal. The public was either unaware or indifferent to these conditions. Despite the good intentions of the early penitentiary supporters, few souls were being saved.

LATE-NINETEENTH-CENTURY PENAL REFORMS

Efforts to reform penal administration in the late nineteenth century led to several innovations. The basic goal of the reforms was to separate those inmates who could be rehabilitated and released back into the community from those who were career criminals. Many of the changes were designed to promote discipline and to encourage rehabilitation through incentives. A major proponent of reform was the National Prison Association (NPA), known today as the American Correctional Association. Established at a meeting in Cincinnati, Ohio, on October 12, 1870, the NPA was a group of prison officials and penologists who supported sentencing reforms. Led by reformers Zebulon R. Brockway and Reverand E. C. Wines, the NPA drafted a Declaration of Principles that advocated the philosophy of reformation as opposed to punishment, the classification of prisoners, the indeterminate sentence, and the cultivation of an inmate's self respect.[13] These principles were put into practice at the Elmira Reformatory, built in 1876.

Among the innovations were "good time" laws. The idea here was simple: a prisoner who stayed out of trouble received time off of his sentence for his or her good behavior. New York's good time statute was enacted around 1817, but most states did not follow suit until after 1850.[14] Every state, including the District of Columbia, had a good time provision on the books by 1916. The use of the indeterminate sentence was another innovation structured to improve prison discipline and make the punishment fit the offender. The idea of the indeterminate sentence has European origins, but the concept was discussed at the first meeting of the NPA. Instead of allowing a judge to sentence a convict to a fixed number of years, the criminal would go to prison for an indefinite period and would only be set free once authorities had decided that he had been rehabilitated. Theoretically, a hardened criminal who showed no signs of reform could remain in prison for life. In practice, pure indeterminate sentences were rare. Most statutes provided for minimum and maximum limits, while others set a minimum and allowed a judge or jury to establish the maximum. These laws were challenged on several grounds, including the claim that they inflicted cruel and unusual punishment. In cases where statutory authority existed for the indeterminate sentence, state courts consistently upheld the laws.[15]

New York enacted the first indeterminate sentence in 1877, and the sentencing scheme was implemented at the Elmira Reformatory under Zebulon Brockway. Elmira housed first-time offenders between the ages of 16 and 30. The board of managers at the reformatory divided the prisoners into categories and evaluated their behavior. Prisoners were moved to higher or lower categories depending on their behavior and effort to improve their character. If a prisoner made substantial progress by earning enough "credits," it was a sign that he was ready to be released back into the community. Other innovative features of the Elmira program included religious, educational, industrial, and athletic programs. All of these programs were designed to improve the character of inmates so that upon release they could become productive members of society.

The Elmira model was praised by reformers and penologists, and other states adopted its methods. By the turn of the century, most state prisons were managed according to the Elmira model. Although there were some variations from state to state, most indeterminate sentence laws provided for a minimum sentence of one year. At the end of the one-year minimum, a prison board would determine how much longer the inmate would serve. The decision was based primarily on behavior while in prison, but other factors such as character development, an inmate's peers, and early social influences would be taken into consideration.[16] Prison boards exercised a significant amount of discretion in weighing these factors.

Parole was another reform introduced during this period. The concept has its origins in Alexander Maconochie's "ticket of leave plan" used in Australian penal colonies in the 1840s.[17] In the United States, parole did not gain widespread acceptance until the late nineteenth century. Parole provides for the early release of an offender from prison under the continued supervision of state authorities, and under conditions that allow the offender to be sent back to prison if the parole conditions are violated. Like indeterminate sentences, there was a lot of discretion in deciding who was going to be paroled, but the reform was a way to encourage good behavior among inmates and to correct some of the inequities of sentencing that were typical of the nineteenth century.

Probation was another penal innovation that was adopted around the turn of the century by many states. Probation allows a convicted criminal to be released conditionally before he is incarcerated. John Augustus of Massachusetts introduced the idea of probation in the United States in the 1840s. From 1841 until he died in 1859, Augustus posted bail for about 2,000 convicts and monitored their progress.[18] States were slow to adopt the practice, however. By 1900, only six states had statutes providing for probation.[19] During the Progressive period the idea caught on, and by 1915 all Northern states except New Hampshire passed probation statutes, and every Western state had a law on the books governing probation.

The effectiveness of these reforms would be debated for decades. By the late 1970s, attempts to rehabilitate inmates were largely abandoned, replaced by penal philosophies that emphasized deterrence and incapacitation. Ironically, all of the innovative measures developed in the late nineteenth century would come under attack a century later. Today, indeterminate sentences have been replaced by determinate ones, and some states are abolishing "good-time" early release programs and parole. Habitual offender statutes, however, achieved renewed popularity in the early 1990s in the form of "three strikes" laws.

PRISONERS AS SLAVES OF THE STATE

As far as efforts to use the courts to improve prison conditions, the expansion of judicial authority into prison administration and the protection of the rights of convicted persons have a short history. For most of the nineteenth century through the mid-twentieth century, prisoners possessed few legal rights. Prison administrators could grant privileges if they wished, but few statutory or constitutional rights existed. In a frequently cited decision that represents the conventional view of prisoners from the late nineteenth century to the mid-twentieth century, the Virginia Court of Appeals declared in *Ruffin v. Commonwealth* (1871) that prisoners were essentially "slaves of the state."[20] The case involved inmate Woody Ruffin who, while serving his sentence, had been contracted by the prison to work on the Chesapeake and Ohio Railroad. While at the work site Ruffin attempted to escape, and in the process he killed a guard. He was tried within the jurisdiction of the prison rather than where the offense occurred, convicted of murder, and sentenced to be hanged. Ruffin appealed, arguing that he was guaranteed a trial within the jurisdiction of the offense under a state constitutional provision that trials be held within a defendant's vicinage.

The state court rejected that argument, however, holding that the vicinage of a prisoner is the prison, even if that person's labor had been contracted to an employer in another county. The court ruled that a convicted felon has, as a consequence of his crime, not only forfeited "his liberty, but all his personal rights except those which the law in its humanity accords to him. He is for the time being the slave of the state."[21]

The "slave of the state" rhetoric used by the court was not entirely accurate, because prison inmates possessed more rights than slaves and some state courts were willing to consider complaints about custodial treatment. In a review of nineteenth- and early twentieth-century cases, Donald Wallace found numerous decisions recognizing limited rights for prisoners, including the right to personal security against unlawful invasion, property interests, and a right to sue.[22] Though state courts may have recognized some rights for prisoners, the *Ruffin* decision represents the general view of prisoners' rights through the early twentieth century. Prisoners were not necessarily slaves, but for all practical purposes, they died a civil death upon conviction, and the federal courts were reluctant to intervene in state prison administration.

EMERGING LEGAL PROTECTIONS

Not until after the Civil War, with the passage of federal legislation and constitutional amendments, did civil rights become recognized as a general legal concept. For prisoners, the Federal Habeas Corpus Act of 1867, the Fourteenth Amendment, the Civil Rights Act of 1871, and several federal court decisions were important developments in providing a foundation for prisoners' rights. It would take decades to build upon this foundation, however.

As discussed in Chapter 1, the Constitution provides for a writ of habeas corpus, which allows a convicted person to challenge the legality of his or her confinement in reference to decisions made during trial and sentencing. The purpose of the writ is to ensure that no one is unjustly imprisoned. During the nineteenth century, legislation and court decisions gradually expanded the writ of habeas corpus beyond its common law meaning. Early in the century, the Supreme Court and lower federal courts followed the common law principle that the writ was not available to someone convicted of a crime by a court of competent jurisdiction.[23] Courts were reluctant to interfere with the authority of prison and jail officials unless it appeared that they had used their authority for oppression.[24] The reluctance of the federal courts to issue writs can be explained in part by disagreement over the scope of habeas corpus review. It was unclear whether the constitutional writ of habeas corpus was intended to give federal courts the power to review custody of state prisoners, or whether it was designed to provide relief to federal prisoners held by the states. In *ex parte Watkins* (1830), the Supreme Court adopted a narrow interpretation of habeas corpus, ruling that unless a federal law was violated, the courts did not have the constitutional or statutory power to issue a writ.

The Habeas Corpus Act of 1867 was the first significant change in habeas corpus. The act made habeas corpus available to state as well as federal prisoners by authorizing federal courts and judges to grant writs "in all cases where any person may be restrained of his or her liberty in violation of the constitution, or of any treaty or law of the United States."[25] The Habeas Corpus Act and other civil rights laws expanded the power of the national government over the states. During the late nineteenth century, federal courts became more willing to review state prisoner petitions. After Reconstruction, support moderated for a strong central government, and the release of prisoners under federal habeas corpus review became a point of contention for state officials. The Supreme Court restricted habeas corpus review in *ex parte Royall* (1885), the first case decided by the Court under the Habeas Corpus Act. Federal courts had long recognized the authority to review state criminal cases before or during a trial. In *Royall*, the Court created the "exhaustion of state remedies" doctrine. Except in extreme circumstances, federal courts must wait until state courts have ruled on a matter before jurisdiction can be established.[26] State prisoners had to exhaust all state remedies before pursuing relief in the federal courts. The exhaustion doctrine still applies to habeas corpus litigation.

Another development in the expansion of civil rights was the Fourteenth Amendment, which would become an important vehicle for nationalizing most of the Bill of Rights. In *Barron v. Baltimore* (1833), Chief Justice John Marshall refused to apply the Bill of Rights to the states, arguing that the framers only intended for the prohibitions found in the first ten amendments to apply to the federal government, not the states. The *Barron* decision effectively ended attempts to use the Bill of Rights as a protection from state power until the passage of the Fourteenth Amendment. Ratified in 1868, the purpose of the amendment was to guarantee civil rights for black Americans. Section One reads:

All persons born or naturalized in the United States, and subject to the jurisdiction thereof, are citizens of the United States and of the State wherein they reside. No state shall make or enforce any law which shall abridge the privileges or immunities of citizens of the United States; nor shall any State deprive any person of life, liberty, or property, without due process of law; nor to deny to any person within its jurisdiction the equal protection of the laws.[27]

Even after the Fourteenth Amendment was passed, the Supreme Court refused to use it to incorporate the Bill of Rights. In the *Slaughterhouse Cases* (1873), the Supreme Court rejected the contention that the privileges and immunities clause incorporated the entire Bill of Rights, and in *Davidson v. New Orleans* (1878), the Court reached a similar result regarding the due process clause. Subsequent Supreme Court decisions explicitly rejected the application of the Eighth Amendment to the states.[28]

Despite these legal developments at the federal level, prisoners were reluctant to challenge the conditions of their confinement in court. Inmates knew that the courts would not be receptive to their claims, and they feared retribution from prison administrators. From 1865 to 1900, fewer than two dozen prison-related civil rights suits were filed in the federal courts, and most of these were dismissed on the merits or for lack of jurisdiction.[29] Prisoner petitions would increase in the early 1900s, but it would take almost a century before a body of law could be constructed protecting the rights of prisoners.

DEFINING CRUEL AND UNUSUAL PUNISHMENT

In his detailed study of the Eighth Amendment, Larry Berkson found that the first recorded judicial opinion in the United States on the cruel and unusual punishment clause was decided by the Connecticut Supreme Court of Errors in 1811.[30] In *State v. Smith* (1811), the state supreme court rejected a claim by Gibson Smith that a consecutive sentence of three years' imprisonment for each of two separate offenses was "novel" and "cruel and illegal." Of the more than 200 decisions involving a claim of cruel and unusual punishment in the next 100 years, most were rendered in state courts under state constitutional law. During the late nineteenth century, the Supreme Court decided several cases concerning the methods of capital punishment and the severity of punishment in noncapital cases. All but one of these opinions supported the government. The Court under Chief Justice Melville W. Fuller (1888–1910) was generally conservative, and a majority of justices respected state authority in criminal law administration and were reluctant to apply the Eighth Amendment to the states. Although the Court's decisions did little to expand prisoners' rights, they were important in helping define the meaning of cruel and unusual punishment under the Eighth Amendment.

In *Wilkerson v. Utah* (1878), the Court ruled that death by firing squad for a murder conviction was not a violation of the Eighth Amendment. Admitting that it was difficult to "define with exactness the extent of the constitutional provision which provides that cruel and unusual punishments shall not be inflicted," the Court felt that the provision prohibited such barbarous punishments as disembowelment, beheadings, public dissections, and burning alive at the stake.[31] Death by shooting, the Court reasoned, simply did not fall into the same category as the cruel punishments mentioned. The Court also noted that death by firing squad was not an unusual punishment, because soldiers convicted of desertion and citizens convicted of treason often were shot.

Twelve years later, the Supreme Court addressed the constitutionality of a new form of capital punishment—the electric chair. After a careful study of the matter, a New York state advisory board concluded that death by electrocution was less barbaric than hanging, and the state legislature passed a law in 1888 providing, "The punishment of death must, in every case, be inflicted by causing to pass through the body of a convict a current of electricity of sufficient intensity to cause death, and the application of such current must be continued until such convict is dead."[32] In *In re Kemmler* (1890), a unanimous Supreme Court upheld death by electrocution.[33]

Mr. Kemmler was convicted of murdering his former wife and was sentenced to death. He filed a writ of habeas corpus, claiming that his sentence of death by electrocution was cruel and unusual punishment in violation of state law and of the U.S. Constitution. A judge on the New York Supreme Court granted a stay of execution, while Kemmler's attorneys attempted to prove that the sentence was cruel and unusual. A hearing on the matter produced over 1,000 pages of testimony, but a county judge denied Kemmler's habeas corpus petition. Kemmler appealed two more times but lost in both the New York Supreme Court and the New York Court of Appeals, the state's highest court. His only hope was an appeal to the U.S. Supreme Court.

However, Kemmler's appeal was soundly rejected by the Court. Chief Justice Fuller's per curiam opinion emphasized judicial restraint in matters of state criminal sentencing. According to the Court, "The Fourteenth Amendment did not radically change the whole theory of relations of the state and Federal government to each other, and of both governments to the people."[34] The Court noted that the state legislature had broad authority to pass criminal laws and impose punishments for the protection of its citizens, and that all of the state courts upheld the law. The punishment may have been new, but as far as the Court was concerned, that did not make it cruel.

Justice Fuller stated that death as a penalty was not prohibited by the Eighth Amendment; rather, the prohibition implied "something inhuman and barbarous, and something more than the mere extinguishment of life."[35] According to Fuller, the goal of the New York legislature was to adopt the most humane method of execution known to modern science, not to inflict a painful or lingering death. As such, Kemmler's punishment did not violate the privilege and immunities clause or the due process clause of the Fourteenth Amendment. Kemmler became the first man in the United States to die in the electric chair.

One issue the Court failed to discuss in the *Kemmler* case was the constitutionality of solitary confinement. Under the New York law, a condemned prisoner was to be placed in solitary confinement while awaiting his execution. Only prison officials and the prisoner's lawyer, physician, a priest or minister, and family members were allowed to visit.[36] Kemmler argued that this isolation was cruel and unusual punishment. By ignoring his claim, the Court implicitly upheld the practice of solitary confinement. Two years later, it was more explicit in upholding the constitutionality of this punishment. In *McElvaine v. Brush* (1891), and *Trezza v. Brush* (1891), a companion case decided on the same day, a unanimous Court concluded that solitary confinement does not restrain a prisoner's liberty in violation of the Constitution and laws of the United States.

THE DOCTRINE OF EXCESSIVENESS

As discussed in the previous chapter, the original meaning of the prohibition on cruel and unusual punishment under the English Bill of Rights was that it restricted not just brutal and tortuous punishments but excessive punishments as well. Criminal sanctions were to be proportionate to the crime. As the concept was transplanted to the American colonies, emphasis was placed on prohibiting certain types of barbarous punishments.[37] For nearly a century after the Eighth Amendment was passed, the courts emphasized the later meaning, and the proportionality requirement was found by many jurists to not have any relation at all to the ban on cruel and unusual punishments. During this period, courts at all levels interpreted the clause to prohibit certain modes of punishment.[38] There was consensus that the clause banned torture and the barbaric punishments associated with English common law, even though none of those types of punishments was in use. Generally, state courts took the position that as long as a punishment was within the statutory limits, it was beyond the review of the courts. The courts, however, could always reserve the right to review a claim of excessive punishment that was not statutorily sanctioned or one that was so outrageously disproportionate that it called into question the motives of the sentencer.

The Supreme Court first considered the issue of proportionality under the Eighth Amendment in *O'Neil v. Vermont* (1892). John O'Neil was convicted on 307 separate counts by a justice of the peace in Vermont for selling intoxicating liquor unlawfully. He was fined $6,140 ($20 for each count) and had to pay court and commitment costs. The total came to $6,638.72, and if not paid, O'Neil was to be imprisoned for three days for each dollar owed—a total of 19,914 days or more than 54 years of hard labor. The Vermont Supreme Court upheld the penalty on the grounds that O'Neil had committed a "great many" offenses, therefore, he was subject to a severe penalty. O'Neil appealed on the grounds that the punishment was excessive and in violation of the Eighth Amendment.

The U.S. Supreme Court agreed with the reasoning of the state supreme court. Rejecting the argument that the penalty was unreasonable, the Court said, "the unreasonableness is only in the number of offenses which the respondent has committed."[39] The Court held that it would not rule on the cruel and unusual punishment claim for technical reasons and because the Eighth Amendment did not apply to the states.

Though the Court would effectively overturn the *O'Neil* decision years later, the case is known more for Justice Stephen Field's dissenting opinion, where he makes a forceful argument in favor of a proportionality requirement under the Eighth Amendment. Justice Field could not find any court decision during the century that had exceeded the severity of O'Neil's punishment. He pointed out that if O'Neil had been "found guilty of burglary or highway robbery, he would have received less punishment than for the offenses for which he was convicted."[40] Considering that the penalty given to O'Neil was six times as great as punishments imposed for manslaughter or forgery in Vermont, Justice Field felt that the sentence was cruel and unusual.

While acknowledging that the designation "cruel and unusual" commonly applied to punishments that inflicted torture, Field argued that the Eighth Amendment prohibition was directed against "all punishments which by their excessive length or severity are greatly disproportioned to the offenses charged."[41] He read the Eighth Amendment as a complete clause, suggesting that the inhibition applied to excessive bail, fines, or punishment inflicted. Justice Field rejected the way the sentencing court arrived at such a harsh sentence:

It [the punishment] does not alter its character as cruel and unusual, that for each distinct offence there is a small punishment, if, when they are brought together and one punishment for the whole is inflicted, it becomes one of excessive severity.[42]

Contrary to the majority opinion, Justice Field believed that the Court had jurisdiction in the case, because the state action infringed on the power of Congress to regulate interstate commerce, and because the Fourteenth Amendment guaranteed privileges and immunities of U.S. citizenship that states could not infringe. He reasoned that the privileges and immunities of U.S. citizenship were those guaranteed by the Constitution and Bill of Rights, and that among these was the guarantee that "every citizen of the United States was protected from punishments which are cruel and unusual."[43] Justice Field felt that a sentence of 54 years of hard labor was excessively severe for the nature of the offenses committed.

In a separate dissenting opinion, Justice John Marshall Harlan, joined by Justice David Brewer, echoed the sentiments of Justice Field by arguing that the Court had jurisdiction in the case. He felt that the state law under which O'Neil was charged infringed upon Congress's power to regulate interstate commerce, and that the Fourteenth Amendment prohibited states from denying or abridging constitutional rights, including immunity from cruel and unusual punishments. Justice Harlan concluded that a judgment of a state court "even if rendered pursuant to a statute, inflicting or allowing the infliction of a cruel and unusual punishment, is inconsistent with the supreme law of the land."[44] This interpretation of the Eighth Amendment requires the Court to exercise independent judgment to determine if a penalty is excessive, regardless of whether the punishment was sanctioned by state law.

Almost two decades later, the views of Justices Field, Harlan, and Brewer would gain majority support on the Court. In *Weems v. United States* (1910), the Supreme Court for the first time used the Eighth Amendment to invalidate a punishment.[45] Paul Weems, a federal disbursing officer, was convicted under Philippine law of falsifying documents. He was sentenced to fifteen years *cadena temporal* (imprisonment at hard labor with a chain strapped from wrist to ankle at all times). Accessory penalties included loss of civil rights, a fine of 4,000 pesos, and police surveillance after the completion of his sentence.[46] Weems argued that the penalty amounted to cruel and unusual punishment. At the time, the Philippines were under American control. The Philippine Bill of Rights contained much of the wording of the American Bill of Rights, including the Eighth Amendment's ban on cruel and unusual punishment. The similarity was not lost on the Supreme Court—the justices knew that any interpretation of the Philippine provision also would give meaning to the Eighth Amendment of the U.S. Constitution.

In a 4-to-2 decision (Lurton and Moody not participating and one seat vacant because of the death of Justice Brewer), the Court ruled that Weems's punishment violated the Eighth Amendment. The rationale of the majority was similar to Justice Field's dissent in *O'Neil*. Writing for the majority, Justice McKenna, joined by Chief Justice Fuller and Justices Harlan and Day, appealed to the framers' intent, yet at the same time he argued against a rigid interpretation of the Eighth Amendment. He said that English common law history as well as the intention of the framers suggested that excessively severe punishments were restricted by the prohibition. Justice McKenna reasoned that the protections of the Eighth Amendment could not have been intended to prohibit only those barbarous punishments that went out of practice following the reign of the Stuarts in England. The framers were men of action who distrusted power, and "it must have come to them that there could be exercises of cruelty by laws other than those which inflicted bodily pain or mutilation."[47] In an explicit rejection of framers' intent or a fixed meaning of the clause, McKenna suggested that "time works changes, brings into existence new conditions and purposes. Therefore a principle, to be vital, must be capable of wider application than the mischief which gave it birth."[48] Adopting a "progressive" interpretation of the Eighth Amendment, McKenna stated that the meaning of cruel and unusual should be determined by current sensibilities and not fixed by "impotent and lifeless formulas."[49]

Justice McKenna was sensitive to the separation of powers issue. He conceded that legislatures have the power to define crimes and their punishment, and he urged courts to respect that legislative power unless it confronted a constitutional prohibition. Only then did the courts have a legal duty to judge the constitutionality of a legislative action.

Having substantiated the Court's authority to set aside excessive punishments, McKenna concluded that Weems's sentence was extremely severe and therefore unconstitutional. Compared with punishments authorized for more serious crimes, the harsh penalty prescribed by Philippine law was unnecessarily severe and amounted to cruel and unusual punishment. The Court seemed to focus on the accessory penalties, which were "not as tangible as iron bars and stone walls, [but] oppress as much by their continuity."[50] But McKenna felt that even the minimum principal penalty of imprisonment was excessive and contrary to the Bill of Rights. It is a precept of justice, he argued, that punishment for crime should be graduated and proportioned to the offense.

Justice Edward White, joined by Justice Oliver Wendell Holmes, authored a vigorous dissenting opinion. Advocating a restrained approach, Justice White argued that the majority opinion

rests upon an interpretation of the cruel and unusual punishment clause of the Eighth Amendment, never before announced, which is repugnant to the natural import of the language employed in the clause, and which interpretation curtails the legislative power of Congress to define and punish crime by asserting the right of judicial supervision over the exertion of that power.[51]

White wrote that the punishment had not been considered cruel or unusual by the custom that had been in force during the Spanish reign of the Philippines. He argued that Congress did not intend for the Eighth Amendment to require proportionality in punishment. His reading of English history led him to conclude that the amendment was only designed to prohibit Congress from "authorizing or directing the infliction of cruel bodily punishments of the past."[52]

The *Weems* decision established the principle that the Eighth Amendment did more than prohibit torture or barbaric punishments—there was a proportionality requirement. Legal commentary on the case suggests that many scholars were both surprised and disappointed by the decision. Such a reaction seems odd, because the doctrine of proportionality was nothing new. It had a firm basis under English common law, and state courts had long applied a proportionality principle under state constitutional prohibitions against cruel and unusual punishment.[53] Though controversial, the *Weems* decision had only a limited impact on criminal punishment, because the Supreme Court did not apply the Eighth Amendment to the states until the 1960s. Therefore, state courts were not obliged to follow the *Weems* precedent, and few did.

Even the Supreme Court seemed to back away from the *Weems* decision in subsequent cases. Two of the four justices who composed the majority in *Weems*, Chief Justice Fuller and Justice William Rufus Day, passed away in 1910 and 1911, respectively. President William Howard Taft, a conservative Republican, nominated Associate Justice Edward Douglas White, the dissenter in *Weems*, as Chief Justice, and he appointed Charles Evans Hughes as associate justice. In the next two years, Taft would appoint three more justices to the Court—Willis Van Devanter (1911), Joseph R. Lamar (1911), and Mahlon Pitney (1912). These justices took a more restrained view of the Eighth Amendment.

In *Collins v. Johnston* (1915), a unanimous Court held that a fourteen-year prison term for perjury was not a violation of due process of the Fourteenth Amendment, and that the Eighth Amendment did not apply to the states. Mr. Collins had claimed that the fourteen-year sentence for perjury was "grossly excessive" and therefore illegal under the Fourteenth Amendment. Writing for the Court, Justice Pitney noted that the case did not involve a sentence exceeding the limit authorized by law. He concluded that

To establish appropriate penalties for the commission of crime, and to confer upon judicial tribunals a discretion respecting the punishment to be inflicted in particular cases, within limits fixed by the law-making power, are functions peculiarly belonging to the several States.[54]

As for the Eighth Amendment, Pitney declared that it is a limitation upon the federal government, not upon the states.

In *Badders v. United States* (1916), the Court returned to the issue that it had considered in *O'Neil v. Vermont*—multiple sentences in a single prosecution. Badders had been charged with placing letters in the mail to defraud. He was convicted on seven counts, each resulting from placing seven different letters in the mailbox. He was sentenced to five years' imprisonment, to run concurrently, and a fine of $1,000 on each count.

Badders argued that the sentence was cruel and unusual and that the fines were excessive. Justice Oliver Wendell Holmes, in a brief unanimous opinion, rejected the claims. Without discussion, Justice Holmes stated that, "There is no doubt that the law may make each putting of a letter a separate offence [sic]."[55] In dismissing the Eighth Amendment argument, he said "there is no ground for declaring the punishment unconstitutional."[56] The restrained approach by Holmes in *Badders* was indicative of the general treatment of prisoners' rights by the Court during the early twentieth century.

THE DEBATE OVER INCORPORATION

By the late 1940s, the Supreme Court had, in a series of cases, incorporated every provision of the First Amendment to the states through the Fourteenth Amendment.[57] The Court returned to the issue of incorporating the Eighth Amendment to the states in *Louisiana ex. rel. Francis v. Resweber* (1947). A very divided Court seemed to reverse its position that the Eighth Amendment did not apply to the states through the due process clause of the Fourteenth Amendment. Willie Francis was convicted of murder in 1945 and sentenced to be electrocuted for the crime. On May 3, 1946, he was prepared for execution and placed in the electric chair. When the executioner threw the switch, the chair malfunctioned and Francis was still alive. He was returned to prison and a new death warrant was issued for the following week. Seeking to stop the state from a second attempt at his electrocution, Francis filed a writ of habeas corpus. He argued that "two electrocutions" violated Fifth Amendment protection against double jeopardy and amounted to cruel and unusual punishment under the Eighth Amendment. Francis claimed that both protections applied to the states through the due process clause of the Fourteenth Amendment. Concluding that there was no violation of state or federal law, the Supreme Court of Louisiana rejected his application for writs of certiorari, mandamus, and habeas corpus.

Perhaps disturbed by the gruesome nature of the facts, the Court accepted review of the case. At the conference on the merits, only Justices Burton, Rutledge, and Murphy voted to reverse. Justice William O. Douglas originally voted to affirm but changed his mind, so the 6-to-3 vote was now a narrow 5-to-4 majority. There were other signs of strategic interaction. Justice Reed wrote the opinion for the Court, which at first gained the support only of Chief Justice Fred Vinson and Justice Felix Frankfurter. Vinson discouraged the practice of writing concurring opinions, because he felt that multiple opinions only confused lower courts and the bar. Justice Robert Jackson initially penned a concurring opinion emphasizing that due process embodies impersonal standards of law, but he withheld it and supported Justice Reed.[58] Justice Frankfurter, however, decided to author a concurring opinion, in part to lecture the dissenters on the merits of judicial restraint. The conference notes of Justice Douglas indicate that Justice Frankfurter admitted that this was "not an easy case." Though a second attempt to electrocute Francis was "hardly [a] defensible thing for a state to do," it was not so offensive as to "make him [Frankfurter] puke," and therefore does not "shock the conscience."[59]

Justice Reed, joined by Chief Justice Vinson, and Justices Hugo Black and Jackson, announced the judgment of the Court. Justice Reed said that the Court would consider the petitioner's claim, "under the assumption, but without so deciding, that violation of the principles of the Fifth and Eighth Amendments, as to double jeopardy and cruel and unusual punishment, would be violative of the due process clause of the Fourteenth Amendment."[60] Yet just a few paragraphs later, Justice Reed was more explicit, stating, "The Fourteenth would prohibit by its due process clause execution by a state in a cruel manner."[61] The Court, however, held that a second electrocution would not be cruel and unusual. "The fact that an unforeseeable accident prevented the prompt consummation of the sentence cannot, it seems to us, add an element of cruelty to a subsequent execution."[62]

Concurring with the judgment of the Court, Justice Frankfurter criticized the four dissenters by suggesting that they were reading their private views of justice into the Constitution rather than the consensus of society on standards of due process. He stressed the central argument of Justice Jackson's original concurring opinion. Admitting that due process and cruel and unusual punishments involve the application of standards of fairness and justice broadly conceived, Justice Frankfurter nevertheless emphasized that, "They are not the application of merely personal standards but the impersonal standards of society which alone judges, as organs of the Law, are empowered to enforce."[63] True to his philosophy of restraint, Frankfurter urged that the "Court must abstain from interference with State action no matter how strong one's personal feeling of revulsion against a State's insistence on its pound of flesh."[64]

Justice Harold Burton, writing for the dissenters, was joined by Justices William O. Douglas, Frank Murphy, and Wiley Rutledge. Murphy and Rutledge had prepared dissents, but they suppressed them in a strategic show of support for Justice Burton, who often voted with Justice Frankfurter.[65] Burton argued that a second application of an electric current through Francis's body would be cruel, unusual, and a violation of due process. He compared the proposed procedure to a lawful electrocution, which would cause instantaneous death. Interrupted or repeated applications of electric current, whether five applications or two, are "sufficiently 'cruel and unusual' to be prohibited."[66] Citing state law, Burton pointed out that neither "the Legislature nor the Supreme Court of Louisiana has expressed approval of electrocution other than by one continuous application of lethal current."[67] Burton and the other dissenters contended that the ban on cruel and unusual punishment restricted the states through the due process clause. One month after the Court announced its decision, Francis was executed, this time successfully.

The *Resweber* case illustrates the divisions on the Court with respect to incorporation of the Eighth Amendment. During the same term, Justice Black, who joined the majority in *Resweber*, announced that he would apply the entire Bill of Rights to the states.[68] Black, with the four dissenters in *Resweber*, would have provided a five-justice majority in favor of incorporation, but two of the dissenting justices died shortly after the 1947 term.[69] Some constitutional scholars cite *Resweber* as the case that applied the Eighth Amendment "cruel and unusual punishment" clause to the states, while others suggest that formal incorporation did not come until the Warren Court's decision in *Robinson v. California* (1962).[70] In the former case, the Court did not use the clause to overturn a state action, but in the latter case, it overturned a conviction as cruel and unusual punishment.

If the Supreme Court was not explicit in its approach to incorporation of the Eighth Amendment in *Resweber*, the Third Circuit Court of Appeals was in *Johnson v. Dye* (1949). Leon Johnson had been convicted of murder and was sentenced to hard labor for life. He escaped from a Georgia chain gang and ended up in Allegheny County, Pennsylvania. A warrant was issued for his extradition to Georgia, under which he was apprehended. Johnson petitioned for a writ of habeas corpus, arguing that he was the victim of cruel, barbaric, and inhuman treatment while on the Georgia chain gang. He feared that his life would be in danger if he were forced to return to Georgia to finish his sentence. The court noted that eyewitness accounts of brutality against Negro chain gang members by Georgia authorities were introduced in the district court.

The appeals court concluded that Johnson was indeed subjected to cruel and unusual punishment, and it had no problem applying the Eighth Amendment to the states. According to the court, "we entertain no doubt that the Fourteenth Amendment prohibits the infliction of cruel and unusual punishment by a state."[71] Comparing the prohibition to the freedoms guaranteed by the First Amendment, the court said, "We are of the opinion that the right to be free from cruel and unusual punishment at the hands of a State is as 'basic' and 'fundamental' a one as the right of freedom of speech or freedom of religion."[72] The *Johnson* decision was among the first by a federal court to use the Eighth Amendment to strike down an action by state prison officials. In a *per curium* opinion, the Supreme Court reversed the *Johnson* decision on other grounds, holding that Johnson did not exhaust his state remedies.[73]

THE HANDS-OFF DOCTRINE

Prior to the 1960s, federal courts maintained a "hands-off" policy when confronted with lawsuits that challenged the internal operation of prisons. Under this doctrine, federal courts refused to consider inmate claims on the grounds that "it is not the function of the courts to superintend the treatment and discipline of prisoners in penitentiaries, but only to deliver from imprisonment those who are illegally confined."[74] The hands-off policy was not mandated by the Supreme Court in any formal sense, and not all courts followed it, but throughout this period, the Court encouraged a policy of nonintervention. If there was evidence of beatings or other physical abuse, the lower courts would sometimes intervene. During the first half of the twentieth century, a few decisions acknowledged that prisoners retained certain rights. For example, in *Coffin v. Reichard* (1944), the Ninth Circuit Court of Appeals held that,

A prisoner retains all the rights of an ordinary citizen except those expressly, or by necessary implication, taken from him by law. While the law does take his liberty and imposes a duty of servitude and observance of discipline, for his regulation and that of other prisoners, it does not deny his right to personal security against unlawful invasion.[75]

The rationale behind the *Reichard* decision is that inmates cannot be denied fundamental rights unless prison officials can demonstrate that certain policies are necessary to prevent violence and disciplinary problems. Prisoners retain many of the rights of free citizens, and the burden is on prison officials to justify restrictive policies. The residual rights of prisoners must be balanced with the need for prison discipline and security.

Despite precedents like *Reichard* and *Johnson*, practical and political considerations at both the state and federal level promoted a policy of nonintervention in prison administration that endured well into the 1960s. Prisoners had few allies outside of the prison walls who would champion their interests. Two of the most effective groups advocating prisoners' rights in the 1960s, the NAACP and the ACLU, were focusing their resources on other civil rights and liberties issues. The NAACP Legal Defense Fund was engaged in a litigation strategy designed to overturn the "separate but equal" doctrine and to secure civil rights for blacks. With large minority populations in prison, prisoners' rights would eventually be tied to the broader civil rights movement, but that would not happen until progress was made in attacking *de jure* segregation.

Public indifference, even hostility, to inmates also made it difficult to win relief in the courts. State judges, many of whom are popularly elected, reflected the prevailing attitudes of their communities, and they did not welcome prison reform litigation in their courts. Elected judges risked defeat at the polls if their decisions were too favorable to prisoners. At the federal level, judges were sensitive to the concept of separation of powers embodied in the Constitution, and they were cognizant of their lack of expertise in correctional administration. The high Court also was concerned about principles of federalism. In *Sweeney v. Woodhall* (1952), an Alabama prisoner who escaped to Ohio filed a habeas corpus petition claiming that he was mistreated in Alabama.[76] In a *per curium* opinion, the Court rejected the inmate's claim, holding that, "Considerations fundamental to our federal system require that the prisoner test the claimed unconstitutionality of his treatment by Alabama in the courts of that state."[77]

Advocates of the hands-off policy also believed that judicial decrees would weaken the authority of correction officials and undermine discipline among inmates. In *Price v. Johnston* (1948), the Supreme Court established that a person did not lose all of his or her constitutional rights upon conviction of a crime, but "lawful incarceration brings about the necessary withdrawal or limitation of many privileges and rights" because of considerations underlying prison administration.[78] Many federal judges feared that intervention would disrupt prison rules and encourage inmates to defy authorities. As a result, judges deferred to the "considerations underlying prison administration." All of these factors contributed to a general reluctance among federal judges to consider petitions from state inmates that challenged the conditions of their confinement.

Unfortunately, the hands-off doctrine meant that the courts never considered the merits of complaints that were worthy of review. The move to a hands-on approach would come slowly—in the 1960s, federal judges began to address prisoners' petitions on the merits. That movement was hastened by several Warren Court decisions that provided inmates with greater access to the federal courts to advance their claims. The next chapter examines the impact that the Warren Court had on prisoners' rights.

NOTES

1. See Wayne N. Welsh, "History of Prisons: The Jacksonian Era," in *The Encyclopedia of American Prisons*, Marilyn D. McShane and Frank P. Williams III, eds. (New York: Garland Publishing, 1996), 234.

2. Douglas Greenberg, *Crime and Law Enforcement in the Colony of New York, 1691–1776* (Ithaca, N.Y.: Cornell University Press, 1976), 125.

3. Welsh, "History of Prisons," 234.

4. Lawrence Friedman, *Crime and Punishment in American History* (New York: Basic Books, 1993), 77.

5. Harry E. Allen and Clifford E. Simonsen, *Corrections in America: An Introduction*, 7th ed. (Englewood Cliffs, N.J.: Prentice Hall, 1995), 24.

6. Harry Elmer Barnes, "The Historical Origin of the Prison System in America," *Journal of American Criminal Law and Criminology* 11 (1921): 35.

7. Allen and Simonsen, *Corrections in America*, 26.

8. Barnes, "The Historical Origin of the Prison System in America," 45.

9. Ibid., 33.

10. Ibid., 41.

11. Ibid., 44.

12. Friedman, *Crime and Punishment in American History*, 156.

13. Negley L. Teeters, "State of Prisons in the United States: 1870–1970," *Federal Probation* 33 (1969): 21.

14. Friedman, *Crime and Punishment in American History*, 159.

15. For a review of cases upholding indeterminate sentences, see Larry C. Berkson, *The Concept of Cruel and Unusual Punishment* (Lexington, Mass.: D.C. Heath and Company, 1975), 82–83.

16. Friedman, *Crime and Punishment in American History*, 161.

17. Larry E. Sullivan, *The Prison Reform Movement: Forlorn Hope* (Boston: Twayne Publishers, 1990), 29.

18. Friedman, *Crime and Punishment in American History*, 162.

19. Sullivan, *The Prison Reform Movement*, 27.

20. *Ruffin v. Commonwealth*, 62 VA. 790 (1871).

21. Ibid., 796.

22. Donald H. Wallace, "*Ruffin v. Virginia* and Slaves of the State: A Nonexistent Baseline of Prisoners' Rights Jurisprudence," *Journal of Criminal Justice* 20 (1992): 333. The decisions cited include *Westbrook v. Georgia*, 133 Ga. 578, 66 SE 788 (1909) and *Anderson v. Salant*, 38 RI 463, 96 A. 425 (1916).

23. Jim Thomas, *Prisoner Litigation: The Paradox of the Jailhouse Lawyer* (Totowa, N.J.: Rowman and Littlefield, 1988).

24. *Ex parte Taws*, Fed. Case No. 13, 768, 2 Wash. C.C. 353 (1809).

25. 14 U.S. Stat 385.

26. Thomas, *Prisoner Litigation*, 78.

27. U.S. Constitution, Amendment 14, Section One, ratified July 9, 1868.

28. See *O'Neil v. Vermont*, 144 U.S. 323 (1892), *Collins v. Johnston*, 237 U.S. 502 (1915), and *Francis v. Resweber*, 329 U.S. 459 (1947).

29. Thomas, *Prisoner Litigation*, 83.

30. Berkson, *The Concept of Cruel and Unusual Punishment*, 9.

31. *Wilkerson v. Utah*, 99 U.S. 130 (1878), 135–136.

32. *In re Kemmler*, 136 U.S. 436, 444 (1890).

33. *In re Kemmler*, 136 U.S. 436 (1890).

34. Ibid., 448.

35. Ibid., 447.

36. Berkson, *The Concept of Cruel and Unusual Punishment*, 60.

37. Ibid., 65.

38. Ibid.

39. *O'Neil v. Vermont*, 144 U.S. 323, (1892), 331.

40. Ibid., Justice Field dissenting, 339.

41. Ibid., 339–340.

42. Ibid., 340.

43. Ibid., 363.

44. Ibid., Justice Harlan dissenting, 371.

45. *Weems v. United States*, 217 U.S. 349 (1910).

46. The statute under which Weems was convicted provided for: (1) twelve years and one day of "hard and painful labor," which included being chained from wrist to ankle at all times; (2) the loss of civil rights, including permanent loss of the right to vote, hold public office, receive retirement pay, deprivation of rights of parental authority, marital authority, and the right to dispose of one's property; (3) a fine of 1,250 pesetas. See *Weems v. United States*, 217 U.S. 349 (1910), 364.

47. *Weems v. United States*, 217 U.S. 349 (1910), 372.

48. Ibid., 373.

49. Ibid.

50. Ibid., 366.

51. Ibid., 385.

52. Ibid., White dissenting, 397.

53. Berkson, *The Concept of Cruel and Unusual Punishment*, 12.

54. *Collins v. Johnston*, 237 U.S. 502 (1915), 510.

55. *Badders v. United States*, 240 U.S. 391 (1916), 394.

56. Ibid.

57. See *Gitlow v. New York*, 268 U.S. 652 (1925) [freedom of speech]; *Near v. Minnesota*, 283 U.S. 697 (1931) [freedom of the press]; *De Jonge v. Oregon*, 299 U.S. 353 (1937) [freedom of assembly and right to petition]; *Cantwell v. Connecticut*, 310 U.S. 296 (1940) [freedom of religion]; *Everson v. Board of Education*, 330 U.S. 1 (1947) [separation of church and state].

58. J. Woodford Howard Jr., *Mr. Justice Murphy: A Political Biography* (Princeton, N.J.: Princeton University Press, 1968), 438.

59. William O. Douglas Papers, Library of Congress, docket sheets and conference notes, case of *Francis v. Resweber* (1947).

60. *Louisiana ex. rel. Francis v. Resweber*, 329 U.S. 459 (1947), 462.

61. Ibid., 463.

62. Ibid., 464.

63. Ibid., Frankfurter concurring, 470.

64. *Resweber*, 471.

65. Howard, *Mr. Justice Murphy*, 438.

66. Ibid., 476.

67. Ibid., 477.

68. *Adamson v. California*, 332 U.S. 46 (1947), 70–72.

69. Justices Wiley Rutledge and Frank Murphy died in office in 1949.

70. Compare Lee Epstein and Thomas G. Walker, *Constitutional Law for a Changing America: Rights, Liberties, and Justice* (Washington, D.C.: Congressional Quarterly, 1998), 80, with David M. O'Brien's *Constitutional Law and Politics: Civil Rights and Liberties* (New York: Norton, 1997), 296.

71. *Johnson v. Dye*, 175 F.2d 250 (1949), 255.

72. Ibid.

73. *Dye v. Johnson*, 338 U.S. 864 (1949).

74. *Stroud v. Swope*, 187 F.2d 850 (1951), 851–852.

75. *Coffin v. Reichard*, 143 F.2d 443 (1944), 445.
76. *Sweeney v. Woodhall*, 344 U.S. 86 (1952).
77. Ibid., 90.
78. *Price v. Johnston*, 334 U.S. 266 (1948), 285.

Chapter 4

The Warren Court and Prisoners' Rights, 1953–1969

Famous for its activism in the areas of school desegregation and criminal defendants' rights, the Warren Court's most important contribution to prisoners' rights was the expansion of access to the courts for rights violations. Between 1958 and 1969, the Court formally incorporated the Eighth Amendment ban on cruel and unusual punishments to the states, provided a standard for determining when punishments were cruel and unusual, guaranteed legal assistance for inmates, and effectively weakened the so-called hands-off policy of federal court intervention in state prison administration. Beyond those accomplishments, however, the Warren Court did little to expand the substance of prisoners' rights in areas such as religious freedom, medical care, overcrowding, and prison conditions. Lower federal courts would assume that task throughout the 1970s and 1980s.

The failure of the Warren Court to take the lead in prison reform may explain why scholars have generally ignored the record of the Court with regard to prisoners' rights. This gap in the literature is unfortunate. Even though the Court's jurisprudence concerning the constitutional rights of convicted persons was not as revolutionary as its record in criminal procedure cases, the Court did issue a number of opinions that laid the groundwork for the development of prisoners' rights. These decisions established a constitutional foundation for rights claims by extending due process and equal protection guarantees to prisoners. In ruling that inmates may bring civil rights claims against state officials and tort actions against federal administrators in federal courts, the Court provided an opportunity for inmates to secure their rights. In holding that inmates should have access to legal materials, the Court made it easier for prisoners to prepare the necessary legal documents to advance their claims. Also, by formally incorporating the Cruel and Unusual Punishments Clause to the states, the Court set the stage for increased federal judicial oversight of state criminal laws and sentencing procedures. It is important, then, to examine the impact that the Warren Court had in this area.

Strategic decision making, in the form of voting fluidity, substantive opinion revisions, dissents from denial of certiorari, and strategic leadership, was evident in many of the decisions during this period. Some members tried to persuade new appointees to accept their judicial philosophy and notions concerning the proper role of the Court in the American political system. Other justices switched their conference votes because they were either undecided about which way to vote or because they were influenced by the arguments of their colleagues. In several cases, opinion authors revised the language of a draft opinion to accommodate the views of moderate justices and thus to solidify a fragile majority. Finally, some justices dissented from denial of certiorari petitions to make their views public and to send a message to lawyers who were attentive to prisoners' rights. All of these actions suggest that the justices of the Warren Court were not just rigidly voting their policy preferences but were seeking to influence strategically their colleagues and individuals in the broader legal community, or were themselves persuaded by the arguments and lobbying efforts of their fellow justices. In some cases, however, there was little or no evidence of voting fluidity or major opinion revision.

THE COMPOSITION OF THE WARREN COURT

Though known as the most liberal Supreme Court in American history, during the first eight terms under Earl Warren's leadership, the Court was closely divided politically. Warren inherited a Court beset by differences in constitutional philosophy. On one side were the views of Justice Hugo Black, who felt that the Court should play an active role in protecting civil rights and liberties from government power. Justice Black came to believe that the Fourteenth Amendment Due Process Clause incorporated all of the rights and liberties in the Bill of Rights to the states. Opposing Justice Black was Justice Felix Frankfurter, the leading advocate of judicial restraint. Justice Frankfurter resented colleagues who sought to promote their personal sense of "justice and fairness" in individual cases. He opposed the death penalty but deferred to the authority of the states to set appropriate punishments. He was sensitive to the undemocratic nature of the judiciary and believed that the Court should refrain as much as possible from overturning the decisions of Congress and state legislatures.

According to Supreme Court scholar Bernard Schwartz, Justice Frankfurter engaged in a massive effort to persuade new Chief Justice Warren to adopt a philosophy of restraint.[1] Justice Black also attempted to win Warren over to his side. The chief justice was a prime target for these lobbying efforts because he had no previous judicial experience. Warren was a former California district prosecutor, an attorney general, and a governor. President Eisenhower saw him as a moderate Republican with good political skills and common sense.[2] He had a tough law-and-order record as a prosecutor and had forcefully argued for the internment of Japanese Americans after Japan had bombed Pearl Harbor during World War II. During Warren's first few terms, Frankfurter appeared to have the upper hand in influencing him because the chief often voted with the Frankfurter wing of the Court, and the two men had developed a warm personal relationship.[3] Beginning with the 1956 term, Warren moved away from a philosophy of restraint toward Justice Black's activist approach. Consequently, the Warren–Frankfurter personal and professional relationship deteriorated. The strained, even bitter, relationship between Frankfurter and Warren was publicly expressed by Frankfurter in strongly worded dissents and heated exchanges with the chief justice during oral arguments and opinion readings.[4] One such exchange took place during the announcement of *Trop v. Dulles* (1958), a case that will be discussed later. Warren would ultimately lead the Court to a level of judicial activism in civil rights and liberties cases beyond that advocated by Justice Black himself.

By the late 1950s Warren, Black, William O. Douglas and, to a lesser extent, William Brennan, formed a liberal voting bloc, while Frankfurter, John Harlan II, Tom Clark, and Harold Burton were on the right. The indecisive Justice Charles Whittaker often voted with the conservatives. Because of changes in personnel, there were eight different "natural courts" during the sixteen years that Warren presided as chief justice. (A natural court means membership is stable for a period of time; see Table 4.1.) With the retirement of conservative Harold Burton in October 1958 and with the appointment of centrist Potter Stewart, the political balance shifted slightly toward the liberals. Jeffrey Segal and Harold Spaeth point out, however, that the Warren Court did not become liberal on civil liberties issues until the 1961 term.[5]

Justice Goldberg's appointment by Democratic President Kennedy at the beginning of the 1962 term to replace Justice Frankfurter significantly changed the direction of the Court in civil liberties cases. Goldberg was the polar opposite of Frankfurter. He believed that the Court should use the Constitution creatively to address the great social problems of the time. He served only three terms, but his liberal voting record in criminal procedure cases was second only to Douglas's.[6] Compared to Frankfurter, Goldberg was more willing to review state prison practices and assert federal power over state authority if necessary. Also, his deeply

Table 4.1
Natural Courts under Chief Justice Earl Warren

1953–1954	1955	1956
Chief: Warren (R)	*Chief*: Warren (R)	*Chief*: Warren (R)
Black (D)	Black (D)	Black (D)
Reed (D)	Reed (D)	Reed (D)
Frankfurter (I)	Frankfurter (I)	Frankfurter (I)
Douglas (D)	Douglas (D)	Douglas (D)
R. Jackson (D)	Burton (R)	Burton (R)
Burton (R)	Clark (D)	Clark (D)
Clark (D)	Minton (D)	Harlan (R)
Minton (D)	Harlan (R)	Brennan (D)

1957	1958–1961	1962–1965
Chief: Warren (R)	*Chief*: Warren (R)	*Chief*: Warren (R)
Black (D)	Black (D)	Black (D)
Frankfurter (I)	Frankfurter (I)	Douglas (D)
Douglas (D)	Douglas (D)	Clark (D)
Burton (R)	Clark (D)	Harlan (R)
Clark (D)	Harlan (R)	Brennan (D)
Harlan (R)	Brennan (D)	Stewart (R)
Brennan (D)	Whittaker (R)	B. White (D)
Whittaker (R)	Stewart (R)	Goldberg (D)

1965–1967	1967–1969
Chief: Warren (R)	*Chief*: Warren (R)
Black (D)	Black (D)
Douglas (D)	Douglas (D)
Clark (D)	Harlan (R)
Harlan (R)	Brennan (D)
Brennan (D)	Stewart (R)
Stewart (R)	B. White (D)
B. White (D)	Fortas (D)
Fortas (D)	T. Marshall (D)

Note: Associate justices are listed in order of seniority, with the most junior justice at the bottom of the list.

Source: Thomas R. Hensley, Christopher E. Smith, and Joyce A. Baugh, *The Changing Supreme Court: Constitutional Rights and Liberties* (St. Paul, Minn.: West Publishing, 1997). © 1997. Reprinted with permission of Wadsworth, a division of Thomson Learning. Fax 800-730-2215.

held religious beliefs convinced him that capital punishment was morally wrong.[7] During his short tenure, Goldberg attempted, without much success, to persuade his colleagues that the death penalty was unconstitutional. Another Kennedy appointee, Justice Byron White, headed in the other direction. More often than not, White supported the government's position in criminal procedure and prisoners' rights cases, and his voting record became more conservative during his remaining years on the bench. Even without White, by 1962 the Court had a liberal majority consisting of Warren, Black, Douglas, Brennan, and Goldberg.

Justice Abe Fortas, who replaced Goldberg in 1965, was also a dependable vote for the liberal wing of the Court. He resigned from office in 1969, however, when it was reported that he received $20,000 in consulting fees from a foundation working for racial and religious cooperation.[8] Justice Thurgood Marshall, appointed in 1967, provided the reliable fifth vote for the liberal bloc, because Justice Black had begun to distance himself from the more controversial activist decisions of the Court. Over the years Marshall developed one of the most liberal voting records in criminal procedure and prisoners' rights cases. Both he and Justice Brennan would become the only sitting members of the Court who felt that the imposition of the death penalty in all circumstances was cruel and unusual punishment.

A NEW STANDARD FOR EIGHTH AMENDMENT VIOLATIONS

The Warren Court set the tone for its approach to the Eighth Amendment "cruel and unusual punishment" clause in *Trop v. Dulles* (1958). *Trop* and a companion case, *Perez v. Brownell* (1958), involved a challenge to sections of the Nationality Act (1940), which provided for a loss of citizenship in certain circumstances. Both cases were brought to the Court in the context of the anticommunist hysteria of the 1950s. In *Trop*, a citizen had deserted the U.S. Army while on duty in French Morocco during World War II; in *Perez*, a citizen had voted in a Mexican election. Both were expatriated for their actions without the benefit of a trial.

The Court had heard oral arguments a year earlier, but it was so badly divided that it scheduled reargument of the issues. Chief Justice Warren was firm in his belief that government could not take away citizenship for the commission of a crime, and he was concerned about the lack of due process afforded to the petitioners. Justices Harlan, Brennan, and Whittaker were less certain, and they switched their votes in conference, with Whittaker changing several times.[9] The voting alignments were so tenuous that Warren, writing for a plurality of the Court in *Trop*, had to delete a portion of his draft opinion that criticized military courts as improper forums for expatriation in order to keep Whittaker's support.[10] In the end, the Court upheld the punishment in *Perez* by deferring to the implied power of Congress to regulate foreign affairs, but in *Trop* found expatriation for desertion unconstitutional. Of the two cases, the *Trop* decision engendered the most controversy because of its reasoning and treatment of the Eighth Amendment.

Because of the split decisions, Warren first had to distinguish the case from *Perez*. He had two strategies available to him, and his choice says a lot about his approach to the Constitution and sense of fairness.[11] One option (used by Justice Brennan in his concurrence) was to distinguish between the use of congressional power in the two cases. Denationalization in *Trop* was based on the war power rather than on the power to regulate foreign affairs. Expatriation was used to maintain discipline and to deter soldiers from desertion. As Justice Brennan argued, however, there were other less punitive deterrents available, and there was no "rational relation" between expatriation and the legitimate purposes of the war power.

Warren chose not to follow Brennan's line of argument, based as it was on narrow legal distinctions. Instead he framed the issue as whether or not denationalization may be inflicted as punishment. Bypassing contrary legal history, Warren determined that deprivation of citizenship was punishment, not just a regulation governing the proper performance of military obligations, because it was imposed after the act of desertion took place. He concluded that denationalization as a form of punishment violated the Eighth Amendment.

At the time, the Court had conceded that the death penalty was not cruel and unusual punishment. This put Warren in an awkward position. By declaring expatriation cruel and unusual, Warren had to explain how denationalization of a citizen was a fate worse than death. He basically sidestepped the issue. Acknowledging that the death penalty did not violate the Eighth Amendment, Warren said that it was "equally plain that the existence of the death penalty is not a license to the Government to devise any punishment short of death within the limit of its imagination."[12] Though denationalization did not involve physical mistreatment or torture, Warren suggested that it was worse than such punishments because it destroyed the individual's status in the polity: "It is a form of punishment more primitive than torture, for it destroys for the individual the political existence that was centuries in the development. The punishment strips the citizen of his status in the national and international political community."[13]

Warren applied a flexible standard that rejected eighteenth-century notions of cruel and unusual punishments. He said that the concept underlying the Eighth Amendment is "nothing less than the dignity of man," and that the ban on cruel and unusual punishment "must draw its meaning from the evolving standards of decency that mark the progress of a maturing society."[14] Warren cited *Weems v. United States* (1910) for support, where Justice McKenna argued that the meaning of the Eighth Amendment is not "fastened to the obsolete but may acquire meaning as public opinion becomes enlightened by a humane justice."[15] This standard is more subjective in what the Eighth Amendment prohibits, and it forces the courts to make a judgment as to whether a certain punishment meets the standards of a civilized society. For Warren, it was the Court's responsibility to make that judgment. His opinion ends with a bold statement about the Court's obligation to judge congressional enactments "by the standards of the Constitution."[16]

In dissent, Justice Frankfurter warned the Court against encroaching beyond its proper bounds and emphasized deference to the power and judgment of Congress. He disagreed with Warren's theory equating denationalization with punishment. According to Frankfurter, "to insist that denationalization is cruel and unusual punishment is to stretch that concept beyond the breaking point."[17] Moreover, he had no patience for a constitutional argument that "seriously urged that loss of citizenship is a fate worse than death."[18]

The differences between Warren and Frankfurter went beyond the language of their opinions. On the day the *Trop* decision was announced, the tensions between the justices were made public. Court watcher Anthony Lewis described the remarks in the courtroom as "bitter, even waspish."[19] When Warren delivered the opinion of the Court, he argued that the Court's ruling was supported by 81 cases in which the Court had overturned congressional action, although the cases were not mentioned in the published opinion.[20] In presenting his dissenting opinion, Frankfurter caustically remarked that the 81 cases were "nothing to boast about," and he pointed out that "many of the decisions had since been overruled."[21] These comments were not part of his published opinion. The *Trop* decision illustrates how far apart Warren and Frankfurter were in their judicial philosophy and professional relationship.

"STATUS" CRIMES RULED CRUEL AND UNUSUAL

In *Robinson v. California* (1962), the Court struck down a California statute that made it a criminal offense to be addicted to drugs. Two Los Angeles police officers had noticed discolorations and numerous needle marks on Robinson's arm. The officers concluded that this was evidence of drug use. Robinson denied the allegations. He was neither under the influence nor suffering withdrawal symptoms when the officers confronted him. Regardless, Robinson was arrested and charged under the state law. The trial judge instructed the jury that the law made it a misdemeanor for a person "either to use narcotics, or to be addicted to the use of narcotics." Robinson was convicted and faced a minimum of 90 days in jail, but it was not clear which charge the jury used to reach a verdict.

The state supreme court upheld Robinson's conviction, and he appealed. At the conference on April 20, 1962, Justices Black, Clark, and White voted to affirm. Justice Harlan had written a memo to the conference in November urging the Court to accept jurisdiction because he believed that "punishing in this manner of the status of being a drug addict raises serious constitutional questions."[22] At the April conference, however, he was now leaning toward affirmance. Four justices—Warren, Brennan, Stewart, and Douglas—voted to reverse. In a calculated move, Warren assigned the opinion to Stewart, in the hope that he would write a moderate draft that would pick up at least a fifth vote.[23] The strategy worked. By the time the Court announced its decision, both Harlan and Black voted to overturn the state law, with Harlan writing a concurring opinion. Only Justices Clark and White dissented in the case. Justice Frankfurter did not vote on the merits in conference because he had retired at the end of the 1961 term.

Finding a violation of due process, Justice Stewart concluded that the law amounted to cruel and unusual punishment. Comparing drug addiction to mental illness and venereal disease, he said that a

state law which imprisons a person thus afflicted as a criminal, even though he has never touched any narcotic drug within the State or been guilty of any irregular behavior there, inflicts a cruel and unusual punishment in violation of the Fourteenth Amendment.[24]

He pointed out that narcotic addiction is an illness that can be contracted innocently or involuntarily, especially if the mother of a newborn child is a drug addict. "To be sure, imprisonment for ninety days is not, in the abstract, a punishment which is either cruel or unusual," Stewart admitted. "But the question cannot be considered in the abstract. Even one day in prison would be a cruel and unusual punishment for the 'crime' of having a cold."[25] As if to emphasize the limited nature of the holding, Stewart ended his opinion by saying that the case deals "only with an individual provision of a particularized local law as it has so far been interpreted by the California courts."[26] He reassured state law enforcement officials that they retained many options in their efforts to combat the evils of drug addiction.

In a concurring opinion, Justice Douglas devoted more attention to the history of the Eighth Amendment and why drug addiction should not be considered a crime. Characterizing drug addiction as an illness, he cited medical studies, government reports, the Council on Mental Health recommendations, and practices in Great Britain to support his contention that narcotics addiction should not be criminalized. He argued that "the principle that would deny power to exact capital punishment for a petty crime would also deny power to punish a person by fine or imprisonment for being sick."[27] Douglas stated that the addict is a sick person who "may be confined for treatment or the protection of society." The California law amounts to cruel and unusual punishment not from confinement, "but from convicting the addict of a crime."[28] The purpose of the law is to punish the addict rather than to provide a cure for the illness. Describing Robinson's conviction as a "barbarous action," Douglas warned that society "would forget the teachings of the Eighth Amendment if we allowed sickness to be made a crime and permitted sick people to be punished for being sick."[29]

In dissent, Justice Clark argued that the law must be placed in perspective by viewing the statute as part of a "comprehensive and enlightened program for the control of narcotism based on the overriding policy of prevention and cure."[30] He disagreed with the majority's characterization of the law. According to Clark, the "criminal" provision under which Robinson was convicted was designed to cure the less seriously addicted person by preventing further use. Another provision in the law, which the majority suggested was valid, provided for civil commitment in a hospital for addicts who have lost the power of self-control. For Clark, both provisions offered treatment for different levels of addiction, only the means of treatment varied. He argued that the majority erred in instructing the state that "hospitalization is the *only treatment* for narcotics addiction—that anything less is a punishment denying due process."[31] Clark felt that the law provided treatment rather than a punishment, but even if interpreted as penal, he said "the sanction of incarceration for 3 to 12 months is not unreasonable when applied to a person who has voluntarily placed himself in a condition posing a serious threat to the State."[32]

Justice White's dissenting opinion was more critical in attacking the rationale of the Court. Admitting that if Robinson's conviction "rested upon sheer status, condition or illness, or if he was convicted for being an addict who had lost his power of self-control" he might have decided otherwise, White said that the record supported none of those situations.[33] He criticized the Court for not construing state laws in a manner that would uphold their constitutionality, and he was concerned about the consequences of the holding. If it was cruel and unusual punishment to convict Robinson for addiction, "It is difficult to understand why it would be any less offensive to the Fourteenth Amendment to convict him for use [of narcotics] on the same evidence."[34] Justice White could not understand why the Court found "it more appropriate to write into the Constitution its own abstract notions of how best to handle the narcotics problem, for it obviously cannot match either the States or Congress in expert understanding."[35]

The *Robinson* decision formally incorporated the Eighth Amendment cruel and unusual punishment clause to the states, but that was not its only significance. The decision expanded traditional categories of actions that violate the Eighth Amendment. A punishment may be deemed cruel and unusual, not because of the methods used or its proportion to the offense but because the mere fact of punishment may be so inherently cruel as to be unconstitutional. The opinion did not apply to antisocial behavior resulting from a drug addiction. Justice White's concern that the holding would prevent the states and the federal government from criminalizing narcotics use under any circumstances was not realized.

JUSTICE GOLDBERG ARGUES AGAINST THE DEATH PENALTY

One year later, three justices expressed support for expanding the application of the cruel and unusual punishment clause to death penalty cases. During the summer of 1963, Justice Goldberg was reviewing six certiorari petitions involving capital punishment. The cases themselves did not address the constitutionality of capital punishment but instead raised procedural questions such as effectiveness of counsel and race bias in sentencing. For example, the issue in *Rudolph v. Alabama* (1963), an interracial rape case, was whether the defendant's confession was voluntary. Though this case did not directly confront the race issue, some lawyers were considering legal challenges to the death penalty based on equal protection claims because there was a pattern of race discrimination in rape cases. Southern juries usually sentenced to death black defendants who allegedly raped white women, while white rapists or blacks whose victims were black received only a prison sentence.[36] The statistics are disturbing. Between 1930 and 1960, nearly 450 Americans were executed for rape, and almost 90 percent were black.[37]

Before the conference on whether the Court would grant certiorari, Justice Goldberg circulated a memo to his colleagues notifying them that he would raise this question: "Whether and under what circumstances, the imposition of the death penalty is proscribed by the Eighth and Fourteenth Amendments to the U.S. Constitution?"[38] The issue was not raised by the attorneys in their briefs, but Goldberg urged the Court to consider the question because he believed that the "evolving standards of decency that mark the progress of [our] maturing society" now made the death penalty unconstitutional. In support of his argument, Goldberg cited reports on the status of capital punishment in other countries, public opinion polls, scholarly analyses, and court decisions.[39]

Most of the justices were appalled by Goldberg's memo, complaining that it violated institutional norms and exceeded the Court's authority. A majority of the justices rejected his suggestion and refused to accept *Rudolph, Snider v. Cunningham* (1963), and the other cases for review. Justice Goldberg, however, joined by Douglas and Brennan, commented in a rare dissent from denial of certiorari that executing a man for rape "who has neither taken nor endangered human life" might constitute cruel and unusual punishment. Noting that only five countries made rape a capital offense, Goldberg suggested that the death penalty violates "evolving standards of decency" that are "more or less universally accepted," and he urged the Court to consider whether capital punishment for rape might not be excessively severe under the Eighth Amendment.[40] He asked whether the goals of punishment (deterrence, isolation, rehabilitation) could be achieved as effectively by punishing rape with a less severe penalty, such as life imprisonment.[41] If there were effective alternatives, Goldberg wondered whether the death penalty for rape might constitute "unnecessary cruelty."[42]

Goldberg's opinion was intended as a signal to lawyers to challenge the constitutionality of the death penalty in their appeals.[43] Some took up the challenge. The ACLU, for example, publicly renounced capital punishment in 1965 and began a legal campaign against state death penalty statutes and convictions. Lawyers for the NAACP Legal Defense Fund also intensified efforts to bring legal challenges in capital punishment cases.[44] The LDF hired Anthony Amsterdam, a former federal prosecutor and law clerk to Justice Felix Frankfurter, to lead the legal assault on the death penalty. Amsterdam and his lawyers focused their early efforts on cases in which black defendants had received the death penalty for raping white women because the statistical evidence of racial bias was overwhelming.[45] But Goldberg's dissent in *Rudolph* did not raise the issue of racial discrimination in the application of the death penalty in rape cases. Lawyers who followed the Court closely interpreted that to mean that the legal environment was not ready for a constitutional challenge on those grounds.[46] In fact, it would take fourteen years for the Court to declare that capital punishment was disproportionate for the crime of rape.[47]

EXPANDING ACCESS TO THE COURTS

The Warren Court made it easier for state and federal prisoners to sue in the federal courts for rights violations. In *United States v. Muniz* (1963), the Court held that federal prisoners may sue under the Federal Tort Claims Act (FTCA) to recover damages from the U.S. government for personal injuries suffered during confinement and resulting from the negligent actions of prison personnel. Though brought by the government as a single case, the *Muniz* litigation involved two separate suits for personal injuries filed by Henry Winston and Carlos Muniz. The district judge dismissed both suits on the grounds that such suits were not permitted by the FTCA. The Court of Appeals for the Second Circuit, sitting *en banc*, reversed.

Winston was confined in the United States Penitentiary at Terra Haute in April 1959. He began suffering from dizziness, loss of balance, and problems with his vision.[48] Winston complained about his condition to prison officials. A prison medical officer diagnosed his illness as border-line hypertension and recommended losing weight. Winston's symptoms became more severe over the next nine months. He regularly complained to prison officials but was denied further treatment, except for some Dramamine for his dizziness. Winston's attorney became so alarmed by his condition that he had him examined by an outside physician. In 1960, an operation removed a benign brain tumor that had been the cause of all the symptoms, although Winston did not regain his vision.[49]

Muniz was a prisoner in the federal correctional institution in Danbury, Connecticut. One afternoon in August 1959, he was outside a prison dormitory when he was struck by an inmate and then pursued by twelve other inmates into another dormitory.[50] Instead of breaking up the altercation, a prison guard locked the dormitory. Beaten with chairs and sticks until he was unconscious, Muniz sustained a fractured skull and lost vision in one eye. He alleged that prison officials were negligent by not providing enough guards to prevent the assault that led to his injuries and by permitting prisoners, some of whom were mentally unstable, to intermingle without adequate guard supervision.[51]

In a unanimous opinion written by Chief Justice Warren, Justice Byron White not participating, the Court held that federal prisoners can sue for damages under the FTCA. In looking at both the text of the statute and the legislative history of the act, Warren concluded that Congress intended to permit such suits. On its face, the act did not preclude lawsuits by federal prisoners, because they were not among the exceptions under the law. Warren also pointed out that there were six bills introduced in Congress between 1925 and 1946 that "either barred prisoners from suing while in federal prison or precluded suit upon any claim for injury to or death of a prisoner."[52] Those exceptions, however, were not included in the act, and the Court determined that Congress deliberately, rather than inadvertently, omitted such language.

The government tried to argue that prisoner suits would not only be costly but also would undermine prison discipline and security. Warren was not convinced that the federal prison system would be disrupted by tort suits, however. He wrote:

We are also reluctant to believe that the possible abuses stemming from prisoners' suits are so serious that all chance of recovery should be denied. It is possible, as the Government suggests, that frivolous suits will be brought, designed only to harass or, more sinister, discover details of prison security useful in planning an escape. . . . It is also possible that litigation will damage prison discipline, as the Government most vigorously argues. However, we have been shown no evidence that these possibilities have become actualities in the many

States allowing suits against jailers, or the smaller number allowing recovery directly against the States themselves.[53]

Though important, the *Muniz* decision had a limited impact on prisoners' rights, because states incarcerate most offenders. A year later, the Court would expand access to the federal courts for state prisoners as well.

In *Monroe v. Pape* (1961), the Court revived Section 1983 of the Civil Rights Act of 1871. Passed by Congress during the period of Reconstruction, the law enabled blacks to sue on constitutional issues in federal courts, thus bypassing prejudiced state courts. The *Monroe* decision provided a basis for *Cooper v. Pate* (1964), a *per curium* decision with a broad impact because it sanctioned the use of 42 U.S.C. Section 1983 by prisoners in suits against prison officials. In *Cooper*, prison officials denied a group of Black Muslim prisoners their right to associate for religious purposes and to purchase religious publications. The prisoners brought an action under Section 1983, claiming a violation of their civil rights. The District Court dismissed the case and the Court of Appeals affirmed. Without discussing the merits of the case, the Supreme Court reversed, stating that it was an error to dismiss the cause of action.[54] The case was noteworthy because it represented the first time that the Court sanctioned the use of Section 1983 of the Civil Rights Act in prisoner civil rights litigation. By the end of the decade, the federal courts decided more than 2,000 Section 1983 suits a year, and that number would ultimately rise to over 39,000 in 1995.

THE LEADERSHIP OF CHIEF JUSTICE WARREN

As he did in other areas of the Constitution, Chief Justice Warren often used his strong personality and communication skills to convince his colleagues to accept his vision of fairness and due process for prisoners. *Brooks v. Florida* (1967) is a good example. Warren's law clerk, Tyrone Brown, had noticed a number of petitions on the miscellaneous docket coming in from the Raiford State Prison in Florida. From the various petitions, Brown learned that a food riot by black inmates had occurred at the prison. Following the riot, Brooks and the others involved were stripped naked and held in barren punishment cells for more than two weeks. Their daily diet consisted of twelve ounces of thin soup and eight ounces of water.[55] One by one, Brooks and the others were led naked past snapping guard dogs to an interrogation room where they signed confessions to mayhem and rioting.[56] The confession was used to convict Brooks. The state court affirmed the conviction, and Brooks filed an *in forma pauperis* petition for certiorari.

At the conference, the justices voted 8 to 1 to oppose granting certiorari on the grounds that the issue was a matter of internal prison discipline. Warren was the lone dissenter. According to Brown, Warren was so upset that he broke a personal rule and wrote a dissent from denial of certiorari.[57] Warren prepared an outline and asked Brown to fill in the details. Brown completed several drafts, but the chief justice kept telling his young clerk, "That's not strong enough. Doggone it! If those guys do not want to take this case, I want to be sure that every gruesome detail is recorded in those books up there [referring to the Supreme Court Reports] for posterity."[58] Finally, Warren was satisfied with the language, and he circulated his strongly worded dissent on November 9, 1967. Over the next month, the justices one by one switched their vote and joined the dissent. What was once an 8-to-1 vote to *deny* certiorari became a 9-to-0 vote for summary reversal of the convictions for rioting, without oral argument. In a short *per curium* opinion issued on December 18, 1967, the Court stated that the "record in this case documents a shocking display of barbarism which should not escape the remedial action of this Court."[59] Though only a few paragraphs long, the opinion described the abusive treatment that Brooks and his fellow inmates received from the guards in the Raiford Prison. Warren's leadership and determination made the difference.

COUNSEL MUST BE PROVIDED AT PROBATION REVOCATION HEARING

Freshman Justice Thurgood Marshall wrote his first opinion for the Court in *Mempa v. Rhay* (1967). On the advice of his court-appointed lawyer, Mempa pled guilty to the offense of "joyriding." He was placed on probation for two years on the condition that he first spend 30 days in jail.[60] Several months later, the local prosecutor moved to have Mempa's probation revoked on the ground that he had been involved in a burglary. Mempa, who was 17 years old, appeared with his stepfather at the revocation hearing in October 1959. He did not have a lawyer and was not asked whether he wanted to have the same court-appointed counsel that he had had for the initial proceedings to represent him at the hearing.

Mempa admitted that he had been involved in the alleged burglary. Without asking the young man whether he had anything to say or any evidence to bring to the attention of the court, the judge immediately revoked his probation and sentenced him to ten years in the penitentiary.[61] The trial judge then told Mempa that he would recommend to the parole board that he only serve one year. In 1965, Mempa filed a habeas corpus petition claiming that he had been denied his right to counsel at the hearing where his probation was revoked and ten-year sentence was imposed. The Washington Supreme Court denied his petition, so Mempa asked the Court to review his case.

At the conference on whether to grant review, the four liberal justices—Fortas, Douglas, Black, and Warren—agreed to take the case. Between the decision to grant certiorari and the conference following oral arguments, Thurgood Marshall had replaced Tom Clark. The vote on the merits in the case was 8 to 1 to reverse, with only Justice Black affirming, and the Court's newest member, Thurgood Marshall, was given the task of drafting the majority opinion.

Marshall argued that a plea of guilty is sometimes improperly obtained by the promise to have a defendant placed on probation. When the probation is revoked, the defendant may wish to withdraw the plea, but without the assistance of counsel may not be aware of this opportunity. Marshall's opinion was convincing enough to prompt Justice Black to change his vote. In a memo to Marshall on November 9, 1967, Black stated that he originally voted to affirm "on the assumption that the probation here was separate and apart from sentencing," but was "now persuaded by [Marshall's] analysis that the so-called probation was in reality a deferred sentence upon the imposition of which [Mempa] was entitled to a lawyer."[62] Justice Black's vote change did not impact the outcome, but *Mempa* illustrates how a well-written opinion can persuade some justices to rethink their view of a case.

COURT REFUSES TO EXTEND *ROBINSON* HOLDING

In a case raising issues similar to those in *Robinson*, a divided Court in *Powell v. Texas* (1968) refused to overturn the conviction of an alcoholic for public drunkenness. LeRoy Powell had been convicted and fined $20 under a Texas statute that provided "Whoever shall get drunk or be found in a state of intoxication in any public place, or at any private house except his own, shall be fined not exceeding one hundred dollars."[63] Powell appealed his conviction on the grounds that his drunken behavior was "not of his own volition," because he was "afflicted with the disease of chronic alcoholism" and therefore to punish him would be a violation of the Eighth Amendment.[64] Powell had been convicted of the offense approximately 100 times. A trial judge in the county court held that as a matter of law, chronic alcoholism was not a defense to the charge of public drunkenness.

The vote was 5 to 4 in conference to reverse, with Justices Fortas, White, Stewart, Brennan, and Douglas in the majority. Chief Justice Warren and Justice Black urged affirmance on the grounds that the case was different from *Robinson* because Powell was not convicted for merely being an alcoholic but for being drunk in a public place. They were joined by Harlan and Marshall. Fortas was assigned the majority opinion and circulated a first draft on April 23. According to David Rosenbloom, one of Fortas's law clerks, the justice had strong feelings about the case, and the opinion reflected his concern for the poor and disadvantaged.[65] Initial drafts of the majority opinion tried to show that alcoholism was in fact a disease. Fortas referred to numerous medical and sociological studies that suggested that alcoholism was a disease, but he did not stop there. He based the decision squarely upon the *Robinson* precedent.

Fortas, who was not known for pressuring his colleagues, lobbied hard to keep the narrow majority. Justice White was struggling with the case. He suggested numerous changes to the draft opinion, and Fortas incorporated every one of them.[66] But in a memo to the conference on May 8, White informed Fortas that "I am with you part way but I am leaving you in other respects and in the result, the upshot being that I do not join your opinion or those on the other side either."[67] In his memo he said that he had "been back and forth for weeks but it is more than likely that I am at rest, at least for now."[68] White's indecisiveness is surprising, given his strong dissenting opinion in *Robinson*. Because of his vote change, Warren assigned the opinion to Marshall, who took up the task of writing a judgment for the Court. Warren, aware of the slim majority, was so concerned that the opinion be written properly that he assigned one of his own law clerks to assist Marshall and his clerks in the opinion. Warren and his clerk met Marshall on several occasions to discuss the language of the opinion, and Warren even took part in writing a portion of the draft opinion himself.[69] Marshall's plurality opinion, announced on June 17, 1968, was joined by Warren, Black, and Harlan. White ended up writing an opinion concurring in the result, while Fortas recast his original majority opinion as a dissent.

Although the trial court found that "chronic alcoholism" is a disease, Marshall refused to extend the *Robinson* rationale to Powell's condition. He began the opinion by criticizing the "findings" of the trial court and pointing out that the medical community was divided on the question of whether alcoholism was a disease. Marshall argued that the case was different from *Robinson*, because Texas "has not sought to punish a mere status, as California did in *Robinson*; nor has it attempted to regulate appellant's behavior in the privacy of his home. Rather, it has imposed upon appellant a criminal sanction for public behavior which may create substantial health and safety hazards."[70] Marshall was troubled by the potential consequences of extending *Robinson* and articulating a general constitutional doctrine of *mens rea*.[71] If Powell could not be convicted of public intoxication, "it is difficult to see how a State can convict an individual for murder, if that individual, while exhibiting normal behavior in all other respects, suffers from a 'compulsion' to kill, which is an 'exceedingly strong influence,' but not completely overpowering."[72] According to Marshall, "traditional common-law concepts of personal accountability and essential considerations of federalism" must lead the Court to reject Powell's arguments.[73] The process of reconciling the evolving aims of criminal law and changing philosophical, religious, and medical views of the nature of man is best left to the states.

Justice Black, joined by Harlan, agreed with Marshall's opinion but wrote separately to expound on his reasoning. He accused the dissenters of trying to create a constitutional barrier by relying on their own preferences about the wisdom of the law, and he described their arguments as reading "more like a highly technical medical critique than an argument for deciding a question of constitutional law."[74] Like Marshall, Black distinguished the facts of the case from *Robinson* and expressed a desire to leave the issue to the judgment of local lawmakers. In a separate concurring opinion, Justice White acknowledged that the Eighth Amendment might forbid Powell's conviction for public drunkenness, "but only on a record satisfactorily showing that it was not feasible for him to have made arrangements to prevent his being in public when drunk and that his extreme drunkenness sufficiently deprived him of his faculties on the occasion issue."[75] White determined that Powell made no showing that he was unable to stay off the streets on the night in question, thus his conviction did not violate the Constitution.

Justice Fortas, joined by Douglas, Brennan, and Stewart, authored the dissenting opinion. Contrary to what the Court concluded, he stressed that the issue posed in the case was a narrow one; there was no threat to public intoxication statutes in general or to the particular Texas law. In his view, the case dealt with the mere *condition* of being intoxicated in public. Fortas spent the bulk of his opinion discussing the problem of alcoholism and citing medical and psychological evidence to support the notion that chronic alcoholism was a disease. He admitted that Powell's crime was different from Robinson's in that the Texas law covered more than a mere status. Yet Fortas found the constitutional defects in the cases similar, because "in both cases the particular defendant was accused of being in a condition which he had no capacity to change or avoid."[76] He concluded that the imposition of a criminal penalty for public drunkenness violated the cruel and unusual punishment clause of the Eighth Amendment.

GUARANTEEING EQUAL PROTECTION AND ACCESS TO LEGAL SERVICES

Several decisions in the last few terms of the Warren Court expanded equal protection and due process for prisoners. For example, in *Lee v. Washington* (1968), the Court unanimously affirmed a lower Court decision that Alabama statutes requiring the segregation of the races in prisons and jails violated the Fourteenth Amendment. Justices Stewart,

Black, and Harlan, however, refused to sign the *per curium* opinion, because they felt that racial segregation may be necessary in some circumstances to maintain discipline. In a memo to Justice White on February 5, 1968, Justice Black wrote that he favored "an opinion that clearly shows that there are circumstances under which Wardens may consider racial matters in connection with racial strife in prisons."[77] Justices Black, Harlan, and Stewart did not feel that the per curium opinion made it clear that some discretion remained with prison authorities in segregating inmates by race. In a concurrence to the per curium, they emphasized that "prison authorities have the right, acting in good faith and in particularized circumstances, to take into account racial tensions in maintaining security, discipline, and good order in prisons and jails."[78]

In *Johnson v. Avery* (1969), the Court ruled that unless prison officials provide reasonable legal assistance to inmates, they cannot prohibit "writ writers" from helping others with their legal claims.[79] Johnson, a prisoner in the Tennessee State Penitentiary, challenged a prison regulation that prohibited inmates from assisting other prisoners in preparing legal claims.[80] The District Court ruled that the regulation was unconstitutional because it denied illiterate prisoners access to federal habeas corpus. The Court of Appeals, however, reversed, concluding that the regulation did not violate the federal right of habeas corpus. In deference to prison administrators, the Sixth Circuit said that "the interest of the State in preserving prison discipline and in limiting the practice of law to licensed attorneys justified whatever burden the regulation might place on access to federal habeas corpus."[81]

At conference, six justices, including Chief Justice Warren, voted to reverse the Sixth Circuit decision. Only Justices Fortas and Black voted to affirm, while Justice White passed on his vote. Fortas, however, changed his mind shortly after the conference vote and ended up writing the majority opinion. Internal court documents do not clearly reveal why Fortas switched in favor of reversing the lower court. In his conference notes, Justice Brennan wrote that Fortas felt that the regulation was "cruel and unusual punishment, but the case was not argued on that issue."[82] As it turned out, Fortas based the decision on both due process and equal protection grounds, even though he fails to use the specific language of either constitutional provision.

Fortas began his opinion by emphasizing the importance of habeas corpus within our constitutional framework. Because the purpose of the writ is for those unlawfully incarcerated to obtain their freedom, he declared that it is "fundamental that access of prisoners to the courts for the purpose of presenting their complaints may not be denied or obstructed."[83] Tennessee tried to argue that the regulation against inmate-to-inmate legal assistance was necessary to maintain prison discipline. While recognizing that states are responsible for the orderly administration of prison facilities, Fortas asserted that when regulations conflict with fundamental constitutional or statutory rights, they may be invalidated. By adopting the prohibition on legal assistance, without providing alternative sources of legal aid for prisoners, Fortas contended that the state effectively denied illiterate or poorly educated prisoners access to habeas corpus. He compared the Tennessee practice to policies in other states, where public defenders are made available to consult with prisoners regarding their habeas corpus petitions or local bar members make periodic visits to the prison to discuss legal options with prisoners.[84]

In a dissenting opinion, Justice White, joined by Justice Black, conceded that habeas corpus should not be denied simply because one is indigent or ignorant. However, White placed more emphasis on the quality of legal assistance provided by "writ writers" and the burdens placed on the criminal justice system. He was very critical of an unregulated jailhouse lawyer system, expressing doubt that "the problem of the indigent convict will be solved by subjecting him to the false hopes, dominance, and inept representation of the average unsupervised jailhouse lawyer."[85] Justice White concluded that the "disciplinary problems are severe, the burden on the courts serious, and the disadvantages of prisoner clients of the jailhouse lawyer unacceptable."[86]

THE WARREN COURT AND PRISONERS' RIGHTS: AN ASSESSMENT

At first glance, the record of the Warren Court in prisoners' rights cases may seem insignificant. There were only a handful of decisions, and several of them were short *per curium* opinions. But the number and length of the decisions obscure the impact that the Warren Court had in this area of the Constitution. The opinions of the Court contributed little to the substantive nature of prisoners' rights, but they extended due process protections and expanded access to the courts. The decision in *Trop v. Dulles* (1958) provided a flexible standard for Eighth Amendment violations that continues to be applied by the courts. In *Robinson v. California* (1962), the Court grappled with the meaning of the Eighth Amendment in noncapital cases and formally incorporated the cruel and unusual punishment clause to the states. In *Lee v. Washington* (1968) and *Johnson v. Avery* (1969) the Court extended equal protection guarantees to prisoners and helped secure access to legal services, albeit by "writ writers." In *Cooper v. Pate* (1964) and *United States v. Muniz* (1963), the Court permitted state and federal prisoners to sue in the federal courts for rights violations. This led to a spate of prisoner litigation in the 1970s and a concomitant increase in federal court supervision of prison practices. The next chapter describes how the Court under Chief Justice Warren Burger responded to these claims.

Before we turn to the decisions of the Burger Court, a question remains concerning the record of the Warren Court in prisoners' rights cases. Why did the Court fail to take the lead in advancing constitutional protections for those incarcerated in America's prisons, as it did in promoting racial equality and due process guarantees for criminal defendants? There are several possible explanations, and any or all of them may explain the Court's behavior. First, the Court came under a lot of criticism for its school desegregation, school prayer, and criminal procedure decisions during the 1960s. The justices may have wanted to avoid further controversy by not tinkering with death penalty statutes or intervening extensively in the administration of prisons. Chief Justice Warren's response to Goldberg's lobbying effort in the death penalty cases provides some support for this explanation. Justice Douglas summed up Warren's view as "It would be best to let the matter sleep for a while."[87]

Another explanation is that a majority of justices may have been concerned about guaranteeing fairness and due process in criminal trials, but once a defendant was convicted, there was not as much support for scrutinizing prison practices and conditions. The hands-off approach to prison administration was still strong among the conservative justices, and even the more moderate members of the Court were sensitive to federalism and separation of powers issues. Most of the substantive decisions of the Warren Court were not handed down until the late 1960s. Even if a majority of the justices was inclined to take a more active role in advancing prisoners' rights, the election of Richard Nixon and the appointment of four conservative justices in the span of a few years abruptly altered the voting alignments of the Court. It would take a few years, but the Nixon appointees would help move the Court in a more conservative direction in prisoners' rights cases. Finally, the Constitution provides fewer opportunities to examine the treatment of inmates and prison conditions. Both defendants and prisoners may raise due process and equal protection claims, but criminal defendants simply have more constitutional safeguards under the Bill of Rights than do prisoners. The Fourth Amendment prohibition against unreasonable searches and seizures, the Fifth Amendment protection against double jeopardy and self-incrimination, and the Sixth Amendment guarantee of a speedy and public trial, an impartial jury, the right to confront witnesses, and the assistance of counsel provides more opportunities for the Court to review state and federal criminal justice procedures, from arrest through prosecution. Compared to the numerous constitutional protections for individuals accused of a crime, the only constitutional provision that deals specifically with the rights of prisoners is the Eighth Amendment.

NOTES

1. The lobbying effort consisted of Frankfurter submitting notes, memoranda, articles, and books to Warren in order to persuade him to adopt a posture of judicial restraint. See Bernard Schwartz, "Felix Frankfurter and Earl Warren: A Study of a Deteriorating Relationship," in *The Supreme Court Review*, Philip P. Kurland and Gerhard Casper, eds. (Chicago: University of Chicago Press, 1980), 117.

2. Henry J. Abraham, *Justices and Presidents: A Political History of Appointments to the Supreme Court*, 3rd ed. (New York: Oxford University Press, 1992), 256.

3. Ibid., 118.

4. Ibid., 122.

5. Jeffrey A. Segal and Harold J. Spaeth, *The Supreme Court and the Attitudinal Model* (New York: Cambridge University Press, 1993), 245.

6. Ibid., 246.

7. Michael Meltsner, *Cruel and Unusual: The Supreme Court and Capital Punishment* (New York: Random House, 1973), 32.

8. Fortas terminated his relationship with the Wolfson Family Foundation during his first year on the Court and returned the $20,000. He denied any wrongdoing but felt that the controversy hurt the image of the Court and decided that it was best to resign. See David M. O'Brien, *Storm Center: The Supreme Court in American Politics* (New York: W. W. Norton, 1996), 119–120.

9. See Ed Cray, *Chief Justice: A Biography of Earl Warren* (New York: Simon and Schuster, 1997), 358.

10. Ibid. Warren's draft opinion emphasized that civilian courts were the proper tribunals for determining loss of citizenship:

If the priceless right of citizenship is ever to be forfeited in a trial, it should be in a civilian court of justice, where all Bill of Rights protections guard the fairness of the outcome. Military courts are to try soldiers for military crimes and impose punishments that do not encroach on purely civilian rights. Who is worthy of continued enjoyment of citizenship is not the constitutional concern of the Army. Its business is to fight wars.

11. G. Edward White, *The American Judicial Tradition* (New York: Oxford University Press, 1988), 348.

12. *Trop v. Dulles*, 356 U.S. 86 (1958), 99.

13. Ibid., 101.

14. Ibid.

15. *Weems v. United States*, 217 U.S. 349 (1910), 378.

16. Ibid., 103.

17. Ibid., Frankfurter dissenting, 125.

18. Ibid.

19. Schwartz, "Felix Frankfurter and Earl Warren," 129.

20. Ibid.

21. Ibid.

22. See Bernard Schwartz, *Super Chief: Earl Warren and His Supreme Court* (New York: New York University Press, 1983), 438.

23. Ibid., 439.

24. *Robinson v. California*, 370 U.S. 660 (1962), 667.

25. Ibid.

26. Ibid., 668.

27. Ibid., Douglas concurring, 676.

28. Ibid.

29. Ibid., 678.

30. Ibid., Clark dissenting, 679.

31. *Robinson*, 682. Italics in original opinion.

32. Ibid., 685.

33. Ibid., White dissenting, 685.

34. Ibid., 688.

35. Ibid., 689.

36. Meltsner, *Cruel and Unusual*, 75–77.

37. Edward Lazarus, *Closed Chambers: The First Eyewitness Account of the Epic Struggles inside the Supreme Court* (New York: Times Books, 1998), 89.

38. Lee Epstein and Joseph Kobylka, *The Supreme Court and Legal Change: Abortion and the Death Penalty* (Chapel Hill: University of North Carolina Press, 1992), 42.

39. Ibid., 43.

40. Quoted in Harold Spaeth, *The Warren Court: Cases and Commentary* (San Francisco: Chandler, 1966), 348.

41. *Rudolph v. Alabama*, 375 U.S. 889 (1963), 891.

42. Ibid.

43. Justice Goldberg's law clerk mailed copies of the opinion to lawyers and interest groups working on behalf of prisoners. See Epstein and Kobylka, *The Supreme Court and Legal Change*, 43.

44. For a firsthand account written by one of the LDF attorneys, see Meltsner, *Cruel and Unusual*.

45. Lazarus, *Closed Chambers*, 90.

46. Ibid., 29.

47. *Coker v. Georgia*, 433 U.S. 548 (1977).

48. *United States v. Muniz*, 374 U.S. 150 (1963), 151.

49. Ibid.

50. Ibid., 152.

51. Ibid.

52. Ibid., 156.

53. Ibid., 162–163.

54. *Cooper v. Pate*, 378 U.S. 546 (1964).

55. *Brooks v. Florida*, 389 U.S. 413 (1967).

56. See Cray, *Chief Justice*, 446.

57. Ibid.

58. Quoted in Schwartz, *Super Chief*, 719.

59. *Brooks v. Florida*, 389 U.S. 413 (1967), 414.

60. *Mempa v. Rhay*, 389 U.S. 128 (1967).

61. Ibid., 129.

62. Marshall Papers, Library of Congress, conference notes in *Mempa v. Rhay*, 389 U.S. 128 (1967).

63. *Powell v. Texas*, 392 U.S. 514 (1968), 517.

64. Ibid.

65. This account is taken from Laura Kalman, *Abe Fortas: A Biography* (New Haven, Conn.: Yale University Press, 1990), 257–258.

66. Ibid., 259.

67. Brennan Papers, Library of Congress, case file of *Powell v. Texas* (1968).

68. Brennan Papers, case file of *Powell v. Texas*.

69. This account is taken from Bernard Schwartz's biography of Warren, *Super Chief*, 694.

70. *Powell v. Texas*, 532.

71. *Mens rea* means a guilty mind or criminal intent.

72. *Powell v. Texas*, 534.

73. Ibid., 535.

74. Ibid., Black concurring, 539.

75. Ibid., White concurring, 552.

76. Ibid., Fortas dissenting, 568.

77. Brennan Papers, Library of Congress, case file of *Lee v. Washington* (1968).

78. *Lee v. Washington*, 390 U.S. 333 (1968).

79. *Johnson v. Avery*, 393 U.S. 483 (1969).

80. The prison regulation stated:

No inmate will advise, assist, or otherwise contract to aid another, either with or without a fee, to prepare Writs or other legal matters. It is not intended that an innocent man be punished. When a man believes that he is unlawfully held or illegally convicted, he should prepare a brief or state his complaint in letter form and address it to his lawyer or a judge. A formal Writ is not necessary to receive a hearing. False charges or untrue complaints may be punished. Inmates are forbidden to set themselves up as practitioners for the purpose of promoting a business of writing Writs. *Johnson v. Avery*, 393 U.S. 483 (1969), 484.

81. *Avery v. Johnson*, 382 F.2d 353 (1967).

82. Brennan Papers, Library of Congress, conference notes from case file of *Johnson v. Avery* (1969).

83. Majority opinion, *Johnson v. Avery*, 393 U.S. 483 (1969), 485.

84. Ibid., 489.

85. Dissenting opinion, *Johnson v. Avery*, 501.

86. Ibid., 499.

87. *The Douglas Letters*, Melvin Urofsky, ed. (Bethesda, Md.: Adler and Adler, 1987). Quoted in Lazarus, *Closed Chambers*, 88.

Chapter 5

The Burger Court and Prisoners' Rights, 1969–1986

This chapter focuses on the 1970s and the 1980s, a period when the federal courts began to intervene actively in the administration of prisons. Confronted with evidence of horrendous living conditions, abusive guard practices, and inadequate services, district court judges ordered changes in the physical condition of prison facilities, the treatment of inmates, staffing, food and medical care, and prison overcrowding. Initially, the decisions of the Burger Court supported the expansion of prisoners' rights. These decisions protected the religious freedom of prisoners, mail privileges, and due process guarantees in disciplinary actions, and held state death penalty statutes unconstitutional. By 1975, however, Chief Justice Burger and other members of the Court were openly concerned about the scope and volume of prison reform cases. Consequently, the Court began to restrict federal court involvement in prison and jail reform and reinstated state death penalty laws. In some cases the Court refused to address the First Amendment claims made by prisoners, while in others it simply deferred to the discretion of corrections officials. One scholar suggested that the Court was developing a new hands-off policy in correctional litigation.[1] Even some of the justices noted with regret the emergence of a new type of hands-off doctrine.[2] Still, the Burger Court did not return completely to the days when the Court would summarily deny prisoner petitions. When examining prisoner claims, the Court attempted to balance the rights of inmates against institutional needs for security, discipline, and rehabilitation. In the last decade of the Burger Court, however, more weight was given to government authority in prison administration than the rights of inmates. Before we turn our attention to these cases, it is important to review the membership changes and voting alignments on the Burger Court in order to understand the dynamics of the small group decision-making environment.

THE COMPOSITION OF THE BURGER COURT

The Burger Court was clearly a court in political transition. President Nixon had the opportunity to appoint four new justices to the Court, including Chief Justice Warren Burger and Associate Justices Harry Blackmun, Lewis Powell, and William Rehnquist. Nixon was determined to select as judicial candidates "strict constructionists" who would follow a conservative jurisprudence and not act as "super legislators," and who would protect society's "peace forces" against the "criminal forces."[3] These new justices were expected to promote tough law and order policies, and it was widely believed that the Burger Court would narrow or overturn Warren Court decisions that favored prisoners and criminal defendants. Some precedents were narrowed and standards restricted, and all four of his appointees voted to uphold the death penalty in *Furman v. Georgia* (1972), but Nixon must have been a little disappointed because his justices did not bring about a constitutional counterrevolution in criminal justice.[4]

As a judge on the U.S. Court of Appeals for the District of Columbia, Warren Burger was a critic of the Warren Court's criminal procedure decisions of the 1960s. He had developed a pro-government record in many areas of criminal procedure.[5] Nixon described his choice for chief justice as a man who would apply the law rather than legislate from the bench, and he expected Burger to interpret constitutional rights narrowly, especially those protecting criminal defendants and prisoners.[6] For the most part, Burger fulfilled those expectations. Though he did not lead a counterrevolution, Burger did have the second most conservative voting record on criminal justice issues by the time he retired from the bench.

Of the four Nixon appointees, Rehnquist was the most conservative member of the Burger Court. As an associate justice, he consistently voted with the conservative bloc, and he cast the lowest percentage of liberal votes in criminal procedure, due process, and civil liberties cases.[7] Rehnquist had established a conservative record on criminal law issues in the Justice Department as an assistant attorney general for the Office of Legal Counsel from 1969 until 1971. While there, he supported broad authority for law enforcement officials, including "inherent executive authority to issue wiretaps and surveillance without a court order, no-knock entry by the police, preventive detention, abolishing habeas corpus proceedings after trial, and abolishing the exclusionary rule."[8] These positions carried over to his work on the Burger Court—he almost never voted in favor of criminal defendants or prisoners. Rehnquist's constitutional philosophy emphasizes deference toward the power of the states and majority rule; consequently, he does not see the Court as a guardian of individual rights. He does not believe that the Due Process Clause of the Fourteenth Amendment incorporates the Bill of Rights or creates any substantive rights.[9] Rehnquist cannot be described as a true judicial conservative, however, because he supports an active role for the courts in protecting state authority within our federal system and, rather than adhering to the doctrine of *stare decisis*, he is quite willing to over-turn the liberal precedents of the Warren Court on criminal justice matters.

Between 1971 and 1975, the voting alignments in criminal procedure and prisoners' rights cases often consisted of Burger, Rehnquist, and White forming a conservative bloc and Brennan, Marshall, and Douglas anchoring the liberal wing of the Court. Justice Stewart usually joined Burger and the other conservatives in favoring state authority over the rights of inmates. Powell and Blackmun were swing votes. Though Blackmun's jurisprudence became moderately liberal by the end of the Burger Court, on issues of criminal justice he frequently voted with the other Nixon appointees. He preferred to defer to prison administrators but was also concerned that the Court not return to a hands-off policy.[10] As a judge, he upheld state death penalty laws, yet he personally strug-gled with the morality and propriety of capital punishment. He would write in *Furman v. Georgia* (1972) about his "distaste, antipathy, and . . . abhorrence" for the death penalty, believing that it "serves no useful purpose that can be demonstrated."[11] Near the end of his service on the Court, Blackmun decided that the death penalty could never be admin-istered in a fair manner, without error or discrimination, and was therefore inherently cruel and unusual punishment in violation of the Eighth and Fourteenth Amendments.[12]

The natural courts under Burger are presented in Table 5.1. In addition to the Nixon appointees, there were two other personnel changes during the seventeen-year tenure of Chief Justice Burger. Both of these appoint-ments were made by Republican presidents, with Gerald Ford appoint-ing John Paul Stevens and Ronald Reagan selecting Sandra Day O'Connor, the first female member of the Court. Together with the Nixon appointees, Justices Stevens and O'Connor altered the voting alignments and general philosophy of the Court, but not always in predicted direc-tions. Stevens replaced Douglas, one of the most liberal members of the Warren Court, and many court watchers expected a change in direction on constitutional issues. But compared to Chief Justice Rehnquist, Ste-vens established a moderate voting record during his first decade on the Court. He developed a reputation for independence of thought and a tendency to write dissenting opinions criticizing the other justices for misinterpreting constitutional principles.[13] Stevens has shown little

Table 5.1
Natural Courts under Chief Justice Warren Burger

1969	1969–1970	1970
Chief: Burger (R)	*Chief*: Burger (R)	*Chief*: Burger (R)
Black (D)	Black (D)	Black (D)
Douglas (D)	Douglas (D)	Douglas (D)
Harlan (R)	Harlan (R)	Harlan (R)
Brennan (D)	Brennan (D)	Brennan (D)
Stewart (R)	Stewart (R)	Stewart (R)
B. White (D)	B. White (D)	B. White (D)
Fortas (D)	T. Marshall (D)	T. Marshall (D)
T. Marshall (D)		Blackmun (R)

1971	1972–1975	1975–1981
Chief: Burger (R)	*Chief*: Burger (R)	*Chief*: Burger (R)
Douglas (D)	Douglas (D)	Brennan (D)
Brennan (D)	Brennan (D)	Stewart (R)
Stewart (R)	Stewart (R)	B. White (D)
B. White (D)	B. White (D)	T. Marshall (D)
T. Marshall (D)	T. Marshall (D)	Blackmun (R)
Blackmun (R)	Blackmun (R)	Powell (D)
	Powell (D)	Rehnquist (R)
	Rehnquist (R)	Stevens (R)

1981–1986
Chief: Burger (R)
Brennan (D)
B. White (D)
T. Marshall (D)
Blackmun (R)
Powell (D)
Rehnquist (R)
Stevens (R)
O'Connor (R)

Note: Associate justices are listed in order of seniority, with the most junior justice at the
   bottom of the list.
Source: Thomas R. Hensley, Christopher E. Smith, and Joyce A. Baugh, *The Changing Supreme Court: Constitutional Rights and Liberties* (St. Paul, Minn.: West Publishing, 1997).
   © 1997. Reprinted with permission of Wadsworth, a division of Thomson Learning.
   Fax 800-730-2215.

interest in strategically maximizing his policy preferences—he does
not make much of an effort to lobby his colleagues and convince
them to vote with him or support his approach to constitutional issues.
As the Court became more conservative, Stevens established an increas-

ingly liberal voting record in criminal procedure and prisoners' rights cases.

Justice Sandra Day O'Connor, who replaced Potter Stewart, has developed a reputation as a moderate, pragmatic justice who avoids the more ideologically driven jurisprudence of both the liberal and conservative blocs on the Court. Described as a "strategist" who approaches decision making on a case-by-case basis, Justice O'Connor attempts to accommodate competing interests with decisions that are context specific.[14] Her background as an Arizona state legislator influences her views on federalism, and she has consistently voted in favor of enhanced state authority. On criminal justice issues, she has supported greater police discretion and death penalty laws, and she has voted to restrict the use of habeas corpus by prisoners to challenge state court convictions.[15]

ACCESS TO THE FEDERAL COURTS

To the surprise of many conservatives, the Burger Court issued a number of decisions during its first few terms that expanded the rights of prisoners. Several of the early cases involved narrowly focused issues, and they were not decided on the merits of the claims. For example, in *Younger v. Gilmore* (1971), the Court affirmed *per curium* a lower court decision finding an unconstitutional interference by prison officials with an inmate's access to legal materials. In *Cruz v. Hauck* (1971), the Court held that the lower court must consider the merits of a prisoner's complaint alleging violations of First Amendment rights. Also, in *Haines v. Kerner* (1972), the Court decided in a *per curium* opinion written by Chief Justice Burger that a prisoner suit should not be dismissed unless it appears "beyond a reasonable doubt that the plaintiff can prove no set of facts in support of his claim which would entitle him to relief."[16] Haines had been placed in solitary confinement after striking another inmate in the head with a shovel following an argument. He alleged that he suffered physical injuries while in solitary confinement and was denied due process in the steps leading to that confinement. Both lower courts had taken a hands-off approach, with the Court of Appeals emphasizing that "prison officials are invested with wide discretion in disciplinary matters."[17] In reversing the appellate decision, the Court said that even though the allegations asserted by Haines were not as formally presented as those by a lawyer, they were sufficient to require an opportunity to offer supporting evidence. The opinion made it easier for inmates to file *pro se* complaints in the federal courts. Other decisions, discussed below, expanded inmate mail privileges, religious freedoms, procedural guarantees, and access to law libraries. A very divided Court also struck down state death penalty laws on due process and Eighth Amendment grounds.

RELIGIOUS FREEDOM FOR PRISONERS

The Court's first attempt to define the religious freedoms retained by prisoners came in *Cruz v. Beto* (1972). Cruz, a Buddhist, was serving fifteen years in a Texas penitentiary for robbery. While prisoners of the Catholic, Jewish, and Protestant faiths were allowed access to the chapel, Cruz was denied use of the facility to practice his faith. He also alleged that he was prohibited from corresponding with his religious advisor in the Buddhist sect, and that he was placed in solitary confinement for distributing Buddhist material to other prisoners. In a decision typical of the hands-off approach, the District Court denied relief without a hearing or findings, explaining that the complaint was in an area that should be left "to the sound discretion of prison administration."[18] The Court of Appeals affirmed this decision.

In another *per curium* opinion, the Court vacated the judgment and remanded the case for a hearing and appropriate findings. The Court noted that Texas provided at the state's expense chaplains for the Catholic, Jewish, and Protestant faiths, Jewish and Christian Bibles, Sunday school classes, and religious services. If Cruz was denied a reasonable opportunity to practice his faith comparable to the opportunity given other prisoners who followed more conventional religious doctrines, then "there was palpable discrimination by the State against the Buddhist religion" in violation of the First Amendment free exercise clause and Fourteenth Amendment equal protection clause.[19] In a footnote, the Court cautioned that the opinion did not mean that every religious sect or group within a prison, regardless of the number of adherents, must be provided identical facilities or personnel. Rather, reasonable opportunities must be given to all inmates to exercise their religious freedom without fear of reprisals. Chief Justice Burger concurred in the result, even though he thought that the allegations were "on the borderline necessary for an evidentiary hearing," and that some were "frivolous." He wanted to make it clear that there "cannot possibly be any constitutional or legal requirement that government provide materials for every religion and sect."[20] At most, he said, officials cannot deny Buddhist materials to prisoners if someone offers to provide them.

Justice Rehnquist, who had been confirmed by the Senate just four months earlier, wrote a dissenting opinion that would become typical of his jurisprudence in prisoners' rights cases. He was not convinced that there was a First Amendment violation, and he urged deference to prison administrators. Rehnquist argued that because of their status, prisoners are obviously limited in the extent to which they can practice their religion. "The fact that the Texas prison system," he argued, "offers no Buddhist services at this particular prison does not, under the circumstances pleaded in his [Cruz's] complaint, demonstrate that his religious freedom

is being impaired."[21] Rehnquist criticized the Court's opinions in prisoners' rights cases, complaining that neither the full decisions nor those
summarily reversing the dismissal of a prisoner petition "have ever
given full consideration to the proper balance to be struck between prisoners' rights and the extensive administrative discretion that must rest
with correction officials."[22] He said that he would apply the rule of deference to administrative discretion. Aside from any facts showing that
the difference in treatment between Cruz and his fellow Buddhists and
practitioners of religions with more numerous followers could not be
reasonably justified, Rehnquist stated that he would leave the matter to
prison officials.

LEGAL ADVOCACY, PRISONER PROTESTS, AND THE COURT OF PUBLIC OPINION

The early Burger Court decisions favorable to prisoners' claims may
have been a response to external factors. By the early 1970s, litigation
and prisoner activism called attention to prison practices and conditions.
During this period, the NAACP Legal Defense and Educational Fund
(LDF) launched an attack on state death penalty statutes that achieved
success with the decision in *Furman v. Georgia* (1972). Another interest
group, the American Civil Liberties Union (ACLU), declared prison conditions a "prime new area" at its Biennial Conference in 1968.[23] Former
civil rights lawyers Phil Hirschkop and Herman Schwartz began han-
dling numerous complaints from prisoners in the late 1960s, and both of
these men started prisoners' rights projects in Virginia and New York,
respectively. Out of these efforts, the ACLU National Prison Project
formed in 1972 with the goal of sponsoring litigation to improve prison
conditions throughout the country. Lawyers for the Prison Project became involved in many of the major prison reform cases of the 1970s
and 1980s.[24]

Prisoners began to organize and demand more immediate changes as
well. Strikes and riots were common. At San Quentin in 1967, almost
2,000 inmates were involved in what began as a strike by black inmates
but, with some encouragement from the guards, turned into a race riot.
There were 39 prison riots in 1969 and 59 in 1970 alone.[25] On November
3, 1970, approximately 2,000 convicts at Folsom Prison in California
staged a nineteen-day strike—the longest in prison history. The prisoners
issued a manifesto with 31 demands covering issues such as living conditions, legal rights, racism, and guard brutality.[26] Though the strike
ended without incidents of violence, that was not the case with other
prisoner protests. In September 1971, 39 people died and 88 were injured
in a four-day prison riot at Attica, New York, when state police and the
National Guard assaulted the prison.[27] Media coverage of what New

York Governor Nelson Rockefeller described as an "insurrection" against state authority raised public awareness of the desperate conditions within American prisons and the need for reforms.[28] Even Chief Justice Burger, in his public speeches and writings, encouraged prison reform and the establishment of inmate grievance procedures.[29] The reform spirit was short lived, however, and there were few fundamental changes to prison conditions in the early 1970s. Continued overcrowding, public indifference, and the Supreme Court's tendency to defer to prison authorities made reform difficult.

STATE DEATH PENALTY STATUTES HELD UNCONSTITUTIONAL

Lawyers for the NAACP LDF advanced their legal challenge against capital punishment in *Furman v. Georgia* (1972).[30] In a *per curium* opinion, the Court declared that the death penalty, as it was currently administered, violated the Eighth and Fourteenth Amendments. William Furman had received the death penalty for killing the father of five children when the victim discovered Furman in his home one morning. The composition of the Court changed in the months preceding the *Furman* decision. The case was originally scheduled for oral argument during the fall of the 1971 term. Justice Hugo Black resigned on September 17 because of ill health and died a few days later. John Marshall Harlan also retired on September 23. Because of these events, the oral argument in *Furman* had to be postponed until January 17, 1972. In the interim, President Nixon appointed Lewis Powell as a replacement for Black and selected William H. Rehnquist to fill Harlan's vacant seat.

According to his biographer, Thurgood Marshall lobbied hard to convince newcomer Justice Powell to vote against the death penalty, but in the end he was unsuccessful.[31] Marshall did get a 5-to-4 vote in his favor, but the Court could not agree on a rationale. The *per curium* decision was followed by five concurring and four dissenting opinions that ran over 240 pages. Only two of the five justices, Justices Brennan and Marshall, argued that the death penalty was itself cruel and unusual, because the "evolving standards of decency" of contemporary society found capital punishment abhorrent. Marshall's 60-page concurring opinion included an array of historical and sociological evidence supporting the argument that, by modern-day standards, death was an excessive penalty and therefore cruel. He also emphasized the irrevocable nature of capital punishment and the fear that an innocent person may be put to death. Marshall's opinion included documentation to support his argument that capital punishment is imposed more often on minorities and the poor. Following *Furman*, Justice Marshall never retreated from his position that the death penalty was in all cases prohibited as cruel and unusual punishment under the Eighth Amendment.

Justice Stewart believed that the problem was not with the death penalty itself but with the manner in which it was being implemented. He said that death sentences in Georgia and Texas are "cruel and unusual in the same way that being struck by lightning is cruel and unusual."[32] Trial juries were left with almost complete discretion in deciding when to impose a sentence of death. The result, Stewart argued, is that the death penalty is "wantonly and freakishly" imposed.[33] Justices Douglas and White also felt that capital punishment was imposed in an arbitrary and a discriminatory manner.

The four Nixon appointees, Burger, Blackmun, Powell, and Rehnquist, dissented. They argued that the death penalty was constitutional according to the text and the intent of the framers. Chief Justice Burger believed that the infrequency with which the death penalty was imposed did not make the punishment arbitrary or cruel. Still, his opinion counseled state legislatures on how to rewrite their death penalty statutes to address the concerns of the Court, particularly Justices Stewart and White, by limiting the discretion of the decision makers. Burger wrote that "legislative bodies may seek to bring their laws into compliance with the Court's ruling by providing standards for juries and judges to follow in determining the sentence in capital cases or by more narrowly defining the crimes for which the penalty is to be imposed."[34] Many states heeded Burger's advice and began rewriting their death penalty laws. It would take several years for these new laws to reach the Court's docket. Meanwhile, the Burger Court turned its attention to prison practices and conditions.

PRISON PRACTICES COME UNDER SCRUTINY

In 1974, the Supreme Court decided three cases dealing with the day-to-day administration of prisons. Still sensitive to the consequences of constitutionalizing rights for prisoners, the Court in these cases retained a significant amount of deference to the discretion of prison administrators. But the decisions did not simply tip the scales in favor of corrections officials. Arguably, inmate claims triumphed in two out of the three cases. A divided Court, in *Pell v. Procunier* (1974), denied prisoners and the press a right to private interviews under the First Amendment or any other provision of the Constitution because of potential security problems. But in *Procunier v. Martinez* (1974), the Court expanded legal access for prisoners and made it more difficult to censor inmate mail, and in *Wolff v. McDonnell* (1974), it established minimal due process protections in prison disciplinary hearings.

Mail Censorship and Access to Legal Services

Procunier v. Martinez involved a constitutional challenge to California prison regulations relating to the censorship of inmate mail and prohibiting law students and paralegals from conducting interviews with inmates.[35] The District Court held the mail censorship regulations unconstitutional under the free speech clause of the First Amendment, void for vagueness, and in violation of the Fourteenth Amendment. The ban against the use of law students and paralegals to conduct attorney-client interviews was found to abridge the right of access to the courts. During the conference on the merits, Justice Rehnquist had voted to reverse the lower court decision. Justice Powell was assigned to write the opinion for the Court. When Rehnquist read his draft, he sent a memo to Powell commenting that he had written a good opinion and said, "I don't think that the legal literature would be enriched by my dissenting on the basis of my Conference vote."[36] The fact that Rehnquist switched his vote did not impact the outcome of the case, but it is interesting to note because he rarely voted to support First Amendment protections for prisoners. An analysis of Powell's opinion reveals why Rehnquist may have decided to join the Court.

Powell noted that the lower courts had utilized a variety of approaches in reviewing prison regulations restricting freedom of speech. Some adopted a hands-off approach, while others applied a "compelling state interest" standard to justify censorship of prisoner mail. Still other courts used an intermediate approach that held regulations to a rational basis test. These divergent approaches gave either too little protection to First Amendment interests or were so inconsistent as to invite more prisoner litigation. In Powell's view, the task of the Court was to articulate an appropriate standard of review for regulations restricting prisoner correspondence.

But instead of treating the question as a "prisoners' rights" issue, Powell recast the case as one that "implicates more than the right of prisoners."[37] Communication by mail is only accomplished when the letter is read by the addressee. Powell argued that censorship of the communication between a prisoner and an outsider implicates the First and Fourteenth Amendment rights of those who are not prisoners. He said that censorship of prisoner mail is only justified when the following criteria are met:

First, the regulation of practice in question must further an important or substantial governmental interest unrelated to the suppression of expression. . . . [T]hey must show that regulation authorizing mail censorship furthers one or more of the substantial governmental interests of security, order, and rehabilitation. Second, the limitation of First Amendment freedoms must be no greater than is necessary or essential to the protection of the particular government interest involved.[38]

Applying this standard, the Court affirmed the judgment of the lower court. Concluding that the regulations "fairly invited prison officials and employees to apply their own personal prejudices and opinions as standards for prisoner mail censorship," the Court said that the regulations authorized censorship of inmate mail far broader than legitimate interest of penal administration required. By not treating the censorship issue as one implicating prisoners' rights, Powell was able to win the support of Rehnquist.

The Court also struck down the regulation restricting access to prisoners to members of the bar and licensed private investigators. The regulation had the effect of banning the use of law students and paralegals by lawyers to interview clients and sign documents. Because due process requires that prisoners be afforded access to the courts to challenge their convictions and to secure remedies for violations of their rights, "regulations and practices that unjustifiably obstruct the availability of professional representation or other aspects of the right of access to the courts are invalid."[39]

Justice Marshall, joined by Brennan, concurred with the Court but used stronger language to defend the First Amendment rights of inmates. Marshall argued that prisoners are entitled to use the mails "as a medium of free expression not as a privilege, but rather as a constitutionally guaranteed right," and he would hold that "prison authorities may not read inmate mail as a matter of course."[40] Marshall said that even the state's asserted interests in security, discipline, and rehabilitation do not justify a blanket policy of reading all prison mail. He suggested that these goals could be met by less intrusive means. Marshall argued that to "suppress expression is to reject the basic human desire for recognition and affront the individual's worth and dignity," which, if anything, are "more compelling in the dehumanizing prison environment."[41]

Press Interviews with Inmates Restricted

In *Pell v. Procunier* (1974), four California inmates and three journalists challenged the constitutionality of a prison regulation that prohibited "press and other media interviews with specific individual inmates."[42] The inmates argued that the regulation violated their free speech rights, and the journalists claimed that the rule restricted their news-gathering activity in violation of the freedom of the press guarantee of the First Amendment and applicable through the Fourteenth Amendment. The District Court held in favor of the prisoners but granted the defendants' motion to dismiss on the media claim. Justice Stewart wrote the opinion for a divided Court, which held that the prison regulation did not violate the rights of either inmates or journalists. The vote was 6 to 3 on whether the regulation infringed the rights of prisoners and 5 to 4 in regard to the claims by the journalists. Douglas, Brennan, and Marshall dissented, while Powell joined the majority in rejecting the free speech arguments of the inmates. In a memo to the conference in late April, Chief Justice Burger announced his intention to vote for restricting press access, because he feared that "an absolute constitutional holding adverse to [prison] administrators will tend to 'freeze' progress."[43]

Stewart began his opinion by emphasizing the need for deference to prison administrators. He said that First Amendment challenges to prison restrictions "must be analyzed in terms of the legitimate policies and goals of the correctional system."[44] He wrote that the "regulation cannot be considered in isolation but must be viewed in the light of the alternative means of communication permitted under the regulations with persons outside the prison."[45] Since California permitted inmates to communicate by mail and allowed them to receive visits from family members, clergy, lawyers, and friends, Stewart suggested that prisoners could use these contacts to communicate with the media. He distinguished the case from *Procunier v. Martinez*, where the Court could find no legitimate interest to justify the substantial restrictions on written communication by inmates. Because this case involved in-person communication with prisoners, "it is obvious that institutional considerations, such as security and related administrative problems, as well as the accepted and legitimate policy objectives of the corrections system itself, require that some limitation be placed on such visitations."[46] The need for restrictions, according to Stewart, is best left to the professional expertise of corrections officials, and the courts should generally defer to their judgment in such matters.

The same logic was used to uphold the ban on press interviews with individual inmates. Stewart devoted several paragraphs explaining why the regulation was enacted in 1971. Prior to the ban taking effect, a journalist had virtually free access to any inmate whom he or she might wish to interview. Prison administrators argued that this resulted in press attention being focused on a small number of inmates who became "public figures" within the prison community. Officials alleged that these celebrity inmates often became the source of severe disciplinary problems. Stewart concluded that the promulgation of the regulation "did not impose a discrimination against press access, but merely eliminated a special privilege formerly given to representatives of the press" that was not available to the public.[47] He said that the Constitution does not "require government to accord the press special access to information not shared by members of the public generally."[48] Thus the regulation did not abridge the protections of the First and Fourteenth Amendments.[49]

Justice Powell concurred with the portion of the opinion denying the prisoners' free speech rights but dissented on the holding that rejected the freedom of the press claims by representatives of the media. He felt that the state's absolute "ban against prisoner-press interviews impermissibly restrains the ability of the press to perform its constitutionally established function of informing the people on the conduct of their government."[50]

Justice Douglas, joined by Brennan and Marshall, wrote a dissenting opinion that supported First Amendment rights for prisoners and journalists. Citing his concurring opinion in *Procunier v. Martinez*, he emphasized that prisoners are still "persons entitled to all constitutional rights unless their liberty has been constitutionally curtailed by procedures that satisfy all the requirements of due process."[51] Douglas said that the state cannot defend an overly broad restriction on communication by demonstrating that it has not eliminated expression completely. He argued that the regulation was offensive to First Amendment principles, because it "flatly prohibits interview communication with the media on the government's penal operations by the only citizens with the best knowledge and real incentive to discuss them."[52] The state's interest in order and prison discipline cannot justify a total ban on press interviews with individual prisoners.

Douglas pointed out that the free press guarantee protects more than just the interests of the media. He described prisons as public institutions that play an important role in crime control and impose significant costs on taxpayers. Of those individuals incarcerated, most will return to society. For these reasons, Douglas believed that the public has a paramount interest in being informed about the administration of prisons. He said that it is not enough to note that the press is denied no more access than the general public. The average citizen is unlikely to request an interview with an inmate with whom he has no prior relationship in order to learn about prison operations. He is more likely, Douglas argued, "to rely upon the media for information."[53]

It is fair to ask why the Court did not treat the issues in *Procunier v. Martinez* and *Pell v. Procunier* similarly. The ban on press interviews could have been analyzed in the same manner as Justice Powell approached the regulation censoring inmate mail. Instead of treating the case as one involving prisoners' rights, Justice Stewart could have emphasized the rights of outsiders—the journalists and their protected interests in freedom of the press. Instead, he decided to dismiss their claims on the grounds that alternative means of communication were available. At least one scholar has argued that *Pell* was the first sign that the Burger Court was moving toward a philosophy of greater deference to prison administrators.[54] But just two days after *Pell* was announced, the Court issued a decision that was at least a partial victory for prisoners' rights.

Due Process in Prison Disciplinary Hearings

In *Wolff v. McDonnell* (1974), inmates at a Nebraska prison filed a suit in federal court raising three issues: an alleged denial of due process rights in prison disciplinary hearings; a claim that legal assistance provided to inmates was constitutionally deficient; and a claim that regulations governing the inspection of inmates' mail were too restrictive. Under Nebraska law, a prisoner found guilty of "flagrant or serious" misconduct may lose good-time credits (these reduce a prison term for good behavior) or be confined to a disciplinary cell. Charges of misconduct were to be investigated by an Adjustment Committee made up of prison officials. An inmate is permitted to discuss the charges with a supervisor and the accusing party. A conduct report is prepared and sent to the Adjustment Committee. At a hearing before the committee, the report is read to the inmate, the charges are discussed, and if necessary, a punishment is imposed. An inmate was permitted to ask questions but had no right to counsel, to cross-examine adverse witnesses, or to present witnesses in his behalf.[55] As to the other issues, the regulation concerning legal assistance provided that only a legal advisor appointed by the warden could assist prisoners in preparing legal documents. The mail regulation permitted mail to be opened in the presence of an inmate in order to search for contraband but could not be read by prison authorities. Of the three issues, the due process one was the most significant, so the analysis will focus on that question.

The District Court rejected the due process claim and held that restrictions on inmates' legal assistance were not constitutionally defective but found the policy of inspecting all attorney-prisoner mail improper. The Eighth Circuit Court of Appeals reversed on the due process claim, holding that prisoners should be given the same due process protections that apply to parole and probation revocation hearings. The Court of Appeals also ordered further proceedings to determine if the state was meeting its burden under *Johnson v. Avery* (1969) to provide legal assistance to prisoners. At the conference, six justices voted to modify the lower court ruling, while Brennan, Douglas, and Marshall voted to affirm. Justice Byron White authored the majority opinion.

In its decision, the Court stressed that prisoners do have constitutional rights, thus rejecting arguments by prison authorities that their actions were "matter[s] of policy raising no constitutional issues."[56] Justice White wrote:

Lawful imprisonment necessarily makes unavailable many rights and privileges of the ordinary citizen, a retraction justified by the considerations underlying our penal system. But though his rights may be diminished by the needs and exigencies of the institutional environment, a prisoner is not wholly stripped of constitutional protections when he is imprisoned for crime. There is no iron curtain drawn between the Constitution and the prisons of this country.[57]

This lofty rhetoric on the constitutional rights of prisoners, however, was tempered with a balancing approach. As the Court explained, "The fact that prisoners retain rights under the Due Process Clause in no way implies that these rights are not subject to restrictions imposed by the nature of the regime to which they have been lawfully committed."[58] Justice White argued that, "There must be mutual accommodation between institutional needs and objectives" and the rights of those incarcerated.[59] The search for "mutual accommodation" characterized the Court's treatment of the due process claims in *Wolff v. McDonnell* (1974) and represented the general approach the Burger Court used in subsequent prisoners' rights cases.

The prisoners argued that the Court should apply the same procedural safeguards required in parole and probation revocation hearings to a disciplinary hearing involving the loss of good-time credits or solitary confinement. These protections included written notice of the alleged violation, disclosure of evidence, an opportunity to be heard in person and to present witnesses, the right to cross-examine adverse witnesses, a neutral and detached hearing body, a written statement by the fact finders regarding the evidence relied on in making a decision, and a limited right to counsel.[60] But the Court held that only two of these procedures—advance written notice of the claimed violation and a written statement of the fact finder's evidence—were required to satisfy the minimum requirements of procedural due process.[61] The Court also was of the opinion that the accused should have an opportunity to present evidence and to call witnesses as long as these procedures were not "unduly hazardous to institutional safety or correctional goals."[62] As the dissenters noted, this effectively left the opportunity for an inmate to present witnesses to the discretion of prison officials.

Why did the Court not mandate more procedural guarantees? Justice White reasoned that providing a disciplinary defendant with the right to confront and cross-examine witnesses might lead to reprisals against guard or inmate accusers and generate hostility in the prison environment. He also argued that to insert counsel into the disciplinary process would "inevitably give the proceedings a more adversary cast and tend to reduce their utility as a means to further correctional goals."[63] Another concern expressed was that retained or appointed counsel would delay the process and create practical problems in providing enough lawyers. Finally, White said that a hearing board composed entirely of prison officials was "sufficiently impartial to satisfy the Due Process Clause."[64]

As for the other issues, the Court said that the mail regulation did not constitute censorship, because the mail would only be opened in the presence of an inmate and not be read by prison officials. White argued that this was reasonable because it allowed prison authorities to search for contraband. The Court concluded that neither the First, Sixth, or Fourteenth Amendments were infringed by the mail regulations. On the question of legal assistance, prison officials asserted that the precedent in *Johnson v. Avery* (1969) limited legal advice to the preparation of habeas corpus petitions. But the Court said that the

> right of access to the courts, upon which *Avery* was premised, is founded in the Due Process Clause and assures that no person will be denied the opportunity to present to the judiciary allegations concerning violations of fundamental constitutional rights. It is futile to contend that the Civil Rights Act of 1871 has less importance in our constitutional scheme than does the Great Writ.[65]

The Court remanded the issue to the District Court.

Justice Marshall, joined by Brennan, concurred in part and dissented in part. Marshall agreed with the Court on the secondary issues concerning mail inspection and access to legal services, but he dissented on the primary issue of the case—the scope of procedural protections required by the Due Process Clause in prison disciplinary hearings. He wanted to make it clear "that an accused inmate's right to present witnesses and submit other evidence in his defense is constitutionally protected . . . and judicially enforceable."[66] While he agreed with the Court that there is some flexibility in the due process requirement, he argued that the exceptions to the right to present witnesses "must be kept to an absolute minimum." Marshall expressed stronger disagreement with the Court's view that the rights of confrontation and cross-examination are not essential to due process. The Court had held these rights to be fundamental in other settings, and Marshall felt that they were just as crucial, if not more so, in the prison disciplinary context. He also felt that the accused prisoner "has a constitutional right to confront and cross-examine witnesses, subject to a limited exception when necessary to protect the identity of a confidential inmate informant."[67] And he believed that prisoners should have some kind of legal assistance in preparing their defense. Marshall agreed with the Court that it would be inappropriate to require the appointment of a lawyer, but he did say that a prisoner is entitled to the assistance of a competent fellow inmate, a correctional staff member, or law students. Finally, Marshall said that an impartial decision maker is a fundamental requirement of due process, but he saw "no constitutional impediment to a disciplinary review board composed of responsible prison officials," provided that no member of the board "has been involved in the investigation or prosecution of a case, or has had any other form of personal involvement."[68]

In a separate opinion, concurring in part and dissenting in part, Justice

Douglas argued many of the same points as did Marshall. He focused on the need for procedural protections in disciplinary hearings, especially when an inmate faces solitary confinement. He also was more critical of the Court's policy of deference. Citing *Holt v. Sarver* (1970), where a lower court held the entire prison system of Arkansas unconstitutional, Douglas said that the "lesson to be learned is that courts cannot blithely defer to the supposed expertise of prison officials when it comes to the constitutional rights of inmates."[69]

Wolff established minimal procedural requirements but left corrections officials much discretion in the conduct of prison disciplinary hearings. Some lower court judges and prisoners' rights advocates criticized the Court for not requiring more extensive procedural rights. Instead of leaving the matter to the discretion of prison administrators, a few courts expanded the due process protections. One appeals court held that an inmate has a right to legal counsel and prisoners who are denied the right to confront and cross-examine witnesses must be provided with written reasons or the denial will be deemed an abuse of discretion.[70] Another Court of Appeals ruled that when a prisoner before a disciplinary committee faces possible prosecution under state law, he or she must be advised of his Fifth Amendment right to be silent and, if requested, prison authorities should consider permitting legal counsel.[71] In a series of cases decided in 1976, the Burger Court reversed these decisions and restricted the scope of due process guarantees in the prison context.

COURT RESTRICTS DUE PROCESS GUARANTEES

In *Baxter v. Palmigiano* (1976), the Court held that the additional procedural requirements imposed by the Courts of Appeals were inconsistent with the "mutual accommodation" reached in *Wolff* between institutional needs and objectives and the constitutional rights of inmates. The Court saw no reason to alter its holding in *Wolff* that inmates "do not have a right to either retained or appointed counsel in disciplinary hearings," and it refused to extend a Fifth Amendment protection against self-incrimination to disciplinary hearings by ruling that "silence in the face of accusation is a relevant fact not barred from evidence by the Due Process Clause."[72] The Court also criticized the decision by the Ninth Circuit Court of Appeals, which required prison authorities to provide written reasons why an inmate was denied the privilege to cross-examine or confront witnesses against them. The Court said that *Wolff* only characterized as "useful" but not required written reasons for denying confrontation and cross-examination of witnesses. Justice White ended the opinion for the Court by saying that the procedures now mandated in prison disciplinary hearings "represent a reasonable accommodation between the interests of the inmates and the needs of the institution."[73]

The scope of due process guarantees for prisoners was further limited by the Court in *Meachum v. Fano* (1976). Fano and five other inmates were incarcerated at the Massachusetts Correctional Institution at Norfolk. Based on reports from informants that he and the other inmates were involved in a series of fires at the institution, prison officials notified Fano and the others that they were to be transferred to another facility—possibly a maximum-security institution with less desirable living conditions. Each prisoner was notified of the classification hearing and informed that authorities had evidence of criminal conduct. The hearings were held before a Classification Board, and each prisoner had an attorney present. Outside the presence of the inmates, the board heard testimony from Meachum, the prison superintendent. The board told the prisoners that the evidence supported the allegations, but they were not given a copy of the transcript of Meachum's testimony. The respondents denied being involved in the incidents and were allowed to present supporting testimony. The board concluded that Fano and two others should be transferred to Walpole, a maximum-security institution with harsher living conditions.[74] Fano and the other inmates complained that they were being deprived of their liberty without due process of law. Applying *Wolff*, the District Court held that the prisoners were entitled to notice and hearing and that both of these were constitutionally inadequate. The Court of Appeals affirmed, holding that the transfer to a maximum-security prison involved a "significant modification of the overall conditions of confinement," and that the changes were serious enough to require due process protections.[75]

At the conference, six justices voted to reverse, and Justice White was assigned the opinion of the Court. Only Stevens, Brennan, and Marshall dissented. Brennan's conference notes indicate that Powell felt that the reclassification hearing was "a punishment proceeding for a serious crime" and thought due process applied, but he believed that the hearing satisfied the necessary protections.[76] Stewart, White, and Rehnquist argued that unless a state created a statutory entitlement to stay in a prison to which an inmate was initially assigned, there is no liberty or property interest. Since there was no such law in this case, there was no denial of due process. That argument became the rationale for White's opinion.

The Court began by rejecting "the notion that *any* grievous loss visited upon a person by the State is sufficient to invoke the procedural protections of the Due Process Clause."[77] To do so in the prison context, the Court said, would only subject to judicial review a wide variety of discretionary actions that traditionally have been the responsibility of prison administrators. Once a criminal defendant is convicted, there ceases to exist a liberty interest to the extent that a state "may confine him and subject him to the rules of its prison system so long as the conditions of confinement do not otherwise violate the Constitution."[78] Moreover, the Court said that the Due Process Clause does not protect a prisoner against transfer from one institution to another, even if life in one prison is more miserable than the other. Finally, Justice White distinguished the case from *Wolff* by noting that the state in *Wolff* had created a liberty interest by providing for good-time credits. Because Massachusetts had established no statutory right for the inmate to remain in the facility to which he or she was originally assigned, the basis for invoking the "protection of the Fourteenth Amendment as construed and applied in *Wolff v. McDonnell* is totally nonexistent."[79]

In a dissenting opinion, Justice Stevens, joined by Brennan and Marshall, wrote that the Court's reasoning was "more disturbing than its narrow holding" because it rested on a conception of "liberty" that he considered fundamentally flawed.[80] Stevens said that the Court's opinion recognized a liberty interest in either of two sources—the Constitution or state law. "If man were a creature of the State," Stevens acknowledged, the "Court's analysis would be correct," but "law is not the source of liberty, and surely not the exclusive source."[81] He thought it self-evident that liberty was one of the cardinal, unalienable rights bestowed by the Creator and enjoyed by all men and women. But locating the source of liberty was not enough to decide the case. Because prisoners have been convicted of a crime, they may be deprived of their liberty. Historically, the deprivation of liberty was most complete when prisoners were viewed as "slaves of the state" during the nineteenth century. Citing *Morrissey v. Brewer* (1972), Stevens said that the Court has moderated that view of a liberty interest by holding that an "individual possesses a residuum of constitutionally protected liberty while in legal custody pursuant to a valid conviction."[82] He argued that the Court not only demeaned the holding in *Morrissey* but demeaned the concept of liberty itself, "if the inmate's protected liberty interests are no greater than the State chooses to allow, he is really little more than the slave described in the nineteenth-century cases. I think it clear that even the inmate retains an unalienable interest in liberty—at the very minimum the right to be treated with dignity—which the Constitution may never ignore."[83] Stevens admitted that the state has the power to change the status of a prisoner, but if the change amounts to a "grievous loss," it cannot be imposed arbitrarily and due process must be afforded. Under this standard, the task for the courts is to determine what constitutes a grievous loss. Stevens felt that the deprivation was serious enough to warrant constitutional protections.

On the same day that the decision in *Meachum* was announced, the Court applied the holding to another case involving the transfer of prisoners. In *Montanye v. Haymes* (1976), the Court held that the Due Process

Clause of the Fourteenth Amendment does not require a hearing when a prisoner is transferred to another institution, regardless of whether the transfer resulted from the inmate's behavior or was disciplinary in nature, and where under state law a prisoner had no right to remain at a particular institution.[84] The voting alignments were the same as in *Meachum*, with Justice White authoring the opinion of the Court and Stevens writing the dissent.

Haymes had been removed from his assignment as an inmate clerk in the law library of the Attica Correctional Facility in New York on June 7, 1972. That afternoon, he was observed circulating a document prepared by him and signed by dozens of inmates. Among other issues, the signatories complained that they had been deprived of legal assistance because Haymes and another inmate had been removed from the library. The document was addressed to a federal judge, but no relief was requested. On June 8, Haymes was notified that he would be moved to the Clinton Correctional Facility, another maximum-security prison, and the transfer took place the next day. The Court noted that no loss of good time, solitary confinement, loss of privileges, or any other punitive measures accompanied the transfer. Haymes asserted that the seizure of the document violated his right to petition the courts for redress of grievances and that his transfer was a reprisal for rendering legal assistance to various prisoners. The deputy superintendent of Attica responded that the prison had a rule prohibiting unauthorized legal assistance and that Haymes had been warned on several occasions about violating the rule.

The District Court had dismissed the action, but the Second Circuit Court of Appeals reversed, ruling that the summary judgment was erroneous because there were two unresolved issues of fact: whether Haymes's reassignment to Clinton was punishment for violating prison rules and, if so, whether the effects of the transfer were serious enough to require a hearing. Writing for the Court, Justice White said that the decision in *Meachum v. Fano* required a reversal in the case. The Court argued that the Due Process Clause does not by its own force mandate hearings whenever prison authorities transfer inmates from one institution to another because of a violation of prison rules:

As long as the conditions or degree of confinement to which the prisoner is subjected is within the sentence imposed upon him and is not otherwise violative of the Constitution, the Due Process Clause does not in itself subject an inmate's treatment by prison authorities to judicial oversight. The Clause does not require hearings in connection with transfers whether or not they are the result of the inmate's misbehavior or may be labeled as disciplinary or punitive.[85]

Justice White also pointed out that under New York law, Haymes had no right to remain at any particular institution and no justifiable expec-

tation that he would not be transferred unless found guilty of misconduct.

The decisions in *Baxter*, *Meachum*, and *Montanye*, along with others
handed down during this period,[86] reversed lower court decisions that
extended broader due process protections to prisoners. The Burger Court
was unwilling to expand the scope of protections beyond those announced in *Wolff v. McDonnell* and preferred to give more discretion to
prison authorities in disciplinary hearings and inmate transfers. Only
three justices—Stevens, Brennan, and Marshall—favored more extensive
procedural guarantees for inmates, but they were unable to convince
their colleagues that such protections were required by the Constitution.

THE "TOTALITY OF CONDITIONS" CASES

For nearly a decade, the Supreme Court did not offer much guidance
on cases involving state prison conditions under the Eighth Amendment.[87] This silence from the highest court meant that federal judges had
wide discretion in determining the proper scope of their intervention.
Many judges were reluctant to intervene, but the conditions were so bad
in some state prisons that they could not be dismissed. Prisons in Southern states were among the worst violators, because correctional facilities
in states such as Arkansas and Mississippi were managed along a plantation model characterized by work farms and manufacturing industries,
long hours in field labor, overcrowded dormitory wings, and the use of
inmate bosses to maintain order. In a few cases, individual complaints
were grouped together under a class-action lawsuit where a "totality of
conditions" created an environment that violated the Constitution.

The first such case was *Holt v. Sarver* (1970). In this case, the entire
prison system of Arkansas was declared unconstitutional because a "totality of conditions" created an environment that violated the Eighth
Amendment's prohibition against cruel and unusual punishments. The
district judge argued that:

[C]onfinement, even at hard labor and without compensation, is not considered
to be necessarily cruel and unusual punishment, [but] it may be so in certain
circumstances and by reasons of the conditions of confinement. . . . Confinement
itself may amount to cruel and unusual punishment prohibited by the Constitution where confinement is characterized by conditions and practices so bad as
to be shocking to the conscience of a reasonably civilized people.[88]

Viewed in isolation, prison conditions such as idleness or inadequate
sanitation may not violate the Eighth Amendment. When taken as a
whole, however, they can create an environment that amounts to cruel
and unusual punishment. Conditions were so terrible in the Arkansas

prison system that, when viewed in their totality, they could not be ignored by the court. Some of these conditions included armed inmate trustees, open barracks that permitted attacks on inmates, food served in unsanitary conditions, and the lack of a rehabilitation program.[89]

The "totality of conditions" approach was further developed by Judge Frank Johnson in *Pugh v. Locke* (1976).[90] Judge Johnson determined that conditions were so appalling in Alabama prisons that the mere fact of confinement within the state prison system was sufficient to violate an inmate's right to decent conditions. The judge said that the conditions as "a whole create an atmosphere in which inmates are compelled to live in constant fear of violence, in imminent danger to their physical well-being, and without opportunity to seek a more promising future."[91] In order to "remedy the massive constitutional infirmities which plague Alabama's prisons," Judge Johnson issued a controversial system-wide decree that contained 44 major guidelines covering prison populations, staffing, and living conditions. The scope and specificity of this decree became a model for remedies in Rhode Island, Texas, Tennessee, and other states. By 1980, 32 states were either under a court order or had impending litigation in the federal courts.

In *Hutto v. Finney* (1978), the Court refused to overturn the District Court's detailed remedial orders in *Holt v. Sarver* (1970), discussed above, which held that conditions in the Arkansas prison system were in violation of the Eighth and Fourteenth Amendments. These orders included limits on the number of inmates that can be confined to one cell, required that each prisoner have a bunk, and set 30 days as the maximum isolation sentence. In upholding the orders, the Court reasoned that if the state had fully complied with earlier orders, the present limits may not have been necessary. However, since the correctional system of Arkansas refused to comply with the remedial decrees, the District Court was justified in substituting its judgment by entering a comprehensive order to ensure compliance.

Prison administrators and state legislators reacted strongly to these decisions. They argued that the decisions undermined prison discipline and state authority in managing its prisons. The Supreme Court seemed to respond to the criticism. Concerned about the volume and scope of state prison litigation, by 1979 the Burger Court moved to limit federal court involvement in prison and jail reform.

"DELIBERATE INDIFFERENCE" STANDARD FOR MEDICAL CARE

The Court discussed the applicability of the Eighth Amendment to prison conditions in *Estelle v. Gamble* (1976).[92] J. W. Gamble was an inmate in the Texas Department of Corrections. On November 9, 1973, he sustained an injury to his back while doing prison labor. Over the next three months, Gamble complained that he suffered from recurring pain in his lower back and chest, migraine headaches, and high blood pressure. He was sent to the hospital numerous times and given a series of medications. A doctor certified him capable of light work, but Gamble said that he was in too much pain to work so he was moved to administrative segregation. On January 31, 1974, he was brought before a prison disciplinary committee for his refusal to work. One official testified that Gamble was in "first class" medical condition.[93] The committee, without additional medical testimony, placed him in solitary confinement. Days later, Gamble complained of more chest and back pains and returned to the hospital. He received medication and was moved back to administrative segregation. Still experiencing pain, he asked twice to see a doctor, but the guards refused. Gamble alleged that the failure of prison officials to adequately treat his back injury amounted to cruel and unusual punishment in violation of the Eighth Amendment and applicable through the Fourteenth Amendment. The District Court dismissed the complaint, but the Court of Appeals reversed and remanded with instructions to reinstate the complaint.

At the conference on the merits, the justices were divided over the standard to be applied to medical care and whether the case should be remanded. Powell voted for a flat reversal and nothing else, because he felt that the complaint was meritless.[94] Rehnquist and Stewart agreed with Powell, with Stewart saying that the actions may have been malpractice but nothing more. Marshall, who voted to affirm on the medical treatment issue and remand the case with instructions to look into the claims other than the medical ones, was assigned to write the opinion for the Court. He circulated several drafts in response to suggestions by Rehnquist and Powell for substantive changes.[95] His revisions were enough to convince Rehnquist and Powell to join his opinion. In the end, only Justice Stevens dissented.

Marshall began by reviewing the Court's Eighth Amendment jurisprudence. He noted that the drafters of the amendment were primarily concerned with prohibiting torture and other barbarous punishments and early Court decisions "applied the Eighth Amendment by comparing challenged methods of execution to . . . inhumane techniques of punishment."[96] He said that more recent decisions, however, have held that the amendment proscribes more than just barbarous punishments, and that it "embodies broad and idealistic concepts of dignity, civilized standards, humanity, and decency."[97] Those principles, the Court said, "establish the government's obligation to provide medical care for those whom it is punishing by incarceration."[98] The failure to provide medical care to prisoners may at the very least cause pain and suffering, and in the worst cases, result in torture or lingering death. The Court concluded that "deliberate indifference to serious medical needs of prisoners constitutes the unnecessary and wanton infliction of pain" in violation of the Eighth Amendment.[99] This indifference can be demonstrated by prison doctors deliberately ignoring the needs of inmates or by guards intentionally denying or delaying access to medical care.

Marshall warned that not every claim by a prisoner who does not receive adequate medical services states a valid Eighth Amendment violation. A physician's negligence in diagnosing or treating a medical problem does not "constitute an unnecessary and wanton infliction of pain," nor can it be viewed as "cruel and unusual punishment."[100] The fact that Gamble was seen by medical personnel on seventeen different occasions during the three-month period indicated, in Marshall's view, that doctors did not act with deliberate indifference. Gamble had no objections to the treatment received for his high blood pressure and heart problems. The failure of the doctors to cure his back injury, Marshall argued, is at most medical malpractice, actionable in a state court under state tort law. The Court concluded that the Court of Appeals was in error to require reversal and remand on the medical issue, but it did remand on the cause of action stated against prison personnel.

In his dissent, Stevens said that there were three reasons why he could not join the Court's opinion. Two of the reasons were procedural in nature, but the third involved the "deliberate indifference" standard. First, Stevens said that the Court's dismissal of a complaint against the chief medical officer of the prison was not faithful to the guidelines established under *Haines v. Kerner* (1972). He pointed out that three judges on the Fifth Circuit thought that enough had been alleged as to require an inquiry into the actual facts. If an evidentiary hearing was permitted, it could have saved the Court the time consumed by hearing the complaint. Stevens criticized the Court for granting certiorari to a case that in his view involved "no more than the application of well-settled principles to a familiar situation, and has little significance except for the respondent." He said that the opinion of the Court "describes the State's duty to provide adequate medical care to prisoners in ambiguous terms which incorrectly relate to the subjective motivation of persons accused of violating the Eighth Amendment rather than to the standard of care required by the Constitution."[101] The standard for whether the Eighth Amendment has been violated, he argued, should depend on the character of the punishment rather than the motivation of those who inflict it. To illustrate his point, Stevens said that regardless of whether the conditions in Andersonville, the infamous Civil War prison, "were the product of design, negligence, or mere poverty, they were cruel and inhuman."[102]

REVISED DEATH PENALTY STATUTES ARE REVIEWED

Following *Furman*, 35 states revised their death penalty statutes to address the concerns of the Court. Georgia's new death penalty statute came before the Court in *Gregg v. Georgia* (1976).[103] Laws in Texas and Florida were also reviewed by the Court in companion cases.[104] The revised Georgia law required a bifurcated trial for capital crimes: in the first stage, guilt is determined in the usual trial court manner; the second stage determines an appropriate sentence. For a jury to impose the death penalty, it has to find at least one of several statutorily prescribed aggravating factors. Death sentences were automatically appealed to the Georgia Supreme Court. The appellate review was required to consider not only the procedural regularity of the trial but whether the evidence supports a finding of an aggravating factor and whether the death sentence is disproportionate to the penalty imposed in similar cases.

Troy Gregg was charged with committing armed robbery and murder. In accordance with the revised procedures for capital cases, he was convicted on two counts of armed robbery and two counts of murder. Finding two aggravating circumstances, the jury sentenced him to death on both counts of murder. The Georgia Supreme Court affirmed the conviction and death sentences. Gregg claimed that the death sentences were cruel and unusual punishment in violation of the Eighth and Fourteenth Amendments. In a 7-to-2 decision, the Court upheld the revised death penalty statutes in Georgia and the other states. Only Brennan and Marshall voted to reverse.

Justice Stewart's plurality opinion, joined by Powell and Stevens, first addressed the argument, made by the petitioner and advocated by Justices Brennan and Marshall, that the punishment of death for the crime of murder is, under all circumstances, "cruel and unusual" and in violation of the Eighth and Fourteenth Amendments. The plurality opinion concluded that history and precedent support the view that capital punishment for the crime of murder is not a violation of the Constitution. Stewart noted that the "death penalty for the crime of murder has a long history of acceptance both in the United States and England" and the penalty "continued to be used into the twentieth century by most American States."[105] The text of the Constitution suggests that the framers accepted capital punishment because at the time the Eighth Amendment was ratified, capital punishment was a common penalty in every state. Moreover, the language of the Fifth and Fourteenth Amendments explicitly acknowledges the existence of capital punishment as a sanction.[106] For the plurality opinion, the most compelling evidence of society's endorsement of the death penalty for murder was the legislative response to *Furman*—at least 35 states enacted new laws that provide for capital punishment for various crimes that result in the death of another person. Stewart said that all of these post–*Furman* laws "make clear that capital punishment itself has not been rejected by the elected representatives of the people."[107] The value of capital punishment as retribution for a crime and as a deterrent is a complex issue that should be left to the judgment of legislatures. The plurality held that "considerations of federalism, as well as respect for the ability of a legislature to evaluate, in terms of its particular State, the moral consensus concerning the death penalty and its social utility as a sanction, require us to conclude . . . that the infliction of death as a punishment for murder is not without justification and thus is not unconstitutionally severe."[108] Finally, the plurality opinion found that the new laws addressed the concerns raised in *Furman* because they "focus the jury's attention on the particularized nature of the crime and the particularized characteristics of the individual defendant."[109] The bifurcated proceeding, the requirement of finding an aggravating factor, and automatic appellate review helped guide the jury and limit its discretion.

Restating his views expressed in *Furman*, Justice Brennan concluded that the law had progressed to the point where the death penalty was no "longer morally tolerable in our civilized society," and therefore "the punishment of death, for whatever crime and under all circumstances, is 'cruel and unusual' in violation of the Eighth and Fourteenth Amendments."[110] For Brennan, a punishment must not be so severe as to be degrading to human dignity. "The fatal constitutional infirmity in the punishment of death is that it 'treats members of the human race as nonhumans, as objects to be toyed with and discarded.' "[111]

Death penalty statutes in North Carolina and Louisiana did not fare as well. Following *Furman*, both states attempted to solve the problem of jury discretion by mandating the death penalty for first-degree murder. Both laws were struck down by the Court. In *Woodson v. North Carolina* (1976), the Court held that the mandatory death sentence statute violated the Eighth and Fourteenth Amendments.[112] Justice Stewart, joined by Powell and Stevens, wrote the judgment for the Court, while Brennan and Marshall issued short statements concurring with the judgment that referred to their dissents in *Gregg*. Stewart wrote that the "history of mandatory death penalty statutes in the United States . . . reveals that the practice of sentencing to death all persons convicted of a particular offense has been rejected as unduly harsh and unworkably rigid,"[113] and therefore incompatible with contemporary values. Stewart argued that the mandatory death penalty law "cannot be exercised within the limits of civilized standards," and provides "no standards to guide the jury in its inevitable exercise of the power to determine which first-degree murderers shall live and which shall die."[114] A third problem with the law, according to Stewart, was that it does not allow the particularized consideration of relevant aspects of the character and record of each defendant. He concluded that in "capital cases the fundamental respect for humanity underlying the Eighth Amendment . . . requires consideration of the character and record of the individual offender and the circumstances of the particular offense."[115]

Expanding its review of state death penalty laws, the Court in *Coker v. Georgia* (1977) held that death is a disproportionate penalty for rape and is therefore prohibited by the Eighth Amendment as cruel and unusual punishment.[116] While serving more than three consecutive life sentences for murder, rape, kidnapping, and assault, Coker escaped from the Ware Correctional Institution in Georgia. He then broke into a couple's home, tied up the husband, and raped his 16-year-old wife. Except for the intimate physical violation, the woman was unharmed. Coker was apprehended, convicted, and sentenced to death under procedures upheld by the Court in *Gregg v. Georgia* (1976). Both the conviction and the sentence were affirmed by the Georgia Supreme Court.

Justice Brennan's docket sheets reveal that at the conference on the merits, only he and Stevens voted to reverse and vacate the sentence.[117] When the judgment was announced, Justice White delivered the opinion to reverse, joined by Stewart, Blackmun, and Stevens. Brennan and Marshall issued brief statements reiterating their views that the death penalty was always unconstitutional, while Powell wrote an opinion concurring in the judgment but dissenting in part. Only Burger and Rehnquist dissented.

Justice White noted the dramatic difference in public acceptability of capital punishment reflected in the post-*Furman* legislative reaction to the death penalty for murder and rape. Following *Furman*, 35 states reinstituted the death penalty for murder. But of the sixteen states in which rape had been a capital offense, only three states provided for the death penalty for rape of an adult woman in their revised statutes—Georgia, North Carolina, and Louisiana. In the latter two states, the Court struck down the laws in *Woodson* and *Roberts*, and neither state reenacted the death penalty for rape. That left Georgia as the only state in the nation that authorized a sentence of death for the rape of an adult woman. According to Justice White, "the legislative rejection of capital punishment for rape strongly confirms our own judgment, which is that death is indeed a disproportionate penalty for the crime of raping an adult woman."[118] He acknowledged that rape was a serious crime deserving serious punishment, but "in terms of moral depravity and the injury to the person and to the public, it does not compare with murder, which does involve the unjustified taking of human life."[119] For the rape victim, White said, life is not over and is not necessarily beyond repair. He concluded that even with the statutory requirement of an aggravating circumstance, the death sentence was still a disproportionate punishment for rape.

Justices Brennan and Marshall, concurring in the judgment, simply recanted their views that the death penalty is in all circumstances cruel and unusual and prohibited by the Eighth and Fourteenth Amendments. Justice Powell dissented in part because he felt that the plurality opinion did not limit its holding to the case before them but instead went "well beyond what is necessary [because] it holds that capital punishment *always*—regardless of the circumstances—is a disproportionate penalty for the crime of rape."[120] Responding to the plurality's language concerning rape, Powell noted that some rapes are brutal and victims "are so grievously injured physically or psychologically that life *is* beyond repair."[121] He concluded that the death penalty may not be disproportionate for the crime of aggravated rape and that the final resolution of the issue must evaluate the objective indicators of society's "evolving standards of decency" as reflected in state legislation and jury decisions in capital cases.

In his dissent, Chief Justice Burger criticized the Court for exceeding the "bounds of proper constitutional adjudication by substituting its policy judgment for that of the state legislature."[122] Like Justice Powell, Burger believed that the holding was unnecessarily broad. It was obvious to him that Coker demonstrated utter disregard for the safety, welfare, and human worth of others and showed no signs of being deterred by long sentences. He would hold that the death sentence imposed in the case was within the power reserved to the state and would leave the question of its application under other circumstances for another day. Burger also emphasized the victims' rights and disagreed with the Court's contention that rape was a crime "light years" removed from murder in the degree of its heinousness. In his view, rape is a terrible crime that poses a serious potential danger to the life and safety of innocent victims. States should have the discretion to impose a punishment of death for rape if that is the considered judgment of the legislators.

One year later, the Court, in *Lockett v. Ohio* (1978), held that the Eighth Amendment requires individualized consideration of mitigating factors during capital sentencing.[123] Sandra Lockett was charged with aggravated murder and aggravated robbery in Ohio. She had participated in the robbery of a pawnshop with her brother and two other men. Lockett helped plan the robbery, but she did not enter the pawnshop because she knew the owner. When the offenders pulled a gun on the pawnbroker, the weapon discharged, killing him. Lockett and the others fled the scene and were arrested a short time later. The state alleged that the murder was committed for the purpose of escaping detention and while attempting to flee after committing aggravated robbery. The jury found Lockett guilty as charged. The Ohio death penalty statute authorized the trial judge to impose a death sentence unless, after considering the nature and circumstances of the crime and the defendant's history, character, and condition, he found "by a preponderance of the evidence that (1) the victim had induced or facilitated the offense, (2) it was unlikely that Lockett would have committed the offense but for the fact that she was 'under duress, coercion, or strong provocation,' or (3) the offense was primarily the product of [Lockett's] psychosis or mental deficiency."[124] The trial judge asked for a pre-sentence report and a psychiatric and psychological analysis. The reports revealed that Lockett was receiving treatment for a drug problem but that she suffered no psychosis or had any mental problems. With this evidence in hand, the judge determined that the offense had not been the product of a psychological or mental illness, and he sentenced Lockett to death. Lockett challenged her death sentence on the grounds that the state law did not permit the sentencing judge to consider, as possible mitigating factors, her age, criminal record, lack of specific intent to cause the death, or role in committing the crime.

Following oral argument, Chief Justice Burger circulated a memo to the conference discussing his views of the case. Although his initial re-action was to affirm the sentence, he reserved his vote at the conference on the merits. Burger indicated in his memo that he did not think that the Ohio law permitted the sentencing judge to fully consider what he called "comparative culpability."[125] Even though he did not agree with the views of the plurality opinion in *Furman* and other capital sentencing cases, Burger said that he was "prepared to yield with the hope that there can be a majority opinion here," because in his view, the "plurality opinions on the death penalty have created uncertainty and instability in an area which deserves the greatest certainty and stability."[126] He of-fered to write a memo detailing his arguments. On April 10, Burger circulated his memo. He suggested that the Court base its decision on the arguments made by the two- and three-member pluralities in *Furman*, *Gregg*, and *Woodson*, which focused on the need to make certain that the sentencing processes were consistent with "civilized standards."[127] Days later, Justices Stevens, Stewart, and Powell circulated a memo to the chief justice stating that they agreed with the basic argument expressed in Burger's memo and applauded his efforts to demonstrate leadership on the issue. Stewart argued that the opinion should be based on the Eighth Amendment rather than the Fourteenth Due Process Clause, because "a decision based upon Due Process would call into question the constitu-tional validity of literally thousands of sentences imposed upon con-victed defendants throughout the country, and would surely lead to countless habeas corpus petitions attacking those convictions."[128] Rehn-quist, however, wrote that he would likely not join in Burger's opinion, because he was concerned about any "spillover outside the area of the death sentence."[129]

Ultimately, Chief Justice Burger's attempt to pull together a majority failed. On the sentencing issue, Burger announced a plurality opinion, joined by Stewart, Powell, and Stevens. Marshall concurred in the judgment but continued to adhere to his view that capital punishment was always unconstitutional. Blackmun also concurred in the judgment. Justices White and Rehnquist dissented, while Brennan took no part in the case. The plurality opinion concluded that "the Eighth and Fourteenth Amendments require that the sentencer, in all but the rarest kind of capital case, not be precluded from considering, *as a mitigating factor*, any aspect of a defendant's character or record and any of the circumstances of the offense that the defendant proffers as a basis for a sentence less than death."[130] The failure to consider these factors creates a risk that the death penalty may be imposed when a less severe sentence is warranted. "When the choice is between life and death," Burger wrote, "that risk is unacceptable and incompatible with the commands of the Eighth and Fourteenth Amendments."[131]

In *Enmund v. Florida* (1982), the Court had to decide if death was a valid penalty under the Eighth and Fourteenth Amendments for someone who neither took life, attempted to take life, nor intended to take life.[132] On April 1, 1975, Sampson and Jeanette Armstrong approached the back door of Thomas and Eunice Kersey's farmhouse on the pretext of obtaining water for their overheated car. The Armstrongs attempted to rob the couple, gunfire was exchanged, and both of the Kerseys were killed. The Armstrongs dragged the bodies into the kitchen, took Thomas Kersey's money, and fled to a nearby car, where Earl Enmund was waiting to help them escape. A jury found both Enmund and Sampson Armstrong guilty of two counts of first-degree murder and one count of robbery. Both men were sentenced to death, and the Florida Supreme Court affirmed Enmund's conviction and sentence. Enmund claimed that because the evidence did not establish that he intended to take life, the death penalty was prohibited by the Eighth Amendment.

The Court was divided 5 to 4 in holding that the imposition of the death penalty upon Enmund was inconsistent with the Eighth and Fourteenth Amendments. Justice White wrote the opinion of the Court, joined by Brennan, Marshall, Blackmun, and Stevens. Brennan also drafted a short concurring opinion expressing his view that the death penalty was always unconstitutional. Justice O'Connor filed a dissenting opinion in which Chief Justice Burger, Powell, and Rehnquist joined.

Justice White approached the case in a manner similar to the Court's plurality in *Coker v. Georgia* (1977). He began his opinion by reviewing the objective factors the Court has used in determining contemporary standards of criminal punishment. Of the 36 states that authorized the death penalty, only eight jurisdictions permitted the imposition of capital punishment for participation in a robbery in which another robber takes a life. In eleven states that provide for capital punishment, the actors in a felony murder are not subject to the death penalty unless there is proof of a culpable mental state, such as intentional murder, premeditated killing, or extreme indifference to human life. This kind of proof was not required in Enmund's case. Four states did not allow a defendant such as Enmund to be put to death, while in nine others, a defendant could not be executed *solely* for participating in a felony in which a person was killed but the defendant did not directly cause the murder.[133] "Only a small minority of jurisdictions—eight—allow the death penalty to be imposed," the Court said, "solely because the defendant somehow participated in a robbery in the course of which a murder was committed."[134] Although the legislative judgment was not unanimous nor as compelling as considered in *Coker*, the Court concluded that the evidence weighs on the side of rejecting capital punishment where a defendant did not take life, attempt to take life, or intend to take the life of another person.

Justice White also noted that juries have overwhelmingly rejected the death penalty for accomplice liability in felony murders. For example, a survey of death penalty cases from 1954 through 1981 revealed only six cases out of 362 where a nontriggerman felony murderer was put to death.[135] Another survey conducted by the NAACP LDF found that of the 796 inmates on death row for homicide in 1981, only three prisoners, including Enmund, were sentenced to death without any evidence that they hired or solicited someone else to kill or participate in a scheme to kill the victim.[136] The Court said that Enmund's "criminal culpability must be limited to his participation in the robbery, and his punishment must be tailored to his personal responsibility and moral guilt." Because he did not kill or intend to kill, the Court reasoned, Enmund's culpability was "plainly different from that of the robbers who killed; yet the State treated them alike and attributed to Enmund the culpability of those who killed the Kerseys. This was impermissible under the Eighth Amendment."[137]

In her dissenting opinion, Justice O'Connor stated that the Court must base its decision not only on whether Enmund's sentence offends contemporary standards, as reflected in state laws and jury decisions, but also whether it is disproportionate to the harm caused and to the petitioner's involvement in the crime, as well as whether the procedures used to sentence Enmund satisfied the individualized consideration required by the Constitution. Justice O'Connor did not feel that the historical evidence or contemporary standards demonstrated that society has rejected the death penalty for felony murderers. She criticized the Court's interpretation of state laws; according to her calculations, 23 states authorized the imposition of the death penalty, even though the felony murderer has neither killed nor intended to kill his victim. On the question of proportionality in sentencing under the Eighth Amendment, Justice O'Connor distinguished the crime committed by Enmund from the crime of rape in *Coker*, and she concluded that the "death penalty is not disproportionate to the crime of felony murder, even though the defendant did not actually kill or intend to kill his victims."[138] She did concede that the trial judge effectively prevented the consideration of mitigating circumstances and that this made it impossible for the trial court to evaluate the circumstances of the particular offense. Because this error may have had an effect on the sentencing judge's decision, Justice O'Connor said she would vacate the decision and remand for a new sentencing hearing.

COURT REAFFIRMS ACCESS TO LEGAL RESOURCES

In *Bounds v. Smith* (1977), the Court supported its holding in *Younger v. Gilmore* (1971), that prisoners have a constitutional right to legal services.[139] The state of North Carolina argued that precedents such as *Johnson v. Avery* (1969), which involved prisoner access to legal resources, merely required the state to permit inmate "writ writers" to function. The state further argued that as long as inmates were free to communicate with each other about their legal problems, there was no further obligation to spend state funds to effectively guarantee the right of access to the courts. The Court, however, said that those arguments misread previous decisions.

Writing for a six-justice majority, Justice Marshall stated that earlier decisions have "consistently required States to shoulder affirmative obligations to assure all prisoners meaningful access to the courts."[140] Marshall admitted that economic factors may be considered in choosing the methods of providing access, "but the cost of protecting a constitutional right cannot justify its total denial."[141] The question was whether law libraries or other forms of legal assistance were needed to give prisoners a reasonable opportunity to present their claims to the courts. The Court argued that a law library was an important tool to draft a petition. The state suggested that most prisoners were not competent enough to use the materials in a law library, but Marshall said that the Court's experience indicates that *pro se* petitioners are capable of using law books to file cases. In reaffirming *Younger v. Gilmore*, the Court held that the "fundamental constitutional right of access to the courts requires prison authorities to assist inmates in the preparation and filing of meaningful legal papers by providing prisoners with adequate law libraries or adequate assistance from persons trained in the law."[142]

PRESS DENIED ACCESS TO PRISONS

Extending the holding in *Pell v. Procunier* (1974), the Court ruled in *Houchins v. KQED* (1978) that the media and public may be denied any access to prisons.[143] In this case, KQED, a public television station operating out of Oakland, California, was denied permission during a public tour to inspect and take photographs of a portion of the Alameda County Jail known as Little Greystone, an area in which a prisoner's suicide had reportedly taken place, where the physical conditions were so terrible that they were affecting the health of the inmates. Cameras and tape recorders were not allowed on the tour, and the media was prohibited from interviewing inmates. KQED argued that these restrictions violated the First Amendment by denying media access and failing to provide an effective means for the public to be informed of conditions within the jail. The District Court was unpersuaded by the petitioner's contention that the media policy in place was necessary to protect inmate privacy or to minimize administrative and security problems. It issued a preliminary injunction ordering the sheriff to give reporters access to the Little Greystone facility and permit them to interview inmates on a random basis. Houchins appealed the District Court order, invoking *Pell v. Procunier* and arguing that the District Court had abused its discretion by granting the media greater access to the jail than the general public. The Court of Appeals sustained the order, however, holding that *Pell* and *Saxbe v. Washington Post Co.* (1974) were not controlling, and that the public and media had a First Amendment and Fourteenth Amendment right of access to prisons and jails.

Justices Marshall and Blackmun did not participate in the consideration or decision of the case. At the conference on the merits, the vote was 4 to 3 to affirm the Appeals Court decision. The majority consisted of Justices Brennan, Stewart, Powell, and Stevens; Burger, White, and Rehnquist voted to affirm. Stevens circulated a draft of a majority opinion in March to which Brennan and Powell agreed to join. On April 24, however, Stewart sent a memo to the conference that he would not join Stevens's opinion. He wrote, "I cannot bring myself to agree that a county sheriff is constitutionally required to open up a jail that he runs to the press and public."[144] Stewart felt that the television station should have been granted access equal to existing public access, but not the much broader injunctive relief issued by the District Court. Because of the vote change, Chief Justice Burger assumed the task of writing a judgment for the Court, and Stewart filed a concurring opinion. Stevens's majority opinion became a dissent joined by Brennan and Powell.

Burger acknowledged that conditions in prisons and jails are matters of public concern, and he recognized that the media play an important role in providing information about prison conditions. Still, Burger argued that the "public importance of conditions in penal facilities and the media's role of providing information afford no basis for reading into the Constitution a right of the public or the media to enter these institutions, with camera equipment, and take moving and still pictures of inmates for broadcast purposes."[145] The media have a right to gather news, he stated, but there is no First Amendment right to compel private persons or governments to supply information. The chief justice believed that *Pell* and *Saxbe* controlled the outcome, because in "those cases the Court declared, explicitly and without reservation, that the media have 'no constitutional right of access to prisons or their inmates beyond that afforded the general public.' "[146] Finally, Burger argued that the kind of access to prisons and jails sought by KQED is a policy issue more appropriately reserved for the legislative process. He suggested that there are a number of alternatives available to prevent problems in penal facilities from escaping public attention, including citizen task forces, grand jury investigations, and legislative oversight. The choice regarding the most effective method of disclosure was a legislative task. It is difficult to accept, however, that official boards and other government mechanisms can be relied upon to provide objective information about prison conditions.

Decisions such as *Houchins* and *Pell* obviously made it more difficult to scrutinize conditions in jails and prisons. In his study of the Burger Court and prisoners' rights, Herman Schwartz argues that these decisions undermined a central strategy of the prison reform movement: to bring outsiders into the prison and to publicize the conditions within the prison system.[147] Prisons were distant from the general public, both literally and figuratively. Television cameras and one-on-one prisoner-press interviews would make visible problems that for the most part were invisible. Because of the Court's rulings, prison officials could now prevent contact between the press and inmates and could limit public information about the correctional system to what a journalist or scholar could collect on guided tours or through other casual contacts.

DOUBLE-CELLING OF INMATES UPHELD

In *Bell v. Wolfish* (1979), the Court found no constitutional grounds for prohibiting the double-celling of inmates.[148] Because the case involved pretrial detainees incarcerated at the Metropolitan Correctional Center (MCC) in New York City, the Court found compensatory value in the limited hours that detainees were confined to their cells and in their short prison sentences. Writing for the Court, Justice Rehnquist disagreed with the lower courts that there is some sort of "one man, one cell" principle embodied in the Due Process Clause of the Fifth Amendment. "We simply do not believe," he said, "that requiring a detainee to share toilet facilities and [an] admittedly small sleeping place with another person for generally a maximum of 60 days violates the Constitution."[149]

The Court also upheld several regulations, including a prohibition against the receipt of hardback books from anyone except the publisher; a prohibition against the receipt of packages; a provision requiring mandatory body cavity searches following contact visits; and spot searches of cells while the prisoner is absent. Citing *Wolff v. McDonnell* (1974), the Court stated that there must be a "mutual accommodation between institutional needs and objectives and the provisions of the Constitution that are of general application," and that this "principle applies equally to pretrial detainees and prisoners."[150] The Court acknowledged that problems inherent in the management of a prison facility or jail are not easy to solve; therefore, "prison administrators should be according wide-ranging deference in the adoption and execution of policies and practices that in their judgment are needed to preserve internal order and discipline and to maintain institutional security."[151]

In *Rhodes v. Chapman* (1981), the Supreme Court again took up the issue of double-celling.[152] It marked the first time that the Court directly addressed the issue of overcrowding in state prisons. The case involved allegations of overcrowding and double-celling of inmates at the modern Southern Ohio Correctional Facility (SOCF) in Lucasville, Ohio. Based on several considerations, the District Court held that double-celling at the SOCF was cruel and unusual punishment. The District Court noted that the SOCF housed 38 percent more inmates than its design capacity, that double-celling did not provide adequate space per inmate, and that the SOCF had made double-celling a practice rather than a temporary condition.[153] The Sixth Circuit Court of Appeals affirmed on the grounds that the conclusions of law were permissible from the findings and the remedy was a reasonable response to the violations found.

Even though the inmate population far exceeded the rated capacity of the institution, the Court was unable to identify any evidence that double-celling seriously harmed inmates there. Inmates had not been deprived of food, medical care, or adequate sanitation, and there was no measurable increase in violence. In its decision, the Court adhered to its long-standing flexibility test: the Eighth Amendment must draw its meaning from the evolving standards of decency that mark the progress of a maturing society. To be cruel and unusual, a practice or condition must be shown on the facts at hand to violate this standard. While the Court recognized that overcrowded conditions at the Ohio facility may have caused a delay in receiving some services, it concluded that these deprivations did not constitute cruel and unusual punishment. Writing for the Court, Justice Powell argued that "The Constitution does not mandate comfortable prisons," and to the extent that prison conditions are "restrictive and even harsh, they are part of the penalty that criminal offenders pay for their offenses against society."[154]

PROPORTIONALITY IN PUNISHMENT

Over a three-year period, the Court decided several noncapital cases—two by full opinion and one *per curium* decision—involving a proportionality principle under the Eighth Amendment. In *Rummel v. Estelle*

(1980), a very divided Court held that the Eighth Amendment is not violated when a state imposes a mandatory life sentence for someone convicted of three nonviolent felonies.[155] In separate prosecutions over a period of years, Rummel had been convicted of the fraudulent use of a credit card, forging a check, and obtaining money under false pretenses. Under Texas law, Rummel was considered a habitual offender and was sentenced to life in prison. Both the District Court and Court of Appeals rejected Rummel's claim that his sentence was so disproportionate to the crimes that his punishment was cruel and unusual. The Appeals Court thought it significant that Rummel would be eligible for parole within twelve years of his confinement. The certiorari vote was 4 to 4 to accept the case, with Rehnquist not participating. On the merits, Rehnquist joined Chief Justice Burger and Justices Stewart, White, and Blackmun in voting to affirm.

In his majority opinion, Justice Rehnquist did not discuss the history of the Eighth Amendment, the intent of the framers, or even the text.[156] His opinion was based almost entirely on an analysis of case law. Rehnquist said that proportionality analysis applies to the death penalty because of the unique nature of the punishment. He recognized that the Court had in the past stated that the cruel and unusual punishment clause of the Eighth Amendment "prohibits imposition of a sentence that is grossly disproportionate to the severity of the crime."[157] He distinguished the precedent of *Weems v. United States* (1910), however, by stating that the Court's finding of disproportionality could not be disconnected from the extreme facts of the case.[158] Rehnquist argued that the length of punishments for recidivists are "matters largely within the discretion of the punishing jurisdiction," and that the state decides the length of a prison sentence "subject only to those strictures of the Eighth Amendment that can be informed by objective factors."[159] The majority opinion affirmed the proportionality doctrine for the death penalty and extreme noncapital punishments outside of the Anglo-Saxon system, but the Court failed to develop criteria for extreme cases and did not identify the objective factors for a proportionality analysis under the Eighth Amendment.

Justice Powell's dissenting opinion devoted more attention to the history of the Eighth Amendment and intent of the framers. Powell criticized the majority opinion for suggesting that the proportionality principle may be less applicable to noncapital sentences, and he argued that such a "limitation finds no support in the history of Eighth Amendment jurisprudence."[160] He stated that a few basic principles emerge from that history:

Both barbarous forms of punishment and grossly excessive punishments are cruel and unusual. A sentence may be excessive if it serves no acceptable social purpose, or is grossly disproportionate to the seriousness of the crime. The principle of proportionality has been acknowledged to apply to both capital and noncapital sentences.[161]

Powell disagreed with the Court of Appeals, which concluded that with good-time credits, Rummel might be eligible for parole within ten or twelve years. Powell pointed out that Rummel would have "no right to early release; he will be merely eligible for parole. And parole is simply an act of legislative grace."[162] The Eighth Amendment, he said, "commands the Court to enforce the constitutional limitation of the Cruel and Unusual Punishments Clause."[163] He proceeded to identify several objective factors that courts should consider when assessing the proportionality of a sentence: (1) the nature of the offense; (2) the sentence imposed for the same crime in other jurisdictions; and (3) the sentence imposed upon other criminals in the same jurisdiction.[164] Applying these factors, Powell concluded that Rummel had suffered a cruel and unusual punishment. Rummel committed a property-related offense that did not threaten another's person or the peace of society. His sentence was harsher than those given to first-time or second-time offenders convicted of more serious crimes. Finally, the Texas criminal justice system assumes that all three-time offenders deserve the same punishment, regardless of whether they committed three murders or cashed three fraudulent checks.

In *Hutto v. Davis* (1982), the Court returned to the issue of proportionality in punishment. Davis was convicted under Virginia law of possessing with intent to distribute and distribution of nine ounces of marijuana, and he was sentenced to 40 years in prison. The District Court granted a writ of habeas corpus and found the punishment to be cruel and unusual. The Circuit Court of Appeals reversed, but the entire Circuit Court, sitting *en banc*, affirmed the award of habeas corpus relief. The Court granted certiorari and remanded the case in light of its decision in *Rummel*. Refusing to follow the *Rummel* precedent, the Appeals Court again affirmed the District Court. In a *per curium* opinion, the Court, without discussing the facts of the case, held that *Rummel* was controlling, and thus reversed.

The Court said that *Rummel* stands for the proposition that "federal courts should be reluctant to review legislatively mandated terms of imprisonment."[165] It also criticized the Court of Appeals for "having ignored, consciously or unconsciously, the hierarchy of the federal court system created by the Constitution and Congress."[166] The decision rejected the "objective factors" applied by the District Court and effectively extended the *Rummel* holding beyond recidivist statutes to prohibit any attempt to apply the proportionality doctrine to prison sentences.

Justice Powell, author of the dissenting opinion in *Rummel*, concurred with the Court in *Hutto*. He believed that there were features of Davis's case that distinguished it from *Rummel*. He compared Davis's drug conviction to the minor property-related offenses of Rummel. He also noted that Rummel's sentence was more severe than Davis's and that Davis was unable to show, by statutory comparison, that his sentence reflected a greater degree of disproportionality than did Rummel's.

Justice Brennan, joined by Marshall and Stevens, dissented from the *per curium* opinion. He sent a memo to the conference on November 9, arguing that the case was deserving of oral argument because he believed that "there must be some judicial review of disproportionality in sentencing."[167] Discussing the decision in *Rummel*, Justice Brennan said that even if he viewed the decision as properly decided, which he did not, "the per curium, by suggesting that it was improper for the courts below to engage in a disproportionality analysis, represents a serious and improper expansion of *Rummel*."[168] He argued that the Court's policy of deference "cannot justify the complete abdication of our responsibility to enforce the Eighth Amendment."[169] Brennan was upset that the *per curium* opinion made no effort to demonstrate why the case was not one of those "exceedingly rare" cases in which the Eighth Amendment would invalidate the sentence as disproportionate. He said that it was obvious to him, as it was to five judges on the Court of Appeals, that this was one of those "exceedingly rare" cases in which the punishment should be declared disproportionate to the offense.

Brennan came to this conclusion for several reasons. First he noted that the punishment imposed on Davis—40 years and $20,000 in fines— was not only harsh but also exceeded punishments imposed by Virginia courts on other defendants. He pointed out that the case was unique because the prosecutor who brought charges against Davis was forced to admit that the punishment represented a "grave disparity in sentencing" and that his incarceration was "grossly unjust."[170] Finally, Brennan stated that the Virginia legislature implied that the punishment was too severe because in 1979 it reduced the maximum sentence for the two offenses for which Davis was convicted from 40 years to 10 years.

The following year, however, the Court backed away from the *Rummel* precedent, though not explicitly overruling it. In *Solem v. Helm* (1983), the Supreme Court attempted to define the concept of "cruel and unusual" punishment in a noncapital case. By 1979, Jerry Helm had been convicted in South Dakota for the commission of six nonviolent felonies over the years. Helm was charged with another nonviolent offense that year—writing bad checks. He was convicted and received a life sentence without parole. On appeal, the Supreme Court ruled that Helm's sentence *did* constitute cruel and unusual punishment. The difference between *Rummel* and *Solem* was a switch in votes—Justice Blackmun, who cast the deciding fifth vote in *Rummel*, joined *Rummel's* four dissenters (Brennan, Marshall, Powell, and Stevens) in *Solem*.

Writing for the majority in *Solem*, Justice Powell stated that the "principle that a punishment should be proportionate to the crime is deeply rooted and frequently repeated in common-law jurisprudence."[171] Citing the Magna Carta (1215), the English Bill of Rights (1689), and several Supreme Court precedents, such as *Weems v. United States* (1910), Powell concluded that the Eighth Amendment "prohibits not only barbaric punishments, but also sentences that are disproportionate to the crime committed."[172] The state had suggested that the principle of proportionality was limited to capital punishment cases, but Powell rejected that argument, pointing out that the constitutional language makes no exceptions for imprisonment.

Powell proposed that proportionality analysis under the Eighth Amendment should be guided by objective criteria, including "(i) the gravity of the offense and the harshness of the penalty; (ii) the sentences imposed on other criminals in the same jurisdiction; and (iii) the sentences imposed for commission of the same crime in other jurisdictions."[173] Applying these criteria, the Court found that Helms's sentence was significantly disproportionate to the crime. Distinguishing the *Rummel* precedent, the Court in *Solem* noted that Rummel was eligible for parole within twelve years of his confinement, whereas Helm faced life imprisonment without parole. Helm's only recourse was executive clemency, which is more difficult to obtain than parole. The difference between the cases was enough for Justice Blackmun to switch his vote in favor of proportionality.

COURT SHOWS MORE DEFERENCE TOWARD PRISON ADMINISTRATORS

By 1981, there was a solid conservative bloc on the Court consisting of Chief Justice Burger and Justices Rehnquist, White, and O'Connor. Powell was the key swing vote, and more often than not he voted with the conservatives. During the last five years of Warren Burger's tenure as chief justice, the Court consistently rejected the claims of prisoners and granted more discretion to prison and jail administrators. It used strong language in denying the constitutional arguments of prisoners, and on some issues it seemed to suggest that prisoners have virtually no judicially protected rights.[174]

For example, in *Hudson v. Palmer* (1984), the Court held that prisoners have no reasonable expectation of privacy in their prison cells.[175] This case involved a "shakedown" search conducted by Hudson and a fellow officer of Palmer's prison cell. The officers discovered a ripped pillowcase in the trash near Palmer's bunk and initiated charges under prison disciplinary procedures. Palmer claimed that Hudson brought a false charge against him solely to harass him, and that the officer intentionally destroyed some noncontraband personal property during the search. The District Court accepted Palmer's allegations but granted summary judgment in favor of Hudson. The Court reasoned that even if the destruction of property were intentional, it did not violate the Fourteenth Amendment, because state tort remedies were available and the alleged harassment did not amount to a constitutional deprivation. The Court of Appeals reversed the summary judgment on the claim that the shakedown search was unreasonable, holding that an "individual prisoner has a 'limited privacy right' in his cell entitling him to protection against searches conducted solely to harass or to humiliate."[176]

At the conference on the merits, the Court was closely divided. Burger, White, Rehnquist, and O'Connor voted to reverse; Brennan, Marshall, Blackmun, and Stevens voted to affirm. Conference notes indicate that Powell was troubled by the "alleged invidious destruction of personal property" but reflecting his indecisiveness, he decided to pass on his vote.[177] Stevens agreed to write an opinion for the dissenters. On June 1, 1984, he circulated a memo to the conference in which he argued that the Fourth Amendment protects not just privacy interests but possessory interests as well. He concluded that "taking and destroying property a prisoner is entitled to have under relevant prison regulations is an unreasonable seizure prohibited by the Fourth Amendment."[178] But several days later, the chief justice distributed a memo responding to Stevens's argument. He proposed a short textual paragraph to the opinion of the Court, contending that the Fourth Amendment protection against unreasonable seizures is just as inapplicable to prison cells as is the protection on searches. Arguably, Burger wrote, "prison officials could constitutionally deny all possessory interests in material personal possessions" during the period of incarceration.[179] This does not mean that officials can destroy property with impunity; he argued that Palmer had a state remedy, apart from inmate grievance procedures, that satisfied due process requirements. Burger's memo was convincing enough, at least to Justice Powell, who agreed to join Burger's opinion on the day the memo was circulated.

In his opinion for the Court, Burger acknowledged that prisons are not beyond the reach of the Constitution, and that prisoners possess rights not inconsistent with the goals of incarceration or prison administration. Yet he asserted that "society is not prepared to recognize as legitimate any subjective expectation of privacy that a prisoner might have in his prison cell," therefore, "the Fourth Amendment proscription against unreasonable searches does not apply within the confines of the prison cell."[180] In determining whether an expectation of privacy is legitimate or reasonable, Burger said that the Court must balance the interest of society in the security of its penal institutions and the interest of the prisoner in privacy within his cell. Viewed in those terms, Burger concluded that the balance be struck in favor of institutional security. He noted that this does not leave a prisoner entirely unprotected—state tort law and common law provide remedies for calculated harassment unrelated to prison needs.

Stevens concurred with Part II-B of the majority opinion, where the Court held that Palmer's complaint does not allege a violation of his right to procedural due process, but he strongly disagreed with the reasoning in the first part of the opinion. In an unusual move designed to underscore his disagreement with the majority opinion, Stevens read his dissent from the bench. Compared to the conditions that prevail in a free society, neither "the possessions nor the slight residuum of privacy that an inmate retains can have more than the most minimal value," but from the prisoners' perspective, "that trivial residuum may mark the difference between slavery and humanity."[181]

Stevens argued that the Court was fundamentally wrong in suggesting that a societal interest in the security of penal institutions prevents prisoners from having any legitimate possessory interests. First, he noted that Palmer's possession of the material was perfectly legal as a matter of state law. The personal material was not contraband nor was possession of it in conflict with prison regulations. In sum, Palmer had a legal right under both state law and the Due Process Clause to possess the material. Second, Palmer's possessory interests are protected as a matter of constitutional law and to rule otherwise would violate the Eighth Amendment. Stevens wrote that "to hold that a prisoner's possession of a letter from his wife, or a picture of his baby, has no protection against arbitrary or malicious perusal, seizure, or destruction would not . . . comport with any civilized standards of decency."[182]

Citing numerous precedents, Stevens argued that the discretion of prison administrators is not absolute. Prisoners retain constitutional rights not inconsistent with legitimate penological goals. "There can be no penological justification for the seizure alleged here," he said, because Palmer's property did not pose a threat to institutional security. Stevens also criticized the Court's contention that society would not recognize as reasonable the possessory interests of prisoners. This perception was not based on empirical data but merely reflected the perception of the five justices in the majority. He pointed out that nearly every federal judge who has addressed the question over the past decade concluded that the Fourth Amendment does apply to a prison cell. Stevens also suggested that the Court's opinion was not based on legitimate institutional interests, because "depriving inmates of any residuum of privacy or possessory rights is in fact plainly *contrary* to institutional goals. Sociologists recognize that prisoners deprived of any sense of individuality devalue themselves and others and therefore are more prone to violence toward themselves and others."[183] Finally, Stevens closed his dissent with some harsh words for the Court:

Once it is agreed that random searches of a prisoner's cell are reasonable to ensure that the cell contains no contraband, there can be no need for seizure and destruction of noncontraband items found during such searches. To accord prisoners any less protection is to declare that prisoners are entitled to no measure of human dignity or individuality. . . . Yet that is the view that the Court takes today. It declares prisoners to be little more than chattels, a view I thought society had outgrown long ago.[184]

On the same day the *Palmer* opinion was announced, the Court made public its decision in *Block v. Rutherford* (1984).[185] This case involved a challenge to the Los Angeles County Central Jail's policy of denying pretrial detainees contact visits with their spouses, family, and friends, and to the jail's practice of permitting irregularly scheduled searches of cells in the absence of the occupants. The District Court and Court of Appeals held that the complete ban on contact visits was excessive in relation to the security and other interests at stake. Distinguishing *Bell v. Wolfish* (1979), the Court of Appeals confirmed the District Court order requiring that certain detainees be permitted contact visits and that inmates be allowed to watch searches of their cells. The Court granted certiorari, and by a 6 to 3 vote, it reversed on both the contact visit and search issues.

Writing for the Court, Chief Justice Burger stated that the principles articulated in *Wolfish* determine the resolution of this case. He said the question is whether the blanket ban on contact visits is reasonably related to the security of the Central Jail facility. According to Burger, there are many justifications for denying contact visits entirely, rather than creating a program of limited visitations. He mentioned the potential danger of low security risk detainees being used to obtain contraband or weapons. Other problems included the difficulty of identifying inmates who have propensities for violence, escape, or drug smuggling. The Court concluded that the blanket prohibition on contact visits "is an entirely reasonable, nonpunitive response to the legitimate security concerns identified, consistent with the Fourteenth Amendment."[186] Extending the rationale of deference to prison officials used in *Wolfish*, the Court held that "the Constitution does not require that detainees be allowed contact visits when responsible, experienced administrators have determined, in their sound discretion, that such visits will jeopardize the security of the facility."[187] On the search issue, the Court saw no difference between the search practices employed by the Central Jail and those that the Court upheld in *Wolfish*, therefore, it refused to reconsider the issue.

In *Whitley v. Albers* (1986), the Court ruled that the shooting of Albers during a riot at the Oregon State Penitentiary did not violate Albers' Eighth Amendment right to be free from cruel and unusual punishments.[188] The Ninth Circuit Court of Appeals had held that an Eighth Amendment violation would be established if "a prison official deliberately shot Albers under circumstances where the official with due allowance for the exigency, knew or should have known that it was unnecessary," or "if the emergency plan was adopted or carried out with 'deliberate indifference' to the right of Albers to be free of cruel and unusual punishment."[189] To violate the Eighth Amendment, the Court argued that conduct that is not punishment must involve more than ordinary negligence for the prisoner's interests and safety. "Obduracy and wantonness, not inadvertence or error in good faith" characterize the conduct prohibited by the Cruel and Unusual Punishments Clause.[190] The Court said that the "deliberate indifference" standard announced in *Estelle v. Gamble* (1976) was appropriate in the context presented in that case, because the state's responsibility to attend to the medical needs of prisoners did not clash with other important governmental responsibilities. But this case was different. In making and executing decisions to use force, prison administrators must ensure the safety of the prison staff, visitors, and the inmates themselves. The Court argued that "a deliberate indifference standard does not adequately capture the importance of such competing obligations, or convey the appropriate hesitancy to critique in hindsight decisions necessarily made in haste, under pressure, and frequently without the luxury of a second chance."[191] The same deference that was extended to preventive measures intended to reduce breaches of inmate discipline in *Bell v. Wolfish* should be extended to a prison security measure taken in response to an actual confrontation with riotous inmates. When prison officials use force to quell a disturbance, the question of whether their actions inflicted "unnecessary and wanton pain and suffering" should turn on whether "force was applied in a good faith effort to maintain or restore discipline or maliciously and sadistically for the very purpose of causing harm."[192] Viewed in the most favorable light to the plaintiff, the Court did not feel that the evidence demonstrated unnecessary or wanton infliction of pain and therefore did not violate the Eighth Amendment.

Marshall's dissenting opinion, joined by Stewart, Powell, and Stevens, criticized the Court for improperly extending the "unnecessary and wanton" standard for Eighth Amendment claims by requiring express intent to inflict unnecessary pain.[193] He believed that a jury, rather than a judge, should properly assess whether there was a disturbance that caused significant risks to the safety of inmates and prison staff. Marshall also disputed the Court's interpretation of the evidence. The issue of "wantonness in the context of a prison disorder," he said, "is a matter of degree," and "it is precisely in cases like this one, when shading the facts one way or another can result in different legal conclusions, that a jury should be permitted to do its job."[194]

THE BURGER COURT AND PRISONERS' RIGHTS: AN ASSESSMENT

The Burger Court clearly had a mixed record on prisoners' rights. Throughout this period, lower federal courts were actively reviewing prison conditions and practices. In some cases, federal judges issued broad remedial decrees over an entire state prison system. The Burger Court showed some initial support for expanding the rights of prisoners. In several *per curium* decisions, the Court protected an inmate's access to legal materials and ensured that *pro se* complaints would be given adequate review in the lower courts. In *Cruz v. Beto* (1972), the Court said that reasonable accommodations must be made for prisoners to exercise their religious freedom. That same year, the Court determined that state death penalty sentences were being imposed in a "wantonly and freakishly" manner and were unconstitutional. The Court also protected inmate mail privileges and access to legal services in *Pell v. Procunier* (1974) and extended limited due process protections in prison disciplinary hearings in *Wolff v. McDonnell* (1974). Following *Wolff*, lower federal courts tried to impose more procedural requirements on prison administrators, but in *Baxter v. Palmigiano* (1976), *Meachum v. Fano* (1976), and *Montanye v. Haymes* (1976), the Court found the additional due process protections inconsistent with the "mutual accommodation" between the needs and objectives of prisons and the constitutional rights of inmates.

By 1975, however, a shift had occurred in the Court's approach to prisoner litigation. The Court reinstated state death penalty statutes in *Gregg v. Georgia* (1976), although it did strike down such punishments for the crime of rape in *Coker v. Georgia* (1977) and for felony murder in *Enmund v. Florida* (1982). In noncapital punishment cases, the Court weakened the principle of proportionality under the Eighth Amendment in *Rummel v. Estelle* (1980), only to revive proportionality review in *Solem v. Helm* (1983).

In other cases involving prison conditions and practices, claims that had been found meritorious in the lower courts were consistently rejected by the Court. Although the Court used a mutual accommodation approach to balance the rights of prisoners against the institutional interests in security and discipline, the scales were often tipped in favor of prison administrators. In cases such as *Bell v. Wolfish* (1979), *Hudson v. Palmer* (1984), *Block v. Rutherford* (1984), and *Whitley v. Albers* (1986), the prevailing doctrinal message was one of restraint and deference, with the Court urging lower court judges to respect the administrative discretion of prison officials. While the Burger Court rejected the hands-off doctrine as a jurisdictional bar to reviewing inmates' complaints and acknowledged that prisoners have constitutional rights, a policy of deference has the same effect as the original hands-off doctrine because the Court is unwilling to interfere with prison practices, even if those actions threaten the rights of prisoners.[195]

NOTES

1. See Mark Berger, "Withdrawal of Rights and Due Deference: The New Hands Off Policy in Correctional Litigation," *University of Missouri–Kansas City Law Review* 47 (1978): 1.

2. Justices Brennan and Marshall, dissenting opinion, *Jones v. North Carolina Prisoners' Union*, 433 U.S. 119 (1977).

3. Henry J. Abraham, *Justices and Presidents: A Political History of Appointments to the Supreme Court*, 3rd ed. (New York: Oxford University Press, 1992), 298.

4. Vincent Blasi, ed., *The Burger Court: The Counter Revolution That Wasn't* (New Haven, Conn.: Yale University Press, 1983).

5. Charles M. Lamb, "The Making of a Chief Justice: Warren Burger on Criminal Procedures, 1956–69," *Cornell Law Review* 60 (1975): 743.

6. See Charles M. Lamb, "Chief Justice Warren E. Burger: A Conservative Chief for Conservative Times," in *The Burger Court: Political and Judicial Profiles*, Charles M. Lamb and Stephen C. Halpern, eds. (Urbana: University of Illinois Press, 1991), 130.

7. Jeffrey A. Segal and Harold J. Spaeth, *The Supreme Court and the Attitudinal Model* (New York: Cambridge University Press, 1993), 249.

8. Sue Davis, "Justice William H. Rehnquist: Right-Wing Ideologue or Majoritarian Democrat?" in Lamb and Halpern, eds., *The Burger Court*, 316.

9. Davis, "Justice William H. Rehnquist," 323.

10. Stephen L. Wasby, "Justice Harry A. Blackmun: Transition from a Minnesota Twin to an Independent Voice," in Lamb and Halpern, eds., *The Burger Court*, 90.

11. Wasby, "Justice Harry A. Blackmun," 94.

12. Justice Blackmun, dissenting from denial of certiorari, *Callins v. Collins*, No. 93–7054 (1994).

13. Bradley C. Canon, "The Lone Ranger in a Black Robe," in Lamb and Halpern, eds., *The Burger Court*, 348.

14. See Nancy Maveety, *Strategist on the Court: Justice Sandra Day O'Connor* (Lanham, Md.: Rowman and Littlefield, 1996), 29.

15. See Kenneth Jost, *The Supreme Court Yearbook, 1996–97* (Washington, D.C.: Congressional Quarterly, 1998), 308.

16. *Haines v. Kerner*, 404 U.S. 519 (1972), 521. Justices Powell and Rehnquist took no part in the decision.

17. Ibid., 520.

18. *Cruz v. Beto*, 405 U.S. 319 (1972), 321.

19. Ibid., 322.

20. Ibid., Chief Justice Burger concurring, 323.

21. Ibid., Rehnquist dissenting, 324.

22. *Cruz v. Beto*, 325.

23. Sam Walker, *Journal*, National Prison Project, 13 (Fall 1987): 3.

24. See "15 Years of Litigation History," *Journal*, National Prison Project, 13 (Fall 1987): 26–27.

25. Larry E. Sullivan, *The Prison Reform Movement: Forlorn Hope* (Boston: Twayne Publishers, 1990), 94.

26. Ibid., 99–101.

27. Ibid., 106.

28. On January 4, 2000, New York State agreed to pay $8 million to inmates involved in the Attica riot. The money will go to 1,280 inmates (or their heirs) who claimed that they were tortured, beaten, and denied medical treatment by prison authorities in retaliation for the revolt. See the *Washington Post*, January 5, 2000, p. A14.

29. In a law review article, Chief Justice Burger commented that we cannot "continue . . . to brush under the rug the problems of those who are found guilty and subject to criminal sentence. . . . It is a melancholy truth that it has taken the tragic prison outbreaks of the past three years to focus widespread public attention on this problem." Warren Burger, "Our Options Are Limited," *Villanova Law Review* 18 (1972): 167.

30. *Furman v. Georgia*, 408 U.S. 238 (1972).

31. Michael D. Davis and Hunter R. Clark, *Thurgood Marshall: Warrior at the Bar, Rebel on the Bench* (New York: Birch Lane Press, 1992), 322.

32. *Furman v. Georgia*, Stewart concurring, 309.

33. Ibid., 310.

34. Ibid., Burger dissenting, 400.

35. The mail regulations asserted that prisoner correspondence was a privilege, not a right. The regulations proscribed inmate correspondence that "unduly complains," "magnifies grievances," "expresses inflammatory political, racial, religious or other views or beliefs," or contains matter deemed "defamatory" or "otherwise inappropriate." See *Procunier v. Martinez*, 416 U.S. 396 (1974).

36. Memo to the conference, Brennan Papers, Library of Congress, case file of *Procunier v. Martinez* (1974).

37. Opinion of the Court, *Procunier v. Martinez*, 416 U.S. 396 (1974), 408.

38. Ibid., 413.

39. Ibid., 419.

40. Ibid., Marshall concurring, 422–423.

41. *Procunier v. Martinez*, 427–428.

42. *Pell v. Procunier*, 417 U.S. 817 (1974).

43. Chief Justice Warren Burger, memo to the conference, April 22, 1974, Marshall Papers, Library of Congress, case file of *Pell v. Procunier* (1974).

44. *Pell v. Procunier*, 822.

45. Ibid., 823.

46. Ibid., 826.

47. Ibid., 831.

48. Ibid., 834.

49. In a case raising similar issues of press freedom and decided on the same

day, the Court, in *Saxbe v. Washington Post Co.*, 417 U.S. 843 (1974), upheld the constitutionality of a Federal Bureau of Prisons regulation prohibiting personal interviews between the press and individual inmates of federal medium- and maximum-security prisons by applying the rationale used in *Pell v. Procunier.*

50. *Pell v. Procunier*, Powell concurring in part and dissenting in part, 835.

51. Ibid., Douglas dissenting, 837.

52. *Pell v. Procunier*, 839.

53. Ibid., 841.

54. See Herman Schwartz, "The Burger Court and the Prisoner," in *The Burger Years: Rights and Wrongs in the Supreme Court*, Herman Schwartz, ed. (New York: Penguin Books, 1987), 182–183.

55. *Wolff v. McDonnell*, 418 U.S. 539 (1974), 552–553.

56. Ibid., 555.

57. Ibid., 555–556.

58. Ibid., 556.

59. Ibid.

60. Ibid., 559. The due process protections for parole and probation revocation hearings were established in *Morrissey v. Brewer*, 408 U.S. 471 (1972), and *Gagnon v. Scarpelli*, 411 U.S. 778 (1973).

61. *Wolff v. McDonnell*, 563.

62. Ibid., 566.

63. Ibid., 570.

64. Ibid., 571.

65. Ibid., 579.

66. Ibid., Marshall concurring in part and dissenting in part, 583.

67. *Wolff v. McDonnell*, 589.

68. Ibid., 592.

69. Ibid., Douglas concurring in part and dissenting in part, 599.

70. *Clutchette v. Procunier*, 497 F.2d 809 (9th Cir. 1974), rehearing 510 F.2d 613 (9th Cir. 1975), following *Wolff.*

71. *Palmigiano v. Baxter*, 510 F.2d 534 (1st Cir. 1974).

72. *Baxter v. Palmigiano*, 425 U.S. 308 (1976), 315, 319.

73. Ibid., 324.

74. *Meachum v. Fano*, 427 U.S. 215 (1976), 217–218.

75. Ibid., 222.

76. Conference notes, Brennan Papers, Library of Congress, case file of *Meachum v. Fano* (1976).

77. *Meachum v. Fano*, 224.

78. Ibid.

79. Ibid., 227.

80. Ibid., Stevens dissenting, 229.

81. *Meachum v. Fano*, 230.

82. Ibid., 232.

83. Ibid., 233.

84. *Montanye v. Haymes*, 427 U.S. 236 (1976).

85. Ibid., 242.

86. See *Moody v. Daggett*, 429 U.S. 78 (1976), where the Court held that a federal parolee, imprisoned for crimes committed while on parole, was not con-

stitutionally entitled to an immediate parole revocation hearing where a parole violator warrant was issued and filed with the institution of his confinement as a "detainer" but was not executed.

87. In *Burrell v. McCray*, 423 U.S. 923 (1975), the Court granted certiorari raising the issue of whether the Appeals Court correctly decided that prison officials had violated the Eighth Amendment ban on cruel and unusual punishment. But then the Court reversed itself by holding, without further explanation, that the writ had been "improvidently granted." *Burrell v. McCray*, 426 U.S. 471 (1976). In a dissent, Justices Brennan and Marshall argued that the Court was evading the issue.

88. *Holt v. Sarver*, 309 F.Supp. 362 (1970), 373. This case is commonly known as *Holt II*.

89. Ibid., 380.

90. *Pugh v. Locke*, 406 F.Supp. 318 (1976).

91. Ibid., 329.

92. *Estelle v. Gamble*, 429 U.S. 97 (1976).

93. Ibid., 101.

94. Memo from the chambers of Lewis Powell to Thurgood Marshall, Marshall Papers, Library of Congress, case file of *Estelle v. Gamble* (1976).

95. For example, Powell and Rehnquist wanted Marshall to delete a portion of his draft opinion that had referred to the actions of "executives and legislators in failing to provide adequate medical care facilities." Rehnquist noted that the issue was not relevant to the case, and he "did not care to express an opinion on it at this time." See memo from Rehnquist to Thurgood Marshall, November 19, 1976, Marshall Papers, Library of Congress, case file of *Estelle v. Gamble* (1976).

96. *Estelle v. Gamble*, 102.

97. Citing *Gregg v. Georgia*, 428 U.S. 153 (1976), 171; *Trop v. Dulles*, 356 U.S. 86 (1958), 100–101, and *Weems v. United States*, 217 U.S. 349 (1910).

98. *Estelle v. Gamble*, 103.

99. Ibid., 104.

100. Ibid., 105, 107.

101. Ibid., Stevens dissenting, 109.

102. *Estelle v. Gamble*, 117.

103. *Gregg v. Georgia*, 428 U.S. 153 (1976).

104. *Jurek v. Texas*, 428 U.S. 262 (1976), upholding the Texas death penalty statute; *Proffitt v. Florida*, 428 U.S. 242 (1976), upholding the Florida death penalty statute.

105. *Gregg v. Georgia*, 176–177.

106. The Fifth Amendment states: "No person shall be held to answer for a capital, or otherwise infamous crime, unless on a presentation or indictment of a Grand Jury; . . . nor shall any person be subject for the same offense to be twice put in jeopardy of life or limb; . . . nor be deprived of life, liberty, or property, without due process of law." The Fourteen Amendment also contemplates the existence of the death penalty by providing that no state shall deprive any person of "life, liberty, or property" without due process of law."

107. *Gregg v. Georgia*, 180–181.

108. Ibid., 186–187.

109. Ibid., 206.

110. Ibid., Brennan dissenting, 229.

111. *Gregg v. Georgia*, quoting *Furman*, 230.

112. *Woodson v. North Carolina*, 428 U.S. 280 (1976).

113. Ibid., 293.

114. Ibid., 301–303.

115. Ibid., 304.

116. *Coker v. Georgia*, 433 U.S. 548 (1977).

117. Brennan Papers, Library of Congress, case file of *Coker v. Georgia* (1977). Either the vote tabulation on the docket sheet was incorrect or several justices changed their minds. Brennan's notes indicate that Marshall took his same general view expressed in *Furman*—that the death penalty was always cruel and unusual.

118. *Coker v. Georgia*, 597.

119. Ibid., 598.

120. Ibid., Justice Powell dissenting in part, 601.

121. *Coker v. Georgia*, 603. Italics in original text.

122. Ibid., C. J. Burger dissenting, 604.

123. *Lockett v. Ohio*, 438 U.S. 586 (1978).

124. Ibid., 593–594.

125. Chief Justice Warren Burger, memo to the conference, January 24, 1978, Brennan Papers, Library of Congress, case file of *Lockett v. Ohio* (1978).

126. Burger, memo to the conference, January 24, 1978.

127. Burger, memo to the conference, April 10, 1978, Brennan Papers, Library of Congress, case file of *Lockett v. Ohio* (1978).

128. Justice Potter Stewart, memo to the Chief justice, April 13, 1978, Brennan Papers, Library of Congress.

129. William Rehnquist, memo to Chief Justice Burger, April 14, 1978, Brennan Papers, Library of Congress, case file of *Lockett v. Ohio* (1978).

130. *Lockett v. Ohio*, 604. Italics in original.

131. Ibid., 605.

132. *Enmund v. Florida*, 458 U.S. 782 (1982).

133. Ibid., 790–791.

134. Ibid., 792.

135. Ibid., 794.

136. Ibid., citing Brief for the Petitioner, NAACP Legal Defense and Educational Fund, Inc., Death Row U.S.A. (October 20, 1981), 795.

137. *Enmund v. Florida*, 798.

138. Ibid., O'Connor dissenting, 826.

139. *Bounds v. Smith*, 430 U.S. 817 (1977).

140. Ibid., 824.

141. Ibid., 825.

142. Ibid., 828.

143. *Houchins v. KQED*, 438 U.S. 1 (1978).

144. Potter Stewart's memo to the conference, April 24, 1978. Brennan Papers, Library of Congress, case file of *Houchins v. KQED* (1978).

145. *Houchins v. KQED*, 438 U.S. 1 (1978), 9.

146. Ibid., 11. See *Pell v. Procunier*, 417 U.S. 817, and *Saxbe*, 417 U.S. 843 (1974), 850.

147. Schwartz, "The Burger Court and the Prisoner," 182.

148. *Bell v. Wolfish*, 441 U.S. 520 (1979).

149. Ibid., 542–543.

150. Ibid., 546.

151. Ibid., 547.

152. *Rhodes v. Chapman*, 452 U.S. 337 (1981).

153. Ibid., 344.

154. Ibid., 347, 349.

155. *Rummel v. Estelle*, 445 U.S. 263 (1980).

156. See Note, "Interpretation of the Eighth Amendment: *Rummel, Solem,* and the Venerable Case of *Weems v. United States*," *Duke Law Journal* 4 (1984): 794.

157. *Rummel v. Estelle*, 445 U.S. 263 (1980), 271.

158. *Weems v. United States*, 217 U.S. 349 (1910). The Philippine punishment of *cadena temoral*, consisting of imprisonment, hard labor, and indefinite restrictions on liberty, was held to be "cruel and unusual."

159. *Rummel v. Estelle*, 284.

160. Ibid., Powell dissenting, 288.

161. *Rummel v. Estelle*, 293.

162. Ibid.

163. Ibid., 295.

164. Ibid.

165. *Hutto v. Davis*, 445 U.S. 370 (1982), 374.

166. Ibid., 374–375.

167. Justice Brennan, memo to the conference, November 9, 1981, Brennan Papers, Library of Congress, case file of *Hutto v. Davis* (1982).

168. *Hutto v. Davis*, Brennan dissenting, 382–383.

169. Ibid. 383.

170. Ibid., 385.

171. *Solem v. Helm*, 463 U.S. 277 (1983), 284.

172. Ibid., 284.

173. Ibid., 292.

174. See Schwartz, "The Burger Court and the Prisoner," 186.

175. *Hudson v. Palmer*, 468 U.S. 517 (1984).

176. Ibid., 521.

177. Conference notes, Brennan Papers, Library of Congress, case file of *Hudson v. Palmer* (1984).

178. Stevens memo to the conference, Brennan Papers, Library of Congress.

179. Burger memo to the conference, June 4, 1984. Brennan Papers, Library of Congress.

180. *Hudson v. Palmer*, 526.

181. Ibid., Stevens dissenting, 542.

182. Ibid., 546.

183. Ibid., 552.

184. Ibid., 554–555.

185. *Block v. Rutherford*, 468 U.S. 576 (1984).

186. Ibid., 588.

187. Ibid., 589.

188. *Whitley v. Albers*, 475 U.S. 312 (1986).

189. Ibid., 318.

190. Ibid., 319.

191. Ibid., 320.

192. Ibid., 320–321.

193. Stevens joined all but footnote 2 of the dissent. Marshall felt that the evidence precluded a direct verdict on the respondent's due process claim.

194. *Whitley v. Albers*, Marshall dissenting, 334.

195. For an early critical view of this trend, see Emily Calhoun, "The Supreme Court and the Constitutional Rights of Prisoners: A Reappraisal," *Hastings Constitutional Law Quarterly* 4 (1977): 219.

Chapter 6

The Rehnquist Court and Prisoners' Rights, 1986–Present

Beginning in 1986, the Supreme Court experienced the first in a series of personnel changes that would continue through 1994. These changes not only affected the political composition of the bench but also the Court's jurisprudence in many areas of constitutional law. Among the retirees during this period were Justices Brennan and Marshall, two of the most liberal members of the Court on prisoners' rights issues. Republican Presidents Reagan and Bush appointed several justices to the Court who were expected to overturn or narrow the scope of Warren and Burger Court precedents, especially on criminal justice issues. For the most part, the conservative justices of the Rehnquist Court have fulfilled those expectations by redefining constitutional provisions concerning criminal procedure, "cruel and unusual" punishments, the death penalty, and habeas corpus.[1] Although the Court has not returned completely to the hands-off approach, a majority of the justices support deference to prison administrators and a more limited role for the federal courts in judging inmate claims. This chapter reviews the most significant prisoners' rights decisions of the Rehnquist Court.

THE COMPOSITION OF THE REHNQUIST COURT

When Chief Justice Warren Burger announced his retirement in 1986, President Ronald Reagan decided to look within the Court for his nominee by elevating Associate Justice William H. Rehnquist to the new chief justice. Rehnquist had been appointed to the Court by President Richard Nixon in 1971, and during his fifteen years on the bench had earned a reputation as the most conservative justice on the Court in decades. Jus-

tice Rehnquist almost always voted for the government in cases involving the rights of criminal defendants and prisoners. As chief justice,
Rehnquist has attempted to advance his policy agenda on criminal law
issues, but he has not made much of an effort to lobby his colleagues to
win them over to his side. One Court observer has commented that the
current chief justice "does not have Warren's reputation for persuasion,
Brennan's for cajoling, or Burger's for arm twisting."[2]

On the same day that Rehnquist was chosen as the new chief justice,
President Reagan appointed Antonin Scalia to fill the seat vacated by
Rehnquist. Throughout his professional career, Scalia developed his conservative ideology and views of the Constitution. From 1982 until his
appointment to the Supreme Court in 1986, he produced a spate of judicial opinions, law review articles, and speeches that attacked the liberal
decisions of the Warren and Burger Courts.[3] Scalia firmly believed that
the federal courts should give more deference to the co-equal branches
of the federal government and to the states. In practice, this meant that
he would be reluctant to review the actions of state prison administrators. Scalia also prefers an approach to the Constitution and statutes
called "textualism." This approach rejects the use of legislative history
and convention debates in favor of a strict reading of the text. He also
feels that adherence to form and text, especially in constitutional interpretation, is critical; to go beyond the text is to read rights into the Constitution that were not contemplated by the framers. For example, Scalia
has argued that the death penalty is contemplated by the text of the
Constitution and therefore cannot be, as Justices Brennan and Marshall
believed, "cruel and unusual" punishment in violation of the Eighth
Amendment.

Scalia's preference for judicial restraint, textualism, and rejection of
legislative history meant that he would approach the Bill of Rights and
Fourteenth Amendment more narrowly than his predecessors on the
Burger or Warren Courts. Indeed, an empirical study of the first seven
years of the Rehnquist Court found that Justice Scalia voted for the government in 90 percent of the cases involving the Eighth Amendment,
capital punishment, and habeas corpus.[4] Scalia's narrow interpretation
of prisoners' rights is exceeded only by Justice Clarence Thomas, President Bush's second nominee to the Court, who will be discussed more
fully below.

With the appointments of Rehnquist and Scalia, the Court now had a
narrow conservative majority consisting of the chief justice and Justices
Sandra Day O'Connor, Lewis F. Powell, Jr., Byron White, and Antonin
Scalia. Though Justice Powell was known as a "swing justice," he tended
to vote more conservatively in cases involving criminal procedure and
prisoners' rights. Justices Harry Blackmun, William Brennan, Thurgood
Marshall, and John Paul Stevens constituted the liberal bloc on the Court.

Table 6.1
Natural Courts under Chief Justice William Rehnquist

1986–1987	1988–1990	1990–1991
Chief: Rehnquist (R)	*Chief*: Rehnquist (R)	*Chief*: Rehnquist (R)
Brennan (D)	Brennan (D)	B. White (D)
B. White (D)	B. White (D)	T. Marshall (D)
T. Marshall (D)	T. Marshall (D)	Blackmun (R)
Blackmun (R)	Blackmun (R)	Stevens (R)
Powell (D)	Stevens (R)	O'Connor (R)
Stevens (R)	O'Connor (R)	Scalia (R)
O'Connor (R)	Scalia (R)	Kennedy (R)
Scalia (R)	Kennedy (R)	Souter (R)

1991–1993	1993–1994	1994–
Chief: Rehnquist (R)	*Chief*: Rehnquist (R)	*Chief*: Rehnquist (R)
B. White (D)	Blackmun (R)	Stevens (R)
Blackmun (R)	Stevens (R)	O'Connor (R)
Stevens (R)	O'Connor (R)	Scalia (R)
O'Connor (R)	Scalia (R)	Kennedy (R)
Scalia (R)	Kennedy (R)	Souter (R)
Kennedy (R)	Souter (R)	Thomas (R)
Souter (R)	Thomas (R)	Ginsburg (D)
Thomas (R)	Ginsburg (R)	Breyer (D)

Note: Associate justices are listed in order of seniority, with the most junior justice at the bottom of the list.

Source: Thomas R. Hensley, Christopher E. Smith, and Joyce A. Baugh, *The Changing Supreme Court: Constitutional Rights and Liberties* (St. Paul, Minn.: West Publishing, 1997). © 1997. Reprinted with permission of Wadsworth, a division of Thomson Learning. Fax 800-730-2215.

These voting blocs, however, would not last long because over a period of seven years five new justices were appointed to the Court. The natural courts during William Rehnquist's tenure as chief justice are presented in Table 6.1.

Following the promotion of William Rehnquist to chief justice and the selection of Scalia, President Reagan appointed Anthony Kennedy in 1988 to fill the seat of retiring Justice Lewis Powell. Because Powell was a moderate and represented a key swing vote, the confirmation process for his successor became very contentious. Kennedy was actually Reagan's third choice; his first, Robert Bork, was criticized for his rigid jurisprudence of original intent and personal style and was defeated in the Senate; his second nominee, Douglas Ginsburg, had to withdraw amid allegations of past marijuana use.[5] Kennedy was described as a moderate conservative who was closer to Powell in judicial temperament than to

Bork or Ginsburg. Though he was not as ideological as Bork, he clearly favored a philosophy of judicial restraint and deference to the political process.[6] Applied to the constitutional rights of prisoners, this philosophy provided the conservative bloc with a reliable vote on the Rehnquist Court. During his first eight terms, Kennedy has voted for the government's position on Eighth Amendment, death penalty, and habeas corpus claims more than 70 percent of the time.[7]

In 1990, President Bush appointed David H. Souter to fill the seat of Justice Brennan. With Brennan's retirement, the Court was losing one of its most ardent defenders of prisoners' rights. At the time of his nomination, Souter was described as the "Stealth nominee" because little was known about him. Except for 200 opinions on the New Hampshire Supreme Court, Souter had almost no paper trail—he had not authored a book or a major law journal article. Souter's professional background and testimony during his confirmation hearing reflected a moderate, pragmatic judge who lacked an ideological agenda. His first term performance, however, was not characterized by moderation. He provided the crucial fifth vote in support of conservative positions in several criminal justice cases.[8]

Justice Souter has moderated his jurisprudence on criminal justice issues since his first term, but he is still much more conservative than Brennan. With regard to police searches, interrogations, criminal procedure, and sentencing, Souter has had a conservative voting record.[9] He appears to be more willing to expand state authority to arrest, prosecute, and sentence criminal defendants. On post–conviction issues, however, such as the death penalty, habeas corpus, and prison conditions, Souter's voting alignments and opinions have been moderate to liberal.[10] Unlike Brennan, Souter believes that capital punishment is constitutional, but his voting record on death penalty cases has been closely divided between state and individual interests. He also is unwilling to support the views of Clarence Thomas, the second Bush appointee, and Scalia on the Eighth Amendment as applied to prison conditions, and he has not consistently voted to limit federal habeas corpus review of state criminal procedures. It is in these areas of criminal law that Souter has the highest rate of support for the individual's claim. His move toward moderation began about the same time Justices Thomas and Scalia were articulating their Eighth Amendment jurisprudence in cases such as *Hudson v. McMillian* (1992) and *Farmer v. Brennan* (1994), to be discussed below. Souter refuses to disregard precedents that have applied the Cruel and Unusual Punishment Clause to prison conditions. Consistent with his pragmatic judicial philosophy, he has attempted to find a middle ground by balancing the interests of prison administrators in maintaining discipline and security with the constitutional rights of prisoners. In contrast to some of his more conservative colleagues, he does not always tip the scale in favor of prison officials.

President Bush's second nominee is an interesting contrast to Souter. On many constitutional issues, including criminal law, Clarence Thomas has established himself as the most conservative justice on the Rehnquist Court. Thomas almost never votes to support recognition of rights for criminal defendants and prisoners, and his opinions lack any compassion for the plight of prisoners.[11] Along with Justice Scalia, Thomas has expressed the most restrictive views of the Eighth Amendment and habeas corpus review. For example, he has suggested, contrary to decades of precedent, that the Eighth Amendment applies only to criminal sentencing by a judge or jury, not prison conditions.[12] At least one commentator has argued that Justice Thomas's jurisprudence in prisoners' rights cases is influenced by his belief in personal responsibility and a strong desire to distance himself from Thurgood Marshall, his liberal predecessor.[13]

President Clinton had the opportunity to appoint the first Democratic nominees to the Court in 26 years. In 1993, he selected Ruth Bader Ginsburg to fill the seat of Byron White, and in 1994, he appointed Stephen G. Breyer to replace the retiring Harry Blackmun. Both Clinton appointees have been judicial moderates. For example, Breyer, unlike Blackmun, believes that the death penalty is constitutional. Both justices tend to argue cases on narrow grounds rather than issue broad holdings. Ginsburg often votes more conservatively on criminal procedure issues, but in closely divided decisions involving the rights of criminal defendants and prisoners, the two Clinton nominees have voted with Stevens and Souter in what remains of the liberal bloc in upholding precedents more favorable to the rights of prisoners.[14]

FELONY MURDER AND CAPITAL SENTENCING

It did not take long for the Rehnquist Court to make its mark on the constitutional rights of prisoners. The Court handed down several decisions during its first term that narrowed precedents or rejected inmate claims. One such case was *Tison v. Arizona* (1987), where the Court held that "participation in a felony murder, combined with reckless indifference to human life," is sufficient to meet the culpability requirements under capital sentencing.[15] The decision narrowed the Burger precedent in *Enmund v. Florida* (1982).

The Tison brothers helped break their father, Gary Tison, and another convicted murderer out of prison. The brothers entered the prison with a chest full of weapons. During the escape, both brothers helped their father and the other convict abduct and rob a family of four. As the brothers looked for a jug of water, they watched as their father and the other convict murdered the family with shotguns. Gary Tison eventually died of exposure in the desert before authorities could arrest him. The brutal crimes received extensive media attention, and many citizens demanded retribution and justice from the state criminal justice system. Both brothers were convicted under Arizona's felony murder and accomplice liability statutes. The Tison brothers alleged that *Enmund v. Florida* required a reversal. The state supreme court, however, upheld the convictions, arguing that both petitioners could have anticipated the use of force in committing the felony.

In his study of decision making on the Supreme Court, Edward Lazarus describes the interactions of the justices in the *Tison* case. At the conference, Justice White voted to affirm, even though he authored the *Enmund* opinion. Rehnquist and Powell also announced their intention to affirm. Since Scalia was a reliable vote to affirm, and the four liberals were votes to reverse, Justice O'Connor held the decisive vote. According to Lazarus, O'Connor had planned to reverse in the case, given the *Enmund* precedent, but when she saw how White voted, she changed her mind.[16] The conservative justices now had a 5-to-4 majority to affirm. In order to keep O'Connor from wavering, Rehnquist assigned her the majority opinion.

Justice O'Connor finessed the *Enmund* precedent by arguing that even though the Tison brothers neither intended nor directly caused the deaths, the record might demonstrate that "they had the culpable mental state of reckless indifference to human life."[17] She argued that the Tisons' substantial involvement in the crimes further implicated them in the resulting deaths. The Court concluded that a high level of participation in a felony murder, combined with reckless indifference to human life, was enough to meet the *Enmund* culpability requirement.

Writing for the dissenters, Justice Brennan described the felony murder doctrine as "a living fossil from a legal era in which all felonies were punishable by death."[18] He pointed out that most European democracies and many states no longer executed felons for murder who neither committed the act nor intended to commit the crime. He criticized the Court for suggesting, in dictum, that its new standard of mental culpability for felony murder was applicable to the Tison brothers, and he argued that the death penalty was a disproportionate penalty for the crime of felony murder.

One explanation the Court offered for its conclusion that death is a proportionate penalty for persons who act with reckless indifference to human life is "that limiting the death penalty to those who intend to kill is a highly unsatisfactory means of definitively distinguishing the most culpable and dangerous of murderers."[19] The Court cited as examples persons who kill others in situations reflecting extreme indifference to human life. Justice Brennan noted, however, that those circumstances were not relevant to this case because, like *Enmund*, it involves accomplices who did not kill. Brennan admitted that the individual who acts recklessly and is indifferent to the possibility that death may result from his or her actions usually deserves severe punishment. "But because that person has not chosen to kill," Brennan argued, "his or her moral and criminal culpability is of a different degree than that of one who killed or intended to kill."[20] He believed that it was essential to differentiate between reckless and intentional actions, especially in felony murder cases, if the law was to maintain the link between criminal liability and moral culpability necessary for criminal justice.

Brennan also criticized the Court's interpretation of the objective factors used in its proportionality analysis. In surveying state statutes authorizing the death penalty for felony murder, the Court concluded that "only a small minority *of those jurisdictions imposing capital punishment for felony murder* have rejected the possibility of a capital sentence absent intent to kill, and we do not find this minority position constitutionally required."[21] This statement suggests that a majority of American jurisdictions permit capital punishment for felony murder where there is no intent to kill. But Brennan pointed out that this was not true. If the states that have abolished capital punishment and those who authorize it in circumstances different from the *Tison* case are combined with those jurisdictions that require a finding of intent to kill for felony murder, then nearly three-fifths of the states prohibited the imposition of the death penalty on a nontriggerman who did not intend to kill. Finally, Brennan noted that other objective factors were not considered in O'Connor's opinion for the Court. For example, the Court in *Enmund* found that between 1954 and 1982, there were "6 cases out of 362 where a nontriggerman felony murder was executed," and all of those occurred in 1955.[22] Also, no European or Commonwealth country would have executed Enmund because all of those nations have either abolished or never employed a felony murder doctrine. Brennan complained that the Court made no effort to review or update this evidence.

Brennan concluded that the Court's proportionality analysis and its holding could not be reconciled with the analyses and results of *Enmund* and other precedents. He would dissent for that reason alone. But the fact that the Court arrived at different results in analytically similar cases only reinforced his belief that capital punishment could never be imposed in a fair manner. "Arbitrariness continues," he said, "so to infect both the procedure and substance of capital sentencing that any decision to impose the death penalty remains cruel and unusual."[23]

RACE DISCRIMINATION AND CAPITAL SENTENCING

Although the Burger Court played a central role in applying Eighth Amendment standards to state death penalty statutes and ultimately confirming that capital punishment was constitutional, Rehnquist Court decisions have addressed several important capital sentencing issues. One of the most controversial was the issue of race discrimination in the administration of the death penalty. In *McCleskey v. Kemp* (1987), the Court rejected a claim advanced by the NAACP Legal Defense and Educational Fund (LDF) that evidence of systemic racial discrimination denied Warren McCleskey equal protection of the law.[24]

McCleskey, an African American, was on death row in Georgia for killing a white police officer during a furniture store robbery. He filed a habeas corpus petition claiming that the Georgia capital sentencing process was administered in a racially discriminatory manner in violation of the Eighth and Fourteenth Amendments. To support his claim, McCleskey presented a statistical study conducted by Professors David Baldus, George Woodworth, and Charles Pulaski (known as the Baldus study). The study examined over 2,000 murder cases in Georgia in the 1970s and involved data referring to the victim's race, the defendant's race, and 230 other variables. Using a sophisticated multivariate analysis, the research purported to show a disparity in the imposition of the death penalty in Georgia based on the murder victim's race and the defendant's race. Specifically, a death sentence was imposed in 22 percent of the cases where the defendant was black and the victim was white; 8 percent where both the defendant and the victim were white; 1 percent involving black defendants and black victims; and 3 percent involving white defendants and black victims.[25] There also was evidence of racial bias in prosecutorial discretion. Prosecutors sought the death penalty in 70 percent of the cases involving black defendants and white victims but in only 19 percent of the cases where white defendants murdered black victims. When controlling for nonracial variables, the study found that defendants charged with killing white victims were 4.3 times as likely to receive the death penalty as defendants charged with killing blacks, and that black defendants were 1.1 times as likely to receive the death penalty as other defendants.[26] As Justice Brennan noted in his dissent, of the seven prisoners executed in Georgia since the death penalty was reinstated, all were convicted of killing whites, and six of the seven were black. This evidence of systemic racial discrimination raised the question of whether capital punishment in the state of Georgia violated the Equal Protection Clause of the Fourteenth Amendment.

The Eleventh Circuit Court of Appeals had voted to affirm the conviction and sentence. On petition for review, all five conservative justices voted against granting certiorari in the case. In his discussion of *McCleskey*, Lazarus describes how the justices responded to the discrimination claim.[27] In trying to rally the conservative justices, Justice White took the unusual action of circulating a pre-conference memo to all of his colleagues that not only attacked McCleskey's key arguments but also called into question the truthfulness of one of the LDF lawyers concerning McCleskey's rejection of a plea bargain.[28] The effect of the memo is uncertain, but White's goal was realized because the conference vote was 5 to 4 to reject the claims of racial discrimination. The majority consisted of Chief Justice Rehnquist and Justices White, Powell, O'Connor, and freshman Justice Scalia. Justices Brennan, Marshall, Blackmun, and Stevens voted to reverse. Powell was assigned the opinion of the Court, and Brennan, Blackmun, and Stevens filed dissenting opinions.

As the draft opinions were circulating, Justice Scalia sent a memorandum to the conference stating that he planned to join Powell's opinion but that he had two reservations.[29] First he disagreed that the inferences from the Baldus study were weakened by the fact that each jury and trial was unique or by the large number of variables. He also took issue, implied by Powell's opinion, that if only stronger statistical evidence of racial bias could be demonstrated a reversal would be required. He admitted that race plays a role in sentencing, but that did not convince him that there was a valid equal protection claim. "Since it is my view," Scalia wrote, "that the unconscious operation of irrational sympathies and antipathies, including racial, upon jury decisions and (hence) prosecutorial decisions is real, acknowledged in the decisions of this court, and ineradicable, I cannot honestly say that all I need is more proof."[30]

In his opinion for the Court, Justice Powell stated that to prevail under the Equal Protection Clause, McCleskey would have to prove that officials acted with a discriminatory purpose in his particular case. But Powell concluded that McCleskey presented "no evidence specific to his own case that would support an inference that racial considerations played a part in his sentence."[31] Powell also rejected McCleskey's disproportionality claim under the Eighth Amendment, because it was not enough to "prove a constitutional violation by demonstrating that other defendants who may be similarly situated did *not* receive the death penalty."[32] Powell downplayed the significance of the Baldus study. He conceded that it indicates a discrepancy in capital sentencing that appears to correlate with race, but he declared that "apparent disparities in sentencing are an inevitable part of our criminal justice system."[33] Discretion in capital sentencing is a product of the jury's function to make difficult human judgments that defy codification. Powell pointed out that this discretion can work to a defendant's advantage. A jury can always decide not to impose the death sentence, or it can decline to convict.

Two other concerns influenced the Court's decision. Powell warned that if taken to its logical conclusion, McCleskey's claim could undermine the entire criminal justice system. Because the Eighth Amendment is not limited to capital punishments, claims of racial bias could be made against all other types of penalties. Claims of bias could be extended to discrepancies that correlate with other characteristics, such as gender, or to statistical disparities that correlate with other actors in the criminal justice system, such as defense attorneys and judges. In short, Powell said that "there is no limiting principle to the type of challenge brought by McCleskey."[34] Finally, Powell suggested that McCleskey's arguments should be made before legislative bodies, not the courts. Legislatures are composed by elected representatives of the people and are therefore in a better position to "respond to the will and consequently the moral values of the people" and to assess the "results of statistical studies in terms of their own local conditions and with a flexible approach that is not available to the courts."[35]

Justices Brennan, Blackmun, and Stevens all wrote separate dissenting opinions. Brennan repeated his belief that the death penalty was in all circumstances unconstitutional, but he argued that even if he did not hold that view, he would still reverse the Court of Appeals on the grounds that McCleskey had demonstrated that his sentence was imposed in a racially discriminatory manner. He argued that it was irrelevant that McCleskey could not prove that race discrimination influenced his particular case because since *Furman*, the "Court has been concerned with the *risk* of the imposition of an arbitrary sentence, rather than the proven fact of one."[36] The statistical strength of the Baldus study and human experience illustrate, according to Brennan, "that the risk that race influenced McCleskey's sentence is intolerable by any imaginable standard."[37]

Reviewing the history of Georgia criminal law and the role that race and poverty have played in capital sentencing within the state, he noted that the Court had invalidated portions of the state capital sentencing system three times dating back to *Furman v. Georgia* (1972). Brennan criticized the Court's contention that statutory safeguards minimize racial bias because he felt that McCleskey's evidence raised questions about the effectiveness of such safeguards. He refused to accept the Court's slippery slope argument—that a recognition of McCleskey's claim might lead to numerous challenges of all aspects of criminal sentencing. "The prospect that there may be more widespread abuse than McCleskey documents may be dismaying," Brennan retorted, "but it does not justify complete abdication of our judicial role."[38] The evaluation of bias in criminal punishment based on other characteristics is not informed by statistics alone, but by history and experience. Brennan believed that these considerations, combined with the sophisticated analysis of the Baldus study, would create a stringent standard of statistical evidence that would be difficult to meet.

NARROWING FIRST AMENDMENT PROTECTIONS FOR PRISONERS

In *Turner v. Safley* (1987), the Court significantly limited the religious and expressive freedoms for inmates by adopting a new standard for review in prisoners' constitutional rights cases. A closely divided Court held that the proper standard of review in determining the validity of prison regulations that restrict inmates' constitutional rights is whether the regulation is "reasonably related to legitimate penological concerns."[39] This standard came to be known as the "legitimate penological interest" test, or the *Turner* test.

The case concerned two regulations promulgated by the Missouri Department of Corrections. The first regulation prohibited inmate-to-inmate correspondence, and the second permitted an inmate to marry only with the permission of the prison superintendent, which was given only when there was a compelling reason to do so. Testimony revealed that, in most cases, a pregnancy or the birth of an illegitimate child qualified solely as a "compelling" reason.[40] This interpretation of the regulation effectively denied nearly all prisoners the right to marry. Though the regulations were in force throughout the state prison system, the case involved the application of the rules at the Renz Correctional Facility in Cedar City, Missouri. The Renz prison population included both male and female inmates of varying security classifications.

The District Court held both regulations unconstitutional, reasoning that the Supreme Court's decision in *Procunier v. Martinez* (1974) required the application of a strict scrutiny standard of review for resolving the constitutional complaints of prisoners. The Eighth Circuit Court of Appeals affirmed, finding the District Court's application of the strict scrutiny standard appropriate because the regulations prohibited the exercise of fundamental rights.[41] The Circuit Court noted that as long as the exercise of fundamental rights is not inconsistent with either the fact of incarceration or valid penological concerns, the exercise of those rights should be given the highest level of protection under the Constitution.

Writing for a 5-to-4 majority, Justice O'Connor, joined by Rehnquist, White, Powell, and Scalia, ruled that the Court of Appeals erred in applying a strict scrutiny analysis. The Court felt that a lesser standard of scrutiny was appropriate for determining the constitutionality of prison rules. Applying the "legitimate penological interest" test, the majority upheld the validity of the correspondence regulation but concluded that the marriage restriction could not be sustained. While Justice O'Connor acknowledged that the decision in *Procunier v. Martinez* established the principle that prison walls do not separate inmates from the Constitution, she also noted that a second principle established in *Martinez* was that "courts are ill-equipped to deal with the increasingly urgent problems of prison administration and reform."[42] The Court recognized that prison administration was a difficult task traditionally reserved for the executive and legislative branches of government, and that separation of powers concerns favored a policy of judicial restraint. Where a state penal system is involved, principles of federalism provided additional reasons to accord more deference to prison administrators. Citing *Martinez*, Justice O'Connor argued that the Court must formulate a standard of review that balances the need to protect the constitutional rights of prisoners with a policy of judicial restraint toward prison administration.[43]

In *Martinez*, however, the Burger Court did not attempt to answer the question it posed. As discussed in Chapter 5, the case involved a regulation in effect at California penal institutions that prohibited mail containing derogatory remarks against prison personnel or inflammatory political, racial, religious, or other views.[44] The Court overturned the content-based mail regulation, but the decision was predicated solely on the unconstitutional restriction on the First and Fourteenth Amendment Rights of *non-prisoners*. The Court held that where free citizens' rights were implicated by prison censorship regulations, the test of their constitutional validity required a showing by the government that the regulation furthered a substantial government interest and was no greater than necessary to protect that interest.[45] A determination of the proper standard of review in cases where prisoners' rights alone were involved was reserved for another day.[46]

Between *Martinez* and *Safley*, the lower federal courts struggled to find an appropriate standard of review for prisoners' rights claims. The courts applied the strict, two-prong test of *Martinez* unless the court found that the regulation was only a minor restriction on a fundamental right, or if the right was limited only to time, place, and manner and was not a content-based restriction.[47] Justice O'Connor's opinion in *Safley* sent a clear message to lower federal courts. Prison regulations that infringe on inmates' constitutional rights are valid if they are reasonably related to legitimate penological interests. According to O'Connor, "subjecting the day-to-day judgments of prison officials to an inflexible strict scrutiny analysis would seriously hamper their ability to anticipate security problems and to adopt innovative solutions to the intractable problems of prison administration."[48] She expressed concern that a strict standard would distort the decision-making process, because every administrative judgment could fall under the scrutiny of some court that would conclude that it had a less restrictive way of solving the problem faced by prison officials.

O'Connor commented that the Court, in *Martinez*, did not establish a clear standard of review in cases involving questions of prisoners' rights, but she pointed out that the Court had addressed such questions in four subsequent cases. Since all four cases were discussed in the previous chapter, they will receive only brief treatment here. In *Pell v. Procunier* (1974), decided the same term as *Martinez*, the Court specifically ruled on a regulation that applied solely to inmates. The case involved a California penal regulation that prohibited face-to-face media interviews with individual inmates. The Burger Court upheld the regulation on the grounds that prisoners had access to alternative means of communication, and that any potential infringement on free speech rights was outweighed by the state's legitimate interest in maintaining prison security.[49] Aside from substantial evidence that prison officials had exaggerated security concerns, the courts were to defer to the expert judgment of prison administrators. O'Connor also cited *Jones v. North Carolina Prisoners' Union* (1977), where the Court upheld a North Carolina prison regulation that barred union meetings, prohibited inmate solicitation of other inmates to join the union, and banned bulk mailings concerning the union from outside sources. The regulation was found to be a reasonable response to legitimate security concerns.

Two additional cases where the Court addressed questions of prisoners' rights involved regulations restricting the rights of pre-trial detainees. In *Bell v. Wolfish* (1979), the Court significantly expanded its policy of deference to prison officials by upholding several restrictive regulations, including a prohibition on the receipt by prisoners of hardback books unless mailed directly from publishers and bookstores; a prohibition against the receipt of packages; provisions mandating body cavity searches following contact visits; a provision allowing spot searches of cells in the prisoner's absence; and a rule allowing for the double-celling of inmates in rooms designed for one prisoner.[50] All of the rules were upheld as a rational response to legitimate security problems. Likewise, in *Block v. Rutherford* (1984), the Court upheld prohibitions on contact visits between pre-trial detainees and family members on the ground that "responsible, experienced administrators have determined, in their sound discretion, that such visits will jeopardize the security of the facility, and the regulation was reasonably related to these security concerns."[51]

In *Pell, Jones, Wolfish*, and *Block*, the Burger Court upheld all of the challenged regulations as valid restrictions on prisoners' First Amendment rights. Justice O'Connor noted that in none of the four cases did the Court "apply a standard of heightened scrutiny, but instead inquired whether a prison regulation that burdens fundamental rights is 'reasonably related' to legitimate penological objectives, or whether it represents an 'exaggerated response' to those concerns."[52] O'Connor identified several factors relevant in determining a regulation's reasonableness. Prison officials must prove that: (1) there is a valid, rational connection between the policy and some legitimate, content-neutral governmental interest; (2) there are alternative means for the prisoner to exercise the right; (3)

accommodation of an asserted right does not impact significantly on prison resources, prison guards, or other inmates; and (4) no readily available alternatives to the regulation exist.[53]

Applying the declared standard of review and the four-factor analysis to the Missouri regulations, the Court concluded that the correspondence regulation was reasonably related to valid correctional goals because it was content-neutral, advanced legitimate security and safety concerns identified by prison officials, and was not an exaggerated response to those objectives.[54] Thus the correspondence regulation was upheld. The marriage regulation, however, did not fair as well. In their brief, the petitioners conceded that the decision to marry was a fundamental right, but they suggested that a different rule should apply in a prison setting. The Court rejected that argument, holding that the right to marry, though subject to restrictions as a result of incarceration, remained a fundamental constitutionally protected right within the prison context.[55] It noted that substantial attributes of marriage remain after incarceration. Inmate marriages involve expressions of emotional support and public commitment, reflections of religious faith, and expectations of consummation after release, and they are a precondition for government benefits, property rights, and less tangible benefits, such as the legitimation of children.[56] The Court concluded that none of the concerns advanced by Missouri prison officials supported the marriage rule, and that the regulation was an "exaggerated response" to alleged security and rehabilitative goals.

Justice Stevens's dissenting opinion in *Turner*, joined by Justices Brennan, Marshall, and Blackmun, took issue with the majority's standard of review and its application to the correspondence regulation. Stevens did not feel that there was much difference between the "needlessly broad" standard applied by the lower courts and the "reasonable relationship" but not an "exaggerated response" standard announced by the Court.[57] Both standards seemed to require the same type of evaluation; the critical difference appeared to be the amount of evidence necessary to demonstrate that a regulation was "unreasonable." Stevens wrote that the "open-ended 'reasonableness' standard made it much too easy to uphold restrictions on prisoners' First Amendment rights on the basis of administrative concerns and speculation about possible security risks, rather than on the basis of evidence that the restrictions are necessary to further an important government interest."[58] The dissenters preferred a more balanced review of the District Court's findings of fact.

While the dissenters concurred with the majority's finding that the marriage regulation was unconstitutional, they strongly opposed the conclusion that the mail regulation was valid. Stevens argued that the majority erred in judging only the facial validity of the regulation when the issue before the Court was whether the correspondence regulation was unconstitutional as applied at the Renz facility.[59] The dissenters believed that a careful review of the facts indicated that the correspondence regulation was an exaggerated response to security concerns and thus failed even the less stringent "reasonably related" standard applied by the majority.

The decision in *Turner v. Safley* is important for several reasons. First, the Court restated its preference for judicial restraint in the area of prisoners' rights. Lower federal courts were to be sensitive to separation of powers concerns and should defer to the judgments of prison administrators as much as possible. This rationale would inform most Rehnquist Court decisions involving prisoners' rights. Another important feature of *Turner* was the Court's declaration that incarceration does not give prison officials absolute power to prohibit all inmate marriages.[60] Unless the marriage poses some threat, the right of inmates to marry is a fundamental one, subject to time, place, and manner restrictions. Finally, the decision established a clear standard for determining whether prison regulations violate the constitutional rights of prisoners. A "strict scrutiny" standard was firmly rejected in favor of a "rational relation" test. Unlike previous cases, O'Connor's opinion goes beyond a mere statement that prison regulations must be "reasonably related" to legitimate penological concerns; rather, she identifies four factors that must be considered when determining the existence of such a relationship.[61] One of those factors—the cost to prison systems for providing alternatives to challenged regulations—is a consideration that had not been raised in previous Court opinions dealing with First Amendment restrictions on prisoners.[62] Given the fact that state spending on corrections increased significantly during the 1980s, it is understandable that the Court would be more sensitive to the allocation of prison resources.

Although the explication of factors to be used in applying the *Turner* test would be helpful to the lower courts, the majority's preference for judicial restraint and a lower level of scrutiny of prisoners' constitutional claims could have only one consequence—a diminished protection for prisoners' rights. Indeed, the impact of the *Turner* decision was felt almost immediately. Just days after deciding *Turner*, the Court applied the "legitimate penological interests" test in the case of *O'Lone v. Estate of Shabazz* (1987), upholding a restraint on the inmates' free exercise of religion.[63] *O'Lone* involved a prison regulation that prevented Muslim inmates who were part of a work gang on assignment outside of the prison from returning at midday for *Jumu'ah*, a Friday service required by the Qur'an.[64] The District Court held that no constitutional violation occurred, because the prohibition on returns plausibly advanced the goals of security, order, and rehabilitation. It also rejected alternative arrangements, stating that "no less alternative arrangements could be adopted without potentially compromising a legitimate institutional objective."[65]

The Third Circuit Court of Appeals, however, decided that the standard applied by the District Court did not adequately protect the free exercise rights of prisoners and argued that prison regulations could only be sustained if "the state . . . shows that the challenged regulations were intended to serve, and do serve, the important penological goal of security, and that no reasonable method exists by which [prisoners'] religious rights can be accommodated without creating bona fide security problems."[66]

The Supreme Court was divided, 5 to 4, with Rehnquist, White, Powell, O'Connor, and Scalia joining the majority, and Brennan, Blackmun, Marshall, and Stevens dissenting. Writing for the Court, Chief Justice Rehnquist argued that the Court of Appeals was wrong when it "established a separate burden on prison officials" to prove that no reasonable methods exist to accommodate the religious rights of prisoners without creating security risks.[67] Applying the *Turner* standard, the Court found that there was a "logical connection" between the prison work policy and the legitimate penological interests of safety and rehabilitation. It noted that the work policy was necessary to reduce overcrowding and was in part designed to ease the strain on the facilities. The return of prisoners during the day would generate congestion and delays outside of the main gate and would create security risks. Moreover, the Court said that Muslim prisoners were "not deprived of all forms of religious exercise, but instead freely observe a number of their religious obligations."[68] The Court concluded that accommodating religious practices by placing all Muslim prisoners in one or two inside work details or providing weekend labor for the inmates would have an adverse impact on other prisoners, staff, and the allocation of resources.

Dissenting, Justice Brennan preferred an intermediate level of scrutiny that "would require prison officials to demonstrate that the restrictions they have imposed are necessary to further an important government interest, and that [the] restrictions are no greater than necessary to achieve prison objectives."[69] He was very critical of the "reasonableness" standard adopted by the Court for reviewing virtually all constitutional claims by inmates. "Our objective in selecting a standard of review," he argued, is "*not* to ensure appropriate deference to prison officials" but to "provide a bulwark against infringements that might otherwise be justified as necessary expedients of governing."[70] Brennan noted that the reasonableness standard was categorically deferential to prison administrators and did not distinguish among degrees of deprivation—a regulation limiting use of the prison library is subject to the same standard as a total ban on reading material. He warned against broad delegations of power to those who supervise the outcasts of society. "Prisons are too often shielded from public view; there is no need to make them virtually invisible," he said.[71]

Brennan favored a standard developed by a lower court in *Abdul Wali v. Coughlin* (1985). Under this approach, the degree of scrutiny of prison regulations depends on three factors: (1) the nature of the right being asserted by the prisoners; (2) the type of activity in which they seek to engage; and (3) whether the challenged restriction works a total deprivation of an asserted right, as opposed to a mere limitation.[72] Prison officials must persuasively demonstrate the need for the absolute deprivation of inmate rights. Brennan remained unconvinced by state arguments that the religious restriction was necessary to further an important government objective or that less extreme measures were unavailable.

DEFINING ELIGIBILITY FOR CAPITAL PUNISHMENT

Several Rehnquist Court decisions helped determine who can be executed under state death penalty laws. An important principle underlying criminal law is that the culpability of an offender for his or her crime should be based on his or her intent to commit an act and his or her mental state. Age is a factor in assessing the culpability of an offender. Generally, children are believed to be less responsible for their actions because they do not have the same moral development as adults. But where should the criminal justice system draw the line in holding children under 18 responsible for serious crimes? In *Thompson v. Oklahoma* (1988), Thompson was a 15-year-old juvenile who participated in the brutal murder of his former brother-in-law.[73] Because he was a "child" under Oklahoma law, the prosecutor petitioned to have him tried as an adult. The trial court granted the petition, and Thompson was convicted and sentenced to death. The Court of Criminal Appeals in Oklahoma affirmed the conviction. Thompson appealed to the Supreme Court, claiming that his punishment violated the Eighth Amendment. Following oral argument, the Court was very divided in its vote and reasoning. Justice Stevens wrote the judgment for the Court and delivered an opinion in which Brennan, Marshall, and Blackmun joined. The plurality opinion held that the cruel and unusual punishments provision of the Eighth Amendment prohibited the execution of a person under age 16 at the time of his or her offense. Justice O'Connor concurred in the judgment only, while Scalia, Rehnquist, and White dissented. Justice Kennedy did not participate in the consideration or decision of the case.

In his plurality opinion, Stevens argued that the imposition of the death penalty on offenders less than 16 years old violated the contemporary standards of decency that define the Eighth Amendment. He reviewed state death penalty laws and found that in fourteen states, capital punishment was not authorized at all, and in nineteen other states, capital punishment was authorized but no minimum age is specified in the law. In the eighteen states that have expressly established a minimum age in the death penalty statutes, all require that the defendant be at least 16 years of age at the time of the offense. Additional evidence, including the views "expressed by respected professional organizations, by other nations that share our Anglo-American heritage, and by the leading members of the West European community," suggests that it would "offend civilized standards of decency to execute a person who was less than 16 years old at the time of his or her offense."[74] Imposing the death penalty on capital offenders less than 16 years old, Stevens argued, would not make any measurable contribution to the goals of retribution and deterrence and would therefore be "nothing more than the purposeless and needless imposition of pain and suffering."[75] The Court left for another day the issue of whether states could impose the death penalty on persons who commit capital offenses at 16 and 17 years of age.

That issue was addressed the following term. In *Stanford v. Kentucky* (1989), the Court concluded that the imposition of capital punishment on a 16-year-old or 17-year-old offender does not constitute cruel and unusual punishment.[76] The case was a consolidation of two cases from Kentucky and Missouri. The first petitioner, Kevin Stanford, was 17 years old when he sodomized and murdered a convenience store clerk in Kentucky. He was certified for trial as an adult, convicted, and sentenced to death. He argued that he had a constitutional right to treatment in the juvenile justice system and declared that his age and the possibility that he might be rehabilitated were mitigating factors that should be left to a jury. The other petitioner, Heath Wilkins, was 16 years old when he stabbed a convenience store clerk to death in Missouri. He was certified for trial as an adult, pleaded guilty, and was sentenced to death. He argued that the sentence violated the Eighth Amendment. The respective state supreme courts affirmed both sentences.

The Rehnquist Court was divided, 5 to 4, with Justice Scalia delivering the opinion of the Court. O'Connor concurred in part and in the judgment. Justice Brennan, joined by Marshall, Blackmun, and Stevens, authored a dissent. In Part I of his opinion, Scalia reviewed the original meaning of the Eighth Amendment. At the time the Bill of Rights was drafted, he stated, the common law permitted capital punishment for juvenile offenders. The petitioners were probably aware of this original meaning, so they argued that their punishment was contrary to the "evolving standards of decency" of a maturing society. In determining which standards have "evolved," Scalia argued that the Court's judgment should be informed by objective factors as much as possible rather than the subjective policy preferences of the individual justices. These objective factors included laws passed by the states and jury decisions in capital trials. "Of the 37 States whose laws permit capital punishment," Scalia noted, "15 decline to impose it upon 16-year-old offenders and 12 decline to impose it on 17-year-old offenders."[77] In his view, these statistics did not represent the national consensus needed to label a particular punishment cruel and unusual, as the Court did in *Coker v. Georgia* (1977), where it declared the death penalty for the crime of rape in violation of the Eighth Amendment. Scalia also argued that the petitioners failed to establish a consensus against capital punishment for 16- and 17-year-old offenders through federal statutes and the behavior of prosecutors and juries. He refused to accept other indicia urged by the petitioners, including public opinion polls and the views of interest groups. He declined to rest constitutional law upon what he called "such uncertain foundations."

Scalia also rejected the petitioner's argument that the death penalty for such young offenders fails to meet legitimate penological goals. Lawyers for the convicted offenders made two arguments on these grounds: (1) that capital punishment fails to deter juveniles because they have less developed cognitive skills and are therefore less likely to fear death; and (2) the imposition of capital punishment fails to exact just retribution because juveniles are less mature and responsible and therefore less blameworthy. To support these claims the petitioners and *amici* submitted a variety of socioscientific evidence concerning the emotional and psychological development of 16 and 17 year olds. Scalia was not convinced by this evidence and suggested that the arguments were misplaced—the audience should be the American people, not the Court. He said that it is the American public that must be persuaded that capital punishment for 16- and 17-year-old offenders is cruel and unusual.

In a portion of his opinion, Scalia responded to the contention of the dissenters that his approach allows political majorities to define the contours of Eighth Amendment protections and fails to restrict those institutions that the Constitution was designed to limit. In language typical of his jurisprudence, Scalia lectured his colleagues on the value of judicial restraint:

When this Court cast loose from the historical moorings consisting of the original application of the Eighth Amendment, it did not embark rudderless upon a wide-open sea. Rather, it limited the Amendment's extension to those practices contrary to the evolving *standards* of decency that mark the progress of a maturing *society*. It has never been thought that this was a shorthand reference to the preferences of a majority of this Court. By reaching a decision supported by neither constitutional text nor by the demonstrable current standards of our citizens, the dissent displays a failure to appreciate that those institutions which the Constitution is supposed to limit include the Court itself.[78]

Scalia concluded that there was neither a historical nor a modern societal consensus against the imposition of capital punishment on anyone who murders at 16 or 17 years of age. Since there was no consensus based on objective factors, the punishments imposed on these juvenile offenders were constitutional under the Eighth Amendment.

In her concurring opinion, Justice O'Connor applied the two-part standard expressed in *Thompson v. Oklahoma* (1988). She concluded that the death sentences imposed on both petitioners "should not be set aside because it is sufficiently clear that no national consensus forbids the imposition of capital punishment on 16- and 17-year-old capital murderers."[79] The difference between this case and *Thompson*, O'Connor said, "is that every single American legislature that has expressly set a minimum age for capital punishment has set that age at 16 or above."[80] She did not join that portion of the plurality's opinion, however, which rejected as irrelevant to Eighth Amendment considerations an obligation imposed on the Court to judge whether the punishment imposed is proportional to the defendant's blameworthiness.

Justice Brennan, writing for the dissenters, believed that it was cruel and unusual and hence in violation of the Eighth Amendment to impose the death penalty as punishment on a person for a crime committed below age 18. He argued that judgments about the "constitutionality of punishment under the Eighth Amendment [are] informed, though not determined, by an examination of contemporary attitudes toward the punishment, as evidenced in the actions of legislatures and juries."[81] With regard to legislative enactments concerning capital punishment, he felt that the Court's discussion gave a distorted view of the evidence of contemporary standards. Twelve of the states whose statutes permitted capital punishment specifically mandate that offenders under age 18 not be sentenced to death. When these states are combined with the fifteen, including the District of Columbia, in which capital punishment was prohibited, the governments in 27 of the states have determined that no one under age 18 should be sentenced to death. Three other states prohibited the death penalty for offenders under age 17, meaning that 30 states would not authorize the execution of petitioner Wilkins. Brennan also noted that in both "absolute and relative terms, imposition of the death penalty on adolescents is distinctly unusual."[82] Of the 2,186 inmates on death row at the time, only 30, or 1.37 percent, were adolescent offenders.[83] The Court interpreted these statistics to mean that juries have reserved capital sentences for rare cases in which it may be appropriate; Brennan, however, concluded that a sentence so rarely imposed is "unusual" under Eighth Amendment analysis.[84]

Unlike Justice Scalia, who rejected the use of polls and the views of interest groups for discerning contemporary standards of decency, Brennan embraced this evidence. "Where organizations with expertise in a relevant area have given careful consideration to the question of a punishment's appropriateness," he said, "there is no reason why that judgment should not be entitled to attention as an indicator of contemporary standards."[85] Citing the *amicus* briefs of over 30 organizations, Brennan noted that there was "no dearth of opinion" that state-sanctioned killing of minors was wrong. He also argued that legislation in other countries was relevant to Eighth Amendment analysis. Over 50 countries had abolished the death penalty or had limited its use, and of the nations that have retained capital punishment, a majority prohibit the execution of juveniles. Finally, Brennan said that the execution of juvenile offenders "fails to satisfy two well-established and independent Eighth Amendment requirements—that a punishment not be disproportionate, and that it make a contribution to acceptable goals of punishment."[86] He concluded that juveniles generally lack the degree of blameworthiness necessary for the imposition of capital punishment under the Eighth Amendment proportionality principle. Moreover, executing 16- and 17-year old offenders serves no acceptable goals of punishment. Retribution is not served, because adolescent offenders lack culpability for their actions, and juveniles are not likely to be deterred by such punishments.

On the day *Stanford* was decided, the Court issued its opinion in *Penry v. Lynaugh* (1989), where by the same 5-to-4 vote it held that states were not barred from executing mentally retarded persons.[87] In a separate holding decided by the same margin, a different coalition ruled that states must allow jurors to consider evidence of mental retardation as a "mitigating factor" when deciding to impose a sentence of death. Justice O'Connor, the author of *Penry*, was the only member in both majorities. She was joined by Rehnquist, White, Scalia, and Kennedy in holding that executing capital murderers who are mentally retarded does not violate a proportionality principle under the Eighth Amendment. On the issue of jury consideration of mental retardation as a "mitigating factor," O'Connor was joined by Brennan, Marshall, Blackmun, and Stevens.

Johnny Paul Penry was 22 years old when he brutally raped, beat, and stabbed with a pair of scissors Pamela Carpenter in her home in Livingston, Texas. At the trial, a clinical psychologist testified that Penry suffered from organic brain damage and moderate retardation—he had the mental capacity of a 6 ½ year old and the social maturity of a 9 or 10 year old. The jury found Penry competent to stand trial, and the state introduced the testimony of two psychiatrists to rebut the testimony of the clinical psychologist. Both psychiatrists testified that Penry was legally sane at the time of the offense. The jury rejected Penry's insanity defense and convicted him of capital murder. Because the jury was not instructed that it could consider and give effect to the mitigating evidence of Penry's mental retardation and abused background, the Court concluded "that the jury was not provided with a vehicle for expressing its 'reasoned moral response' to that evidence in rendering its sentencing decision."[88]

USE OF VICTIM IMPACT STATEMENTS IN CAPITAL SENTENCING

In another case decided during the Rehnquist Court's first term, the justices considered the constitutionality of Victim Impact Statements (VIS) during capital sentencing. In Maryland, court procedures allowed murder victims' family members to testify before the jury about the loss caused by the defendant's actions. In *Booth v. Maryland* (1987), the Court, by a 5-to-4 vote, said that survivor victim impact statements were irrelevant to the blameworthiness of the defendant, and only evidence relating to the guilt of a defendant is relevant to the capital sentencing decision.[89] Victim impact evidence, the Court observed, could well distract the sentencing jury from its constitutional responsibility "of determining whether the death penalty is appropriate in light of the background and record of the accused and the particular circumstances of the crime." Admitting such statements would create a constitutionally unacceptable risk that the jury may impose the death sentence in an arbitrary, capricious manner.

Two years later, the Court, in *South Carolina v. Gathers* (1989), held that a description of the victim's religious beliefs and patriotism by a prosecutor during closing arguments were indistinguishable from an impact statement and therefore contrary to the Eighth Amendment.[90] In his study of the politics of the Rehnquist Court, Edward Lazarus describes the strategy behind the *Gathers* decision. The vote was a big disappointment for Chief Justice Rehnquist and the conservative justices who expected *Booth* to be overturned when the case was granted review. The lower court had thrown out Gathers's sentence on *Booth* grounds. Justice Kennedy had replaced Powell, *Booth's* author, so Rehnquist thought that he now had the votes to overrule *Booth*. But the plan backfired. Kennedy voted as Rehnquist had hoped, but Justice White, who wrote a dissent in *Booth*, voted to uphold the precedent. *Gathers* became a 5-to-4 liberal victory, affirming the *Booth* precedent.[91] Justice Brennan authored the opinion for the Court, joined by White, Marshall, Blackmun, and Stevens. Justice O'Connor filed a dissenting opinion, which was joined by Rehnquist and Kennedy, and Scalia wrote a separate dissent.

In his opinion for the Court, Justice Brennan remarked that the Court's capital cases have consistently recognized that the punishment must be tailored to the defendant's personal responsibility and moral guilt. The only difference between this case and *Booth*, Brennan said, was that it was the prosecutor who made statements concerning the personal characteristics of the victim rather than the victim's survivors. The *Booth* opinion, he noted, did "leave open the possibility that the kind of information contained in victim impact statements could be admissible if it related directly to the circumstances of the crime."[92] He concluded, however, that the statements did not provide any information relevant to the defendant's moral culpability.

Justice Scalia's dissenting opinion was very critical of the *Booth* holding, arguing that it had no "basis in the common-law background that led up to the Eighth Amendment, in any long-standing societal tradition, or in any evidence that present society, through its laws or actions of its juries, has set its face against considering the harm caused by criminal acts in assessing responsibility."[93] He urged the Court to overrule the precedent, and he was unconcerned about the consequences to the Court's public image of overturning such a recent decision. Scalia even went so far as to admit that the changing political composition of the Court influences the decision to reverse precedents: "I doubt that overruling *Booth* will so shake the citizenry's faith in the Court. Overrulings of precedent rarely occur without a change in the Court's personnel."[94] Scalia believed that it was better to reverse an erroneous decision sooner rather than later, because respect for prior decisions increases the longer they are on the books and as society has a chance to adjust itself to their existence. For one Court scholar, this candid admission of the role of the appointment process in determining legal doctrine seemed to suggest that "Scalia was looking forward to further personnel changes that might advance his preferred outcome."[95] He did not have to wait long, for in 1990, Justice William Brennan retired from the Court and was replaced by Republican appointee David Souter.

In a decision that overturned the precedents in *Booth* and *Gathers*, the Rehnquist Court, in *Payne v. Tennessee* (1991), held that the admission of VIS during the sentencing phase of a capital trial was not barred by the Eighth Amendment.[96] The ruling permitted a murder victim's mother to testify about the impact of the murder on the victim's 2-year-old son. Chief Justice Rehnquist wrote the opinion for the Court, in which White, O'Connor, Scalia, Kennedy, and Souter joined. Rehnquist described VIS as "simply another form or method of informing the sentencing authority about the specific harm caused by the crime in question, evidence of a general type long considered by sentencing authorities."[97] Citing the dissenting opinions in *Booth* and *Gathers*, the Court argued that the ban on VIS turns the victim into a "faceless stranger at the penalty phase of a trial" and "deprives the State of the full moral force of its evidence and may prevent the jury from having before it all the information necessary to determine the proper punishment for first-degree murder."[98] The decision emphasized victims' rights. If the defendant can introduce mitigating evidence during the sentencing phase, it was reasonable to allow the state to submit evidence of the specific harm caused by the convicted defendant. Rehnquist conceded that "adhering to precedent is usually the wise policy," and that "*stare decisis* is the preferred course because it promotes the evenhanded, predictable, and consistent development of legal principles," but "when governing decisions are unworkable or are badly reasoned," the Court has never felt obligated to follow precedent.[99] To strengthen the argument for overruling precedent, the Court noted that *Booth* and *Gathers* were decided by the narrowest of margins, over strong dissents that challenged the rationale of the Court, and have not been consistently applied by the lower courts.

In a concurring opinion, Justice Souter felt that it would be problematic to exclude VIS. He wrote that prohibiting victim impact evidence was unworkable, because details about the impact of a crime on the victim and survivors would most likely be revealed during the guilt phase of the trial. The only way to prevent this would be to have two separate juries, which would be impractical. In a dissenting opinion, Justice Marshall noted that neither the law nor facts supporting *Booth* and *Gathers* had changed since they were decided; the only difference was the composition of the Court—Brennan had been replaced by Souter, who joined the four conservatives in overturning the precedents.

COURT REVISITS PROPORTIONALITY PRINCIPLE UNDER THE EIGHTH AMENDMENT

The Court severely weakened, if not overruled, the *Solem v. Helm* (1983) precedent in *Harmelin v. Michigan* (1991), where it held that a mandatory life term without the possibility of parole for possessing over 650 grams of cocaine did not constitute cruel and unusual punishment.[100] The State Court of Appeals ruled that the sentence did not violate the Eighth Amendment. Justices Brennan, Marshall, Stevens, and Scalia had voted to grant certiorari, but by the time the case reached the Court, Brennan had been replaced by David Souter. The conference vote on the merits was 6 to 3, with Rehnquist, Blackmun, O'Connor, Scalia, Kennedy, and Souter voting to affirm. Justices White, Marshall, and Stevens favored a reversal. By the time the decision was announced, Blackmun had switched his vote in support of a reversal, so the Court was divided 5 to 4 for the third time in this series of Eighth Amendment proportionality cases. If Justice Brennan rather than Souter had participated in the merits of the case, the vote certainly would have been decided differently.

Justice Scalia's opinion deferred to the authority of the states to set penalties for criminal violations. He argued that the words "cruel and unusual" must be read in the conjunctive; in other words, a punishment must be *both* cruel and uncommon to American legal culture to be a violation of the Eighth Amendment. He wrote that "severe, mandatory penalties may be cruel but they are not unusual in a constitutional sense," having been used throughout our history.[101] Scalia spent the first four parts of the opinion criticizing several precedents that provided for a proportionality principle under the Eighth Amendment, but he was joined only by Chief Justice Rehnquist on these sections. Scalia concluded that "Solem was simply wrong; the Eighth Amendment contains no proportionality guarantee."[102] Part B of the opinion is a dissertation on the historical origins of the Eighth Amendment Cruel and Unusual Punishments Clause. Scalia argued that the amendment was intended to prohibit certain barbaric modes of punishment devised by legislative bodies. He noted that the framers, when they drafted and ratified the federal Constitution, chose not to include within it a guarantee against disproportionate sentences. This omission was reasonable, according to Scalia, because of the difficulty of developing standards to apply a proportionality principle. "In the real-world enterprise," he argued, "the standards seem so inadequate that the proportionality principle becomes an invitation to imposition of subjective values."[103] Finally, Scalia argued that proportionality is only required when the Court is considering capital punishment: "Proportionality review is one of several respects in which we have held that 'death is different,' and have imposed protections that the Constitution nowhere else provides."[104] It is difficult to understand, however, how Justice Scalia's conclusion fits with the history and text of the Eighth Amendment or Supreme Court precedent. The text says nothing about limiting the Eighth Amendment to capital punishment, and the *Weems* and *Solem* decisions clearly read a proportionality requirement into the Eighth Amendment in noncapital cases. By distinguishing *Weems* and urging that *Solem* be overturned, Scalia lost the support of the moderate conservatives on the Court.

Concurring in part and in the judgment, Justice Kennedy, joined by O'Connor and Souter, felt that several Court precedents had established a limited concept of proportionality that applied to noncapital punishments. Regardless of the debate over the historical meaning of the Eighth Amendment, Kennedy argued that "*stare decisis* counsels our adherence to the narrow proportionality principle that has existed in our Eighth Amendment jurisprudence for 80 years."[105] Though the Court has recognized a proportionality principle, Kennedy admitted that "its precise contours are unclear." Still, he was able to identify some common principles that define the scope and limits of proportionality review: (1) legislatures have the primary function of setting punishments; (2) the Eighth Amendment does not mandate a particular penological theory; (3) our federal system results in a wide range of criminal punishments; and (4) proportionality review should be informed by objective factors. These four principles, Kennedy stated, inform the final one: the Eighth Amendment does not require strict proportionality between crime and sentence.[106]

In applying the principles, Kennedy pointed out that the sentence imposed in both *Solem* and *Harmelin* was the same; the difference was the seriousness of the crime. The crime of uttering a no account check at issue in *Solem* was minor compared to the more serious conviction of cocaine possession in *Harmelin*. For Kennedy and the others, the severity of Harmelin's crime "brings his sentence within the constitutional boundaries established by our prior decisions."[107] Finally, Kennedy rejected the petitioner's attack on his sentence because of its mandatory nature, declaring that the Court's Eighth Amendment "capital decisions reject any requirement of individualized sentencing in noncapital cases," and that the "sentence comports with our noncapital proportionality decisions as well."[108]

Justice White wrote a dissenting opinion, joined by Blackmun and Stevens, while Marshall and Stevens authored separate dissents. White acknowledged that the Eighth Amendment does not refer to proportionality in so many words, but that it does prohibit excessive fines, language that suggests that a determination must be made about whether the fine imposed is disproportionate to the crime committed. White disagreed with Scalia's historical analysis of the amendment and treatment of Supreme Court precedents that recognized a proportionality principle. He criticized Scalia for declaring that there is no proportionality guarantee in the Eighth Amendment, then backtracking to admit that proportionality is relevant in a special class of cases—sentences of death.[109] Except for capital cases, this interpretation would mean that any "prison sentence, however severe, for any crime, however petty, will be beyond review under the Eighth Amendment."[110] He pointed out the limitations of a purely historical analysis concerning the scope of the prohibition on cruel and unusual punishments. Citing *Trop v. Dulles* (1958), White said that a punishment may violate the amendment if it is contrary to the "evolving standards of decency that mark the progress of a maturing society." In response to Scalia's legislative deference and sensitivity to federalism, White argued that it is the responsibility of the courts "to scrutinze legislative enactments concerning punishment."[111]

White identified two dangers lurking in Justice Scalia's analysis of the Eighth Amendment. First, it provided no mechanism for a situation described in *Rummel*, in which a legislature declares overtime parking a felony punishable by life imprisonment. Scalia dismissed the example as improbable, but White said that without a proportionality guarantee, there would be no basis for deciding such cases should they arise. Second, Scalia's contention that the Eighth Amendment only applies to modes or methods of punishment was inconsistent with the Court's capital punishment cases, White argued, which do not outlaw death as a method of punishment but place limits on its application.

White also criticized Justice Kennedy for reducing the three factors relevant to a proportionality outlined in *Solem* to just one. The opinion in *Solem* contradicts this interpretation, however, because the Court made clear that "no single factor will be dispositive in a given case," but a combination of objective factors can make proportionality analysis workable.[112] If all three factors in *Solem's* proportionality test are applied, White concluded that the mandatory penalty of life imprisonment without parole is unconstitutionally disproportionate and a violation of the Eighth Amendment.

Marshall agreed with White's dissenting opinion, except for its assertion that the Eighth Amendment does not proscribe the death penalty. Citing his dissent in *Gregg v. Georgia* (1976), Marshall adhered to his belief that capital punishment is in all instances unconstitutional. He found White's cental conclusion—that the Eighth Amendment imposes a general proportionality requirement—consistent with his views on both capital and noncapital punishment. Stevens's dissent, and Blackmun's, noted that "a sentence of mandatory life imprisonment without parole does share one important characteristic with a death sentence: the offender will never gain his freedom."[113] White argued that because such a sentence does not even attempt to serve a rehabilitative function, the sentence must rest on a rational determination that drug possession is so "atrocious that society's interest in deterrence and rehabilitation wholly outweighs any considerations of reform or rehabilitation of the perpetrator."[114] He believed that it was irrational to conclude that every perpetrator convicted of cocaine possession was "wholly incorrigible." In his view, the punishment was well beyond anything imposed under the Federal Sentencing Guidelines and laws in most states and did not satisfy any meaningful requirement of proportionality.

THE "DELIBERATE INDIFFERENCE" STANDARD

During the 1990 term, the Court viewed its first prison "conditions of confinement" case in a decade. In *Wilson v. Seiter* (1991), the Court held that in cases alleging cruel and unusual punishment, it is necessary to examine a prison official's state of mind.[115] Wilson was incarcerated at the Hocking Correctional Facility in Nelsonville, Ohio. He complained that his conditions of confinement were in violation of the Eighth and Fourteenth Amendments. His complaint alleged improper living conditions, including overcrowding, excessive noise, inadequate heating and cooling, unclean and inadequate restrooms, unsanitary dining facilities and food preparation, and housing with mentally and physically ill inmates.[116] The Sixth Circuit Court of Appeals agreed with the District Court that even if the allegations were true, they did not establish unconstitutional conditions, and the case therefore should be dismissed. The Supreme Court granted certiorari to decide the question of whether an inmate claiming that prison conditions are cruel and unusual punishment is required to demonstrate that prison officials possessed a culpable state of mind.

Writing for the Court, Justice Scalia was joined by Rehnquist, O'Connor, Kennedy, and Souter. Justice White filed an opinion concurring in the judgment only, in which Marshall, Blackmun, and Stevens joined. The Court rejected the lower court ruling that prisoners must show that corrections officials have acted with "persistent and malicious cruelty" and instead applied a "deliberate indifference" standard. Justice Scalia concluded that an objective approach to unconstitutional prison conditions was not sufficient to analyze the allegations, but rather that an inquiry must be made into the prison officials' state of mind. The Court then had to determine what state of mind should be applied to cases challenging prison conditions. Comparing the standards announced in *Whitley v. Albers* (1986) and *Estelle v. Gamble* (1976), the Court saw "no significant distinction between claims alleging inadequate medical care (in *Estelle*) and those alleging inadequate conditions of confinement."[117]

Newspaper commentators characterized the *Seiter* decision as a setback for prisoner litigants. Some advocates of prisoners' rights acknowledged, however, that the standard announced in the case had routinely been applied in the lower federal courts, though often without using the same terminology.[118] In medical care cases, courts have focused on the actions and omissions of medical and correctional personnel, not on their mental states. Lower federal courts held that deliberate indifference may be established by showing repeated examples of negligent acts which disclose a pattern of conduct by the prison medical staff, or by showing gross deficiencies in staffing, facilities, equipment, or procedures. These criteria do not require plaintiffs to establish evidence of a particular mind-set on the part of prison officials. Nevertheless, a standard based upon the psychological disposition of prison officials requires extensive evidence of a pattern of negligence and places a greater burden on the plaintiffs.

MODIFICATION OF CONSENT DECREES

Seiter was followed by an important ruling concerning the modification of court-approved settlements between plaintiffs and state defendants. In *Rufo v. Inmates of Suffolk County Jail* (1992), the Court made it easier for state and local officials to modify consent decrees that required them to improve conditions at prisons and other public institutions.[119] The case involved litigation dating back 20 years. Corrections officials in Suffolk County, Massachusetts, had entered into a consent decree providing for the construction of a new jail that would provide single-occupancy cells for pre-trial detainees. Work on the jail progressed slowly. The new facility was supposed to be completed by 1983, but construction did not even begin until 1987. Meanwhile, inmate populations had outpaced projections. Jail officials sought a modification of the consent decree to allow double bunking in some cells in order to raise the jail's capacity. The District Court denied relief, holding that "nothing less than a clear showing of grievous wrong evoked by new and unforeseen conditions" should prompt a change in what was decreed after years of litigation and with the consent of all of the parties.[120] This standard was established in *United States v. Swift and Co.* (1932) and was believed to have been codified in the Federal Rules of Civil Procedure. The District Court also rejected the argument that *Bell v. Wolfish* (1979) required modification of the decree. The Court of Appeals affirmed.

The majority opinion, written by Justice White, was joined by Rehnquist, Scalia, Kennedy, and Souter. Justice O'Connor concurred in the judgment. The Court's opinion allowed judges to reconsider the case and determine whether a "significant change" in the factual circumstances or interpretation of the law justified altering the terms of the settlement. In rejecting the *Swift* standard, the Court said that "the 'grievous wrong' language of *Swift* was not intended to take on a talismanic quality, warding off virtually all efforts to modify consent decrees."[121] The Court mentioned that institutional reform litigation had increased significantly since *Brown v. Board of Education, Topeka* (1954). Because some of these decrees remain in place indefinitely, the likelihood of major changes occurring during the life of the decree is enhanced. The Court suggested that a lower court should exercise flexibility in considering requests for modification of a decree. Changes may not always be warranted. "The party seeking modification of a consent decree," the Court declared, "bears the burden of establishing that a significant change in the circumstances warrants revision of the decree."[122] This initial burden can be met by showing a significant change in either the facts or the law.

The Court warned that a modification must not create or perpetuate a constitutional violation, nor should it strive to rewrite the decree so it conforms to a constitutional floor. Within these constraints, the Court said that the public interest and concern for the allocation of power within our federal system require that lower courts "defer to local government administrators, who have primary responsibility for elucidating, assessing, and solving the problems of institutional reform."[123] Perhaps more important, the majority concluded that the financial burdens placed on government are a relevant factor when considering the modification of a consent decree. The Court noted:

Financial constraints may not be used to justify the creation or perpetuation of constitutional violations, but they are a legitimate concern of government defendants in institutional reform litigation and therefore are appropriately considered in tailoring a consent decree modification.[124]

Taken together, *Wilson v. Seiter* and *Rufo v. Inmates of Suffolk County Jail* encourage lower federal courts to yield to the authority of state and local officials in prison and jail administration. These decisions may not represent a return to the hands-off policy, but they are a significant retreat from extensive intervention. District Court judges may choose to ignore or at least to give different interpretations to these precedents, much as they did in the earlier cases on overcrowding. While the overall message of these decisions is one of judicial restraint and respect for state administrative powers, both opinions set unclear standards and allow room for interpretation. As the dissenters in *Rufo* argued, both the "grievous wrong" and "significant change" standards for altering consent decrees invite interpretation. Trial court judges now have to determine if a significant change in law or facts requires modification of a consent decree.

USE OF EXCESSIVE FORCE MAY BE CRUEL AND UNUSUAL PUNISHMENT

In a noncapital punishment case, the Court, in *Hudson v. McMillian* (1992), ruled that the excessive use of force against a state penitentiary prisoner may constitute cruel and unusual punishment under the Eighth Amendment, even if the prisoner does not suffer serious injury.[125] Keith Hudson had been punched and kicked by two guards while he remained handcuffed, and a supervisor instructed the guards not to have "too much fun."[126] He sustained minor bruises and swelling of his face and mouth, some loose teeth, and a crack in his partial dental plate that made it unusable for several months. The decision was a rare victory for prisoners' rights in the Rehnquist Court. The majority opinion, written by Justice O'Connor, was joined by Chief Justice Rehnquist, White, Kennedy, and Souter. Stevens concurred in part and concurred in the judgment, while Blackmun concurred in the judgment. Thomas and Scalia dissented.

Under *Whitley v. Albers* (1986), the standard for excessive use of force is whether guards "unnecessarily and unwantonly" inflict pain. The Court rejected the argument made in Justice Thomas's dissent that inmates must show a "significant injury" in addition to the unnecessary and wanton infliction of pain. O'Connor said that the inquiry set out in *Whitley* is relevant to this case, "whether force was applied in a good-faith effort to maintain or restore discipline, or maliciously and sadistically to cause harm."[127] The respondents argued that a significant injury requirement was mandated by the "objective component" of Eighth Amendment analysis. Quoting *Trop v. Dulles* (1958), O'Connor noted that the Eighth Amendment draws its meaning from the "evolving standards of decency that mark the progress of a maturing society," and the "objective component of an Eighth Amendment claim is therefore contextual and responsive" to contemporary standards of decency.[128] "When prison officials maliciously and sadistically use force to cause harm," she argued, "contemporary standards of decency are always violated . . . whether or not significant injury is evident."[129]

In his concurring opinion, Stevens complained that the Court's reliance on the "malicious and sadistic" standard was misplaced, because there was neither a prison riot or the need to use force, since Hudson was in handcuffs and shackles. In this context, he would apply the less demanding standard of unnecessary and wanton infliction of pain. Blackmun's concurring opinion speculated on the consequences if the Court were to hold that an excessive use of force is actionable only when coupled with "significant injury" that requires medical attention or leaves permanent marks. Such a holding, he warned, might place various kinds of torture and abuse beyond judicial review.[130] Along those lines, Blackmun argued that psychological harm can prove to be just as cruel and unusual as physical injury and may be actionable under the Eighth Amendment.

It was Justice Thomas's dissenting opinion in *McMillian* that drew most of the attention from scholars and journalists. Contrary to decades of precedents, Thomas argued that the ban on cruel and unusual punishment was designed to guard against excessive prison sentences, not to protect inmates from harsh treatment once in prison. Justice Thomas was very critical of the majority's reliance of the standard articulated in *Trop v. Dulles*, and he rejected the Court's conclusion that inmates need not show a significant injury. According to Justice Thomas, "a use of force that causes only insignificant harm to a prisoner may be immoral, it may be tortuous, it may be criminal, and it may even be remedial under other provisions of the Federal Constitution, but it is not cruel and unusual punishment."[131] Thomas argued that the federal Constitution is not to be used to solve all of the problems in our society. "Abusive behavior by prison guards is deplorable conduct that properly evokes outrage and contempt," he said, "But that does not mean that it is invariably unconstitutional. The Eighth Amendment is not, and should not be turned into, a National Code of Prison Regulation."[132] Thomas concluded that if a prisoner wants to claim that he or she was subjected to cruel and unusual punishment, he or she must always show that he or she has suffered a serious injury.

HABEAS CORPUS PETITIONS UNDER ATTACK

The Rehnquist Court has been quite active in trying to reform habeas corpus review. Since the 1980s, Chief Justice Rehnquist has been on a mission to limit state prisoners' access to the federal courts and to reduce the volume of habeas corpus petitions.[133] In a major ruling affecting habeas corpus petitions in death penalty cases, the Rehnquist Court made it much more difficult for death row inmates and other state prisoners to file multiple challenges to the constitutionality of their sentences. By a 6-to-3 vote in *McCleskey v. Zant* (1991), the Court created a new standard for lower federal courts, under which a prisoner's second or subsequent habeas corpus petition must be dismissed only in exceptional circumstances. The decision made it easier for state prosecutors to contest as an abuse of the writ all habeas corpus petitions filed after a prisoner's first one. Under the new definition of the "abuse of the writ" doctrine, second or subsequent petitions may be dismissed as abusive unless the inmate can show: (1) that there was a good reason for not raising the claim earlier; and (2) that the inmate suffered "actual prejudice" from the constitutional error that he or she claimed occurred in his or her trial, conviction, or sentencing.

Applying this same standard, the Rehnquist Court, in *Sawyer v. Whitley* (1992), held that a defendant bringing a successive habeas corpus claim that he or she was "actually innocent" must show by "clear and convincing evidence" that except for a constitutional error at the trial and sentencing, no reasonable juror would have found the defendant eligible for the death penalty under applicable law. *Herrera v. Collins* (1993) is a capital punishment case involving death row inmate Leonel Herrera, who, ten years after his conviction for killing a police officer, filed a habeas corpus petition claiming that newly discovered evidence proved that he was innocent. Herrera argued that the state's denial of his petition was a violation of the Eighth Amendment prohibition of "cruel and unusual" punishment and the Fourteenth Amendment's Due Process Clause.

Rehnquist's majority opinion concluded that a death row inmate is not ordinarily entitled to habeas corpus relief based solely on the claim that he or she is actually innocent. Rehnquist argued that inmates also must have an independent claim of constitutional error in state trial proceedings. He dismissed the due process claim by saying that the refusal of the state of Texas to consider the new evidence ten years after Herrera's conviction did not violate "principles of fundamental fairness."[134] If Herrera wanted fairness, Rehnquist suggested that he seek executive clemency. Souter and Stevens joined a strongly worded dissenting opinion by Justice Blackmun. The dissenters felt that the majority opinion violated prevailing standards of decency under the Eighth Amendment and that this was a violation of due process. "The execution of a person who can show that he is innocent," Blackmun argued, "comes perilously close to simple murder."[135]

Subsequent decisions on habeas corpus review had mixed results for prisoners' rights. In *Withrow v. Williams* (1993), Justice Souter's majority opinion ruled that federal courts in habeas corpus cases may throw out state convictions where police do not advise a suspect of his or her Miranda rights before interrogation. In *Brecht v. Abrahamson* (1993), the Court upheld the first-degree murder conviction of a man who claimed at trial that the shooting of his brother-in-law was an accident. The vote was 5 to 4, but the coalitions were unusual for the Rehnquist Court. Chief Justice Rehnquist, joined by White, Blackmun, O'Connor, and Souter, wrote the opinion for the Court, which announced a less stringent rule for reviewing trial-related errors in habeas corpus cases. Under the old rule, errors had to be proved harmless beyond a reasonable doubt. With the new standard, habeas corpus relief is available only if an error had "substantial and injurious effect or influence in determining the jury's verdict."

JUSTICE BLACKMUN ANNOUNCES HIS OPPOSITION TO THE DEATH PENALTY

Late in his career on the Court, Justice Blackmun declared his opposition to the death penalty in a dissent from denial of certiorari in *Callins v. Collins* (1994).[136] Blackmun had become convinced that the death penalty could never be administered in a fair, unbiased, and error-free manner. This conclusion took on greater significance, given the Rehnquist Court's movement to restrict habeas corpus petitions that effectively limited federal court oversight of capital trial procedures.

Blackmun began his dissent with a description of how Callins was to be executed by lethal injection by the state of Texas. "Twenty years have passed since this Court declared that the death penalty must be imposed fairly, and with reasonable consistency, or not at all," Blackmun recalled, "and, despite the effort of the States and courts to devise legal formulas and procedural rules to meet this daunting challenge, the death penalty remains fraught with arbitrariness, discrimination, caprice, and mistake."[137] The central problem, according to Blackmun, was that the constitutional goal of eliminating arbitrariness and discrimination from capital trial procedures "can never be achieved without compromising an equally essential component of fundamental fairness—individualized sentencing."[138] In other words, the rationale of *Furman v. Georgia* (1972) was in conflict with the holding in *Lockett v. Ohio* (1978). Sentences should be rational and consistent, but fundamental fairness also requires the sentencer to consider any mitigating evidence that would warrant a sentence less than death.

Blackmun argued that the Court had engaged in a futile effort to balance the constitutional demands of rationality and consistency with individualized sentencing. Citing *McCleskey v. Kemp* (1987), he said that the Court has conceded that fairness and rationality cannot be achieved in the imposition of the death penalty, and he criticized the Court for "abdicating its statutorily and constitutionally imposed duty to provide meaningful judicial oversight to the administration of death by the States."[139] Justice Blackmun concluded that:

From this day forward, I no longer shall tinker with the machinery of death. For more than 20 years I have endeavored—indeed, I have struggled—along with a majority of this Court, to develop procedural and substantive rules that would lend more than the mere appearance of fairness to the death penalty endeavor. Rather than continue to coddle the Court's delusion that the desired level of fairness has been achieved and the need for regulation eviscerated, I feel morally and intellectually obligated simply to concede that the death penalty experiment has failed.[140]

The Court's decision in *Herrera v. Collins* (1993) only strengthened Blackmun's belief that the death penalty can never be constitutional. In his view, the opinion in *Herrera* demonstrated just how far the Court would stray from its obligation to evaluate and correct claims of constitutional error on federal habeas corpus review.

Justice Scalia responded to Blackmun's dissent with a strongly worded opinion of his own. He noted that Blackmun's rationale for rejecting the death penalty was based on intellectual, moral, and personal perceptions, not on the text or the tradition of the Constitution. "It is the latter rather than the former that ought to control," he said.[141] Scalia argued that the incompatible demands attached to the death penalty were the product of justices reading their personal policy preferences into the Eighth Amendment rather than adhering to the text or historical evidence. He felt that Blackmun drew the wrong conclusion from his acknowledgment of the competing demands of *Furman* and *Lockett*. The correct conclusion, Scalia suggested, was that at least one of the commands was wrong. Finally, Scalia criticized Blackmun for selecting a case involving one of the less brutal murders to announce his opposition to the death penalty. Callins's death by injection looked a lot better, he said, than some of the other murder cases that had come before the Court, including "the case of the 11-year-old girl raped by four men and then killed by having her panties stuffed down her throat. . . . How enviable a quiet death by lethal injection compared with that!"[142]

SECONDHAND SMOKE AND INMATE HEALTH

In another rare victory for prisoners' rights during Chief Justice Rehnquist's tenure, the Court, in *Helling v. McKinney* (1993), allowed prison inmates to sue for involuntary exposure to environmental tobacco smoke (ETS).[143] In a 7-to-2 ruling, with only Justices Scalia and Thomas dissenting, the Court concluded that confining a prisoner in a cell with another inmate who smoked five packs of cigarettes a day posed an unreasonable risk to an inmate's health and may be a cause of action under the Eighth Amendment's ban on cruel and unusual punishment. The petitioners tried to argue that unless McKinney could prove that he was currently suffering serious medical problems caused by exposure to ETS, there was no violation of the Eighth Amendment. The Court, however, said that the Amendment protects against future harm to inmates resulting from "deliberate indifference" to their health and safety, as well as current health problems.[144] The case was remanded to the District Court so that McKinney could prove his allegations, which the Court said would require him to prove both an objective and subjective elements necessary for an Eighth Amendment violation. For example, he must show that he was being exposed to unreasonably high levels of ETS to meet the objective requirement. The Court said that the subjective factor, deliberate indifference, "should be determined in light of the prison authorities' current attitudes and conduct, which may have changed considerably."[145] Indeed, they had. Because the prison had established a formal smoking policy since the Court of Appeals decision, McKinney would have a difficult time proving deliberate indifference.

Justice Thomas believed that the majority opinion was an unwarranted extension of the *Estelle* precedent to a "prisoner's mere *risk* of injury."[146] *Stare decisis*, he said, may require the Court to be "cautious in overruling a dubious precedent, but it does not demand that such a precedent be expanded to its outer limits."[147] Reiterating his views first expressed in *Hudson v. McMillian* (1992), Thomas criticized the premise of each conditions of confinement case—that the deprivations suffered by a prisoner constitute "punishment" for Eighth Amendment analysis, even when the deprivations are not part of the formal sentence. He argued that the text and history of the Eighth Amendment, along with 185 years of pre-*Estelle* precedents, support the view that judges or juries—but not jailers—impose punishments. Thomas doubted that *Estelle* was correctly decided, and he announced that he might vote to overrule it if the right case were to come before the Court.

COURT CLARIFIES THE "DELIBERATE INDIFFERENCE" STANDARD

In *Farmer v. Brennan* (1994), Justice Souter authored the opinion for a unanimous Court, which ruled that a prison official may be "held liable under the Eighth Amendment for acting with 'deliberate indifference' to inmate health or safety only if he knows that inmates face a substantial risk of serious harm and disregards that risk by failing to take reasonable measures to abate it."[148] The case involved a preoperative transsexual inmate who was incarcerated with other male inmates in federal prison and then transferred to a higher security penitentiary and placed in the general population. The transsexual inmate claimed to have been beaten and raped following the transfer. The petitioner alleged that prison officials had acted with "deliberate indifference" because they knew that the penitentiary had a history of inmate assaults and that a transsexual inmate would be particularly vulnerable to a sexual attack.

Applying the holdings in *Wilson v. Seiter* (1991) and *Helling v. McKinney* (1993), Souter rejected a purely objective test for liability based on inhumane prison conditions and wrote that the Eighth Amendment requires a subjective component. Arguing that the Eighth Amendment outlaws only cruel and unusual "punishments" and not "conditions," the Court ruled that "subjective recklessness as used in the criminal law" was a workable standard for "deliberate indifference" under the Eighth Amendment.[149] To win an Eighth Amendment claim, an inmate would have to demonstrate that a prison official acted or failed to act despite his or her knowledge of a substantial risk of serious harm. Knowledge of a substantial risk, Souter explained, was a question of fact that would have to be determined at trial with the usual evidentiary methods, including circumstantial evidence.

Though all of the justices signed the opinion of the Court, there were three concurring opinions in *Farmer* that illustrate the differences among the justices on cases involving prison conditions. The broadest interpretation was taken by Justices Blackmun and Stevens who argued that "inhumane prison conditions violate the Eighth Amendment even if no prison official has an improper, subjective state of mind."[150] Both justices felt that constitutional violations should be determined by the character of the punishment rather than by the subjective intentions of those who inflict it. A more conservative approach was followed by Justice Thomas, who adhered to his belief, expressed in dissenting opinions in *Hudson v. McMillian* and *Helling v. McKinney*, that the Eighth Amendment applies only to punishments imposed by judges or juries, not conditions of confinement.[151] Souter's position falls somewhere between Blackmun's objective standard and Thomas's refusal to apply the Eighth Amendment to prison conditions, and it is typical of his pragmatic approach to judicial decision making. His subjective recklessness standard is an attempt to balance the interests of prison administrators in prison discipline and security with the right of prisoners to be protected from abuse.

COURT WEAKENS DUE PROCESS GUARANTEES

Led by Justice Rehnquist, a conservative majority, in *Sandin v. Conner* (1995), attempted to limit federal court intervention of prisons and jails by narrowing due process guarantees for inmates. The 5-to-4 decision severely weakened a 21-year-old precedent set in *Wolff v. McDonnell* (1974) by establishing a new standard for determining when due process protections apply to the inmate disciplinary process. Under *Wolff*, due process protections (notice, hearing, calling witnesses, impartial hearing officer, etc.) applied any time that either good-time credit or segregation was at risk. In *Sandin*, however, the Court ruled that the Fourteenth Amendment due process protections come into play only when inmates face the loss of good-time credits or other extraordinary results that impose an "atypical and significant hardship." For the majority, the decision to place an inmate in disciplinary segregation for 30 days does not require due process, but the Court made no effort to define an "atypical and significant hardship."

Justice Breyer's dissent in *Sandin*, joined by Souter, questioned the meaning of the "atypical and significant hardship" and asserted that Conner was deprived of "liberty" within the meaning of the Due Process Clause. Breyer noted that the disciplinary punishment had led to a major change in Conner's conditions. In the absence of the punishment, Conner would have been able to leave his cell and work, take classes, or mingle with other prisoners for eight hours a day. Because of the disciplinary segregation, he was confined to his cell alone for 30 days, with the exception of 50 minutes for shower periods and exercise, and was constrained by leg irons and waist chains.[152] Both Breyer and Souter believed that under existing precedents, Conner had been deprived of procedurally protected liberty.

INMATE ACCESS TO LEGAL RESOURCES LIMITED

In *Lewis v. Casey* (1996), inmate access to prison law libraries was restricted. The Court overturned a federal judge's broad remedial order that was designed to correct deficiencies in prison law libraries and in legal services.[153] In *Bounds v. Smith* (1977), the Burger Court ruled that a "fundamental right of access to the courts requires prison authorities to assist inmates in the preparation and filing of meaningful legal papers by providing prisoners with adequate law libraries or adequate assistance from persons trained in the law."[154] In *Casey*, Justice Scalia, writing for the majority, argued that *Bounds* did not create an "abstract, free-standing right to a law library or legal assistance." Rather, *Bounds* acknowledged a right of access to the courts. In order "to establish a *Bounds* violation," Scalia said, "the 'actual injury' that an inmate must demonstrate is that the alleged shortcomings in the prison library or legal assistance program have hindered, or are presently hindering, his efforts to pursue a nonfrivolous legal claim."[155] Though *Bounds* made no mention of an actual injury requirement, Scalia said that it was consistent with the doctrine of standing.

Justice Souter wrote an opinion, concurring in part and dissenting in part, that was joined by Ginsburg and Breyer. Although he felt that the scope of the injunction had not been justified by the factual findings of the Court to date, and that it did not give proper deference to prison officials under *Turner v. Safley* (1987), Souter disagreed with the Court's treatment of the standing doctrine and other points. He argued that standing principles could not be applied to review challenges to the orders aimed at providing access for illiterate prisoners. He also took issue with the Court's determination that the prisoner claim be "nonfrivolous." He pointed out that, "It is the existence of an underlying grievance, not its ultimate legal merit, that gives a prisoner a concrete interest in the litigation," and that "*Bounds* recognized a right of access for those who seek adjudication, not just for sure winners or likely winners or possible winners."[156] In his study of the Rehnquist Court's criminal punishment decisions, Christopher E. Smith has commented that the "injury in fact" requirement can place prisoners in a "Catch-22" situation, because it requires knowledge of the law and legal procedures in order to demonstrate that they need legal assistance.[157] Most prisoners do not have the requisite knowledge of the law to press their claims for legal assistance.

CONGRESS AND HABEAS CORPUS REFORM

Congress joined in the movement to reform habeas corpus when it enacted the Anti-Terrorism and Effective Death Penalty Act in 1996. The law raises the standards for federal courts habeas corpus review of state criminal proceedings, imposes strict filing deadlines, limits successive petitions, tightens the requirements for a successful petition, and requires greater deference by the federal courts to decisions made in state criminal courts.[158] These restrictions work to hasten the execution of inmates on death row. Under the statute, federal judges cannot grant a writ of habeas corpus unless a state court decision upholding a prisoner's conviction is "unreasonably wrong" or flatly contradicts clearly established Supreme Court rulings. In addition to the more stringent standards, the law for the first time imposes a statute of limitations on the filing of habeas corpus petitions. Inmates have one year from the time their conviction becomes final to file, but if the state provides counsel in a post–conviction proceeding, the state prisoner has only six months to file a habeas corpus petition. In many ways this legislation simply codified decisions by the Rehnquist Court that placed limits on habeas corpus petitions.

The constitutionality of the Anti-Terrorism and Effective Death Penalty Act was challenged, and the five conservative justices, over the objections of Souter, Stevens, Ginsburg, and Breyer, voted to expedite review of the law. Ultimately, a unanimous Court, in *Felker v. Turpin* (1996), upheld the act. Chief Justice Rehnquist narrowed the law somewhat by arguing that the statute did not abolish the Court's power to hear habeas corpus petitions filed under its original jurisdiction. In concurring opinions, Souter, Stevens, and Breyer deferred to Congress as the appropriate forum for limiting habeas corpus procedures, but they also said that state inmates could find other ways to present a habeas corpus challenge to the Court.[159] Justice Souter helped narrow the impact of the law with his majority opinion for a Court divided 5 to 4 in *Lindh v. Murphy* (1997). This case involved the application of the act to cases pending in the courts when the statute became effective. The law contained a variety of new restrictions on federal habeas corpus petitions in capital and non-capital cases. The text of the statute specified that some provisions were to apply to pending capital cases, but Congress did not state whether the rest of the law was retroactive. The Court held that the law does not apply to all cases pending when the law took effect.

THE REHNQUIST COURT AND PRISONERS' RIGHTS: AN ASSESSMENT

The Reagan–Bush appointments to the Court created a conservative majority that has clearly been more restrained in its treatment of prisoners' religious freedom, due process protections, habeas corpus, and prison conditions cases. While advocating restraint, the conservative majority has been active in narrowing or overturning many Warren and Burger Court precedents that were favorable to the rights of prisoners. At least through 1991, there was less evidence of strategic interaction as the justices tended to hold consistent and in some cases strong policy preferences on prisoners' rights issues. There were fewer examples of vote changes or major opinion revisions. On both the merits of the prisoners' claims and the standards applied by the Court, the emphasis of the Rehnquist Court has been concern for issues of federalism and deference to institutional needs and objectives.

In *Turner v. Safley* (1987), the Court rejected a strict scrutiny standard for prisoners' fundamental rights in favor of a less stringent "legitimate penological interest" test. In *McCleskey v. Kemp* (1987), it rejected evidence of racial bias in capital sentencing. In *Harmelin v. Michigan* (1991), it virtually eliminated a proportionality principle under the Eighth Amendment Cruel and Unusual Punishment Clause. The decision diminishes any judicial responsibility to protect prisoners from a legislature or a sentencing judge who could impose a severely disproportionate sentence. A conservative majority, in *Payne v. Tennessee* (1991), did not hesitate to overturn precedents that had prohibited VIS during capital sentencing. The Court favored the interests of state and local officials by making it easier to modify consent decrees in *Rufo v. Inmates of Suffolk County Jail* (1992), and it restricted due process protections for prisoners in *Sandin v. Conner* (1995) by requiring that inmates demonstrate an "atypical and significant hardship" when deprived of liberty interests under the Fourteenth Amendment. Finally, the Court has launched a successful attack on habeas corpus petitions that makes it more difficult for federal courts to review state trial court procedures.

There were only a handful of decisions over the last twelve years that favored the claims of the individual prisoner, and most of these were decided on narrow grounds. In *Hudson v. McMillian* (1992), the Court ruled that excessive use of force against a prisoner may constitute cruel and unusual punishment, even if the inmate suffered no significant injury. The Court also held that involuntary exposure to secondhand tobacco smoke could create an unreasonable risk to an inmate's health and may be grounds for a claim of cruel and unusual punishment under the Eighth Amendment. In *Farmer v. Brennan* (1994), the Court attempted to find a middle ground in applying a "deliberate indifference" standard to prison conditions. These few decisions pale in comparison to the many Rehnquist Court opinions that have narrowed or overturned precedents more favorable to the rights of prisoners.

NOTES

1. Christopher E. Smith, *The Rehnquist Court and Criminal Punishment* (New York: Garland Publishing, 1997), 8.

2. Joan Biskupic, "The Rehnquist Court: Justices Want to be Known as Jurists, Not Activists," *Washington Post*, Sunday, January 9, 2000, B3.

3. James F. Simon, *The Center Holds: The Power Struggle inside the Rehnquist Court* (New York: Touchstone, 1996), 141.

4. See Christopher E. Smith, "The Constitution and Criminal Punishment: The Emerging Visions of Justices Scalia and Thomas," *Drake Law Review* 43 (1995): 593.

5. Henry J. Abraham, *Justices and Presidents: A Political History of Appointments to the Supreme Court*, 3rd ed. (New York: Oxford University Press, 1992), 358–359.

6. Ibid., 361.

7. Smith, "The Constitution and Criminal Punishment," 597. In subsequent

terms, Justice Kennedy has regularly voted with the conservative bloc, especially in closely divided cases.

8. See Christopher E. Smith and Scott P. Johnson, "Newcomer on the High Court: Justice David Souter and the Supreme Court's 1990 Term," *South Dakota Law Review* 37 (1992): 901.

9. John A. Fliter, "Justice David Souter and Criminal Law," paper presented at the Southern Political Science Association Conference, Savannah, Ga., November 5, 1999.

10. Ibid., see Table 1. During his first seven years on the Court, Justice Souter participated in eleven cases involving prison conditions and voted for the individual seven times.

11. Smith, "The Constitution and Criminal Punishment," 596–598. In Eighth Amendment, capital punishment, and habeas corpus cases, Justice Thomas votes for the government's position 95 percent of the time.

12. *Hudson v. McMillian*, 503 U.S. 1 (1992), Thomas dissenting, at 18. ("Until recent years, the Cruel and Unusual Punishments Clause was not deemed to apply at all to deprivations that were not inflicted as part of the sentence for a crime. For generations, judges and commentators regarded the Eighth Amendment as applying only to torturous punishments meted out by statutes or sentencing judges, and not generally to any hardship that might befall a prisoner during incarceration.")

13. Note, "Lasting Stigma: Affirmative Action and Clarence Thomas's Prisoners' Rights Jurisprudence," *Harvard Law Review* 112 (1999): 1348.

14. See *Sandin v. Conner*, 515 U.S. 472 (1995); *Kansas v. Hendricks*, 95–1649 (1997).

15. *Tison v. Arizona*, 481 U.S. 137, 158 (1987).

16. Edward Lazarus, *Closed Chambers: The First Eyewitness Account of the Epic Struggle inside the Supreme Court* (New York: Times Books, 1998), 209.

17. *Tison v. Arizona*, 137.

18. Ibid., Brennan dissenting, 159.

19. Ibid., 169.

20. Ibid., 171.

21. Ibid., 175.

22. Ibid., citing *Enmund*, 176.

23. Ibid., 184–185.

24. *McCleskey v. Kemp*, 481 U.S. 279 (1987).

25. Ibid., 287.

26. Ibid.

27. Lazarus, *Closed Chambers*, 204.

28. Memo to the Conference, Chambers of Justice White, October 16, 1986, Marshall Papers, Library of Congress, case file of *McCleskey v. Kemp* (1987).

29. Memo to the Conference, Chambers of Justice Scalia, January 6, 1987, Marshall Papers, Library of Congress, case file of *McCleskey v. Kemp* (1987).

30. Ibid.

31. *McCleskey v. Kemp*, 292.

32. Ibid., 306–307.

33. Ibid., 312.

34. Ibid., 318.

35. Ibid., 319.

36. Ibid., Brennan dissenting, 322.

37. Ibid., 325.

38. Ibid., 339.

39. *Turner v. Safley*, 482 U.S. 78 (1987).

40. Ibid., 78.

41. *Safley v. Turner*, 777 F.2d at 1313–14 (8th Cir. 1985).

42. *Turner v. Safley*, 84 (citing *Procunier v. Martinez*, 416 U.S. 396 (1974), 405.

43. Ibid., 85 (citing *Martinez*, 406).

44. *Procunier v. Martinez*, 416 U.S. 405 (1974), 399.

45. Ibid., 413–415. The Court reasoned that the extreme prohibition on freedom of speech, though it was related to the important government objective of prison security, was much more encompassing than necessary to advance government interest.

46. *Procunier v. Martinez*, 408. "[W]e have no occasion to consider the extent to which an individual's right to free speech survives incarceration, for a narrower basis of decision is at hand."

47. See Ellen Bigge, "Prisoners' First Amendment and Marriage Rights in Conflict with Prison Regulations," *University of Missouri–Kansas City Law Review* 56 (1988): 595.

48. *Turner v. Safley*, 89.

49. *Pell v. Procunier*, 417 U.S. 817 (1974), 827.

50. *Bell v. Wolfish*, 441 U.S. 520 (1979), 550–560.

51. *Turner v. Safley*, 482 U.S. at 87 (citing *Block v. Rutherford*, 468 U.S. 576 (1984), 589.

52. Ibid., 87.

53. Ibid., 89–90. See also Mark Lopez, "Decisions in *Safley* and *O'Lone* Undo Years of Progress," *National Prison Project Journal* 15 (Spring 1988): 8.

54. *Turner v. Safley*, 93. Officials testified at trial that the correspondence regulation was necessary to curb prison gangs and to prevent inmates from planning escapes.

55. Ibid., 95.

56. Ibid., 96.

57. Ibid., 100.

58. Ibid., 101.

59. Ibid., 102. The distinction is important because a statute or regulation declared *facially* invalid is void and must be rescinded, whereas a statute declared unconstitutional as *applied* does not void the statute but requires modification of the application.

60. Bigge, "Prisoners' First Amendment and Marriage Rights in Conflict with Prison Regulations," 600.

61. Rebekah Whiteford, "Newly Minted Standard of Review for Prison Regulations Has Bittersweet Impact on Prisoners' Rights," *Washburn Law Journal* 27 (1988): 669.

62. Bigge, "Prisoners' First Amendment," 601.

63. *O'Lone v. Estate of Shabazz*, 482 U.S. 342 (1987).

64. *Jumu'ah* is the central and only obligatory service of the Muslim religion.

65. *O'Lone v. Estate of Shabazz*, 347.

66. Ibid.

67. Ibid., 350.

68. Ibid., 352.

69. Ibid., Brennan dissenting, 354.

70. Ibid., 356.

71. Ibid., 358.

72. Ibid.

73. *Thompson v. Oklahoma*, 487 U.S. 815 (1988).

74. Ibid., 830.

75. Ibid., 838.

76. *Stanford v. Kentucky*, 492 U.S. 361 (1989).

77. Ibid., 370.

78. Ibid., 378–379. Italics in original.

79. Ibid., O'Connor concurring in part and in the judgment, 381.

80. Ibid., 381.

81. Ibid., Brennan dissenting, 383.

82. Ibid., 386.

83. Ibid.

84. In footnote 3, Brennan commented that capital sentences for juveniles would likely be more unusual if capital juries were drawn from a true cross section of society rather than excluding jurors who opposed the death penalty.

85. *Stanford v. Kentucky*, 388.

86. Ibid., 390–391.

87. *Perry v. Lynaugh*, 492 U.S. 302 (1989).

88. Ibid., 328.

89. *Booth v. Maryland*, 482 U.S. 496 (1987).

90. *South Carolina v. Gathers*, 490 U.S. 805 (1989).

91. Lazarus, *Closed Chambers*, 445.

92. *South Carolina v. Gathers*, 811.

93. Ibid., Scalia dissenting, 825.

94. *South Carolina v. Gathers*, 824.

95. Smith, *The Rehnquist Court and Criminal Punishment*, 81.

96. *Payne v. Tennessee*, 501 U.S. 808 (1991).

97. Ibid., 825.

98. Ibid.

99. Ibid., 827.

100. *Harmelin v. Michigan*, 501 U.S. 957 (1991).

101. Ibid., 994–995.

102. Ibid., 965.

103. Ibid., 986.

104. Ibid., 994.

105. Ibid., Kennedy concurring, 996.

106. *Harmelin v. Michigan*, 998–1001.

107. Ibid., 1004.

108. Ibid., 1006.

109. Ibid., White dissenting, 1014.

110. *Harmelin v. Michigan*, 1014.

111. Ibid., 1017.

112. Ibid., 1019.

113. Ibid., Stevens dissenting, 1028.

114. *Harmelin v. Michigan*, 1028, quoting Blackmun, concurring in *Furman v. Georgia*, 408 U.S. 238 (1972), 306.

115. *Wilson v. Seiter*, 501 U.S. 294 (1991).

116. Ibid., 296.

117. Ibid., 303.

118. John Boston, "Highlights of Most Important Cases," *National Prison Project Journal* 6 (1991): 6.

119. *Rufo v. Inmates of Suffolk County Jail*, 502 U.S. 367 (1992).

120. Ibid., 367.

121. Ibid., 380.

122. Ibid., 383.

123. Ibid., 392.

124. Ibid., 392–393.

125. *Hudson v. McMillian*, 503 U.S. 1 (1992).

126. Ibid., 4.

127. Ibid., 7.

128. Ibid., 8.

129. Ibid., 9.

130. Ibid., Blackmun concurring, 15. Blackmun used examples such as lashing prisoners with leather straps, whipping them with rubber hoses, shocking them with electric currents, intentionally exposing them to undue heat or cold, or forcibly injecting them with psychosis-inducing drugs.

131. *Hudson v. McMillian*, Thomas dissenting, 18.

132. Ibid., 28.

133. Smith, *The Rehnquist Court and Criminal Punishment*.

134. *Herrera v. Collins*, 506 U.S. 390 (1993), 411.

135. Ibid., Blackmun dissenting, 446.

136. *Callins v. Collins*, 998 F.2d 269 (5th Cir. 1993), cert. denied, 93-7054, at 510 U.S. 1141 (1994).

137. Ibid., Blackmun dissenting, 1144.

138. *Callins v. Collins*, 1144.

139. Ibid., 1145.

140. Ibid.

141. Ibid., Scalia concurring, 1141.

142. *Callins v. Collins*, 1143.

143. *Helling v. McKinney*, 509 U.S. 25 (1993).

144. Ibid., 33–35.

145. Ibid., 35–36.

146. Ibid., Thomas dissenting, 37.

147. *Helling v. McKinney*, 42.

148. *Farmer v. Brennan*, 511 U.S. 825 (1994).

149. Ibid., 839–840.

150. Ibid., 851.

151. Ibid., Thomas concurring, 859.

152. *Sandin v. Conner*, 515 U.S. 472 (1995), Breyer dissenting, 95.

153. Among other requirements, the remedial order specified the times that

libraries were to be kept open, the number of hours of use to which each inmate was entitled (ten per week), the minimal educational requirements for prison librarians, the content of a videotaped legal research course for inmates, and direct assistance from lawyers or paralegals for illiterate and non-English-speaking inmates. See *Lewis v. Casey*, 518 U.S. 343 (1996), 347.

154. *Bounds v. Smith*, 430 U.S. 817 (1977), 828.

155. *Lewis v. Casey*, 351.

156. Ibid., Souter concurring in part and dissenting in part, 402–403.

157. Smith, *The Rehnquist Court and Criminal Punishment*, 115.

158. Ibid., 115.

159. Kenneth Jost, *The Supreme Court Yearbook, 1996–97* (Washington, D.C.: Congressional Quarterly, 1998), 91.

Chapter 7

Prisoners' Rights, the Supreme Court, and Evolving Standards of Decency

The rights of prisoners have changed drastically since the beginning of the twentieth century. In 1900, prisoners had few rights recognized by the judiciary, and the federal courts generally assumed a hands-off policy in reviewing inmates' claims. From the late 1800s through the middle of the twentieth century, the Supreme Court did not decide very many prisoners' rights cases. Almost all of those cases that were reviewed were decided in favor of the government. The most significant decisions during this period concerned particular methods of capital punishment under the Cruel and Unusual Punishments Clause of the Eighth Amendment. For example, the Court upheld execution by firing squad, the electric chair, and the gas chamber. These punishments were unusual in the sense that they were new methods of execution, but the Court did not find them to be cruel or barbaric. Beyond issues of modes of punishment, the Court promoted a policy of nonintervention in prison administration in reviewing lower court decisions.

ASSESSING THE ROLE OF THE COURT IN DEVELOPING PRISONERS' RIGHTS

Inmate claims did not receive significant consideration at the Supreme Court level until late in the Warren Court period. Most of the activism of the Court during the 1960s in the area of criminal law was focused on criminal procedure and the rights of defendants. Most of the Warren Court justices exercised restraint in reviewing state prison practices and conditions and there was little support for overturning state death penalty statutes. By the time the Court began considering inmate claims, the political composition of the bench had changed with the addition of the four Nixon appointees—Warren Burger, William Rehnquist, Potter Stewart, and Lewis Powell.

The Warren Court did not decide many cases with full written opinions and therefore had little influence on the substantive meaning of prisoners' rights. Although it did not lead a revolution in prisoners' rights, as it did with the rights of criminal defendants, the Warren Court did make important contributions. The Court announced a flexible standard for claims of cruel and unusual punishment under the Eighth Amendment, formally incorporated the Eighth Amendment Cruel and Unusual Punishment Clause to the states, and expanded prisoner access to legal resources and to the federal courts for claims of rights violations. These decisions laid the groundwork for a spate of prisoner litigation in the 1970s.

Spurred by the civil rights movement, media coverage of violent prison riots, and the emergence of a prisoners' rights bar, federal courts began to take a more active role in reviewing prison practices and conditions in order to improve the treatment and living conditions of inmates. During the 1970s, the federal judiciary actively promoted the reform of our nation's prisons and jails. Confronted with cases involving violence and intimidation, denial of due process, prison overcrowding, and severely inadequate facilities and services, federal judges intervened in the administration of state prisons and local jails to correct what they determined to be violations of constitutional rights. The courts expanded the legal protections afforded to inmates and formulated remedies, some extremely detailed, to secure those rights. Judges ordered changes in prison staffing and procedures, reductions in inmate populations, and capital improvements, and they have extended significant due process guarantees to inmates. In some states, entire prison systems were declared unconstitutional and placed under court order, while in others, one or more facilities were targeted for reforms.

The justices appointed by President Nixon altered the voting alignments on the Burger Court and helped move the Court in a more conservative direction. The Burger Court issued several early decisions that expanded prisoners' rights, but by 1975 the Court attempted to limit lower court intervention in prisons and jails. The Rehnquist Court continued this trend and has been even more deferential to state authority and the institutional objectives of prison administrators. With few exceptions, the justices appointed by presidents Reagan and Bush have been more restrained in reviewing inmate petitions. The conservative majority on the Court, consisting of Rehnquist, O'Connor, Scalia, Kennedy, and Thomas, is now openly hostile to inmate appeals that question the legality of their conviction or the conditions of their confinement. The Court has narrowed or overturned a number of Warren and Burger

Court precedents in the areas of capital sentencing, due process, legal resources, habeas corpus, and proportionality in punishment.

EVIDENCE OF STRATEGIC INTERACTION ON THE COURT

As in many areas of constitutional law, justices on the Supreme Court have been divided over the nature and scope of prisoners' rights. Although justices often hold strong policy preferences on criminal punishment issues, they must work within certain internal constraints and external pressures. Of the three strategic relationships (colleagues, political institutions, and public opinion), the most important has been the small group dynamics among the justices. Strategic interaction in the form of vote changes, opinion revisions, dissents from denial of certiorari, and strategic lobbying were evident in many prisoners' rights cases. The incidents of strategic interaction are presented in Table 7.1. Because of the secrecy surrounding Supreme Court decision making, it is impossible to identify every possible example of strategic interaction. The public papers of the justices provide a glimpse into the dynamic decision-making environment, but even those resources are limited. The papers of the justices do not record efforts that may occur in the halls of the Supreme Court building or in the justice's chambers to lobby or persuade colleagues to vote in a particular fashion. The Marshall Papers, which are the most current, only cover the first five years of the Rehnquist Court.

Despite these limitations, the preceding analysis of prisoners' rights cases illustrates that at least some of the justices use strategy to advance preferred policy outcomes. At times the strategic event altered the outcome of a case, while at other times a vote change simply added to the majority coalition. One of the most dramatic changes involved Chief Justice Earl Warren's circulation of his dissent from denial of certiorari in *Brooks v. Florida* (1967). An 8-to-1 vote to deny certiorari became a 9-to-0 vote for summary reversal. In *Powell v. Texas* (1968), Justice White's decision to vote against Powell despite Fortas's efforts to keep him in the majority altered the judgment in the case. What began as a 5-to-4 decision to reverse the conviction of an alcoholic for public drunkenness on Eighth Amendment grounds became a vote to affirm by a similar margin. In several other cases, a vote change on the merits did not affect the judgment but only strengthened the majority coalition. And in at least one case, the strategic move did not achieve its policy goal. In *South Carolina v. Gathers* (1989), Chief Justice Rehnquist's strategy of using the case to overturn the *Booth v. Maryland* (1987) precedent backfired when Justice White voted in *Gathers* to uphold *Booth*. Rehnquist may have lost the policy battle in *Gathers* but he ultimately won the war because both

Table 7.1
Incidents of Strategic Interaction in Prisoners' Rights Cases, 1957–1991

Case	Strategic Event	Impact
Warren Court		
Trop v. Dulles (1958)	vote change on the merits / substantive opinion revision	Whittaker stays in majority coalition
Robinson v. California (1962)	majority opinion assignment	Harlan and Black join majority coalition
Rudolph v. Alabama (1963)	Goldberg's memo to Conference / dissent from denial of certiorari	sent signal to lawyers to challenge death penalty laws
Brooks v. Florida (1967)	Warren's dissent from denial of certiorari	vote to deny certiorari became summary reversal
Mempa v. Rhay (1967)	vote change on the merits	8-to-1 decision became unanimous
Powell v. Texas (1968)	substantive opinion revision / vote change on the merits	5-to-4 vote to reverse becomes judgment to affirm
Lee v. Washington (1969)	concur with *per curiam*	clarified Court's position on racial segregation
Johnson v. Avery (1969)	vote change on the merits	strengthened majority coalition

Burger Court

Procunier v. Martinez (1974)	vote change on the merits	strengthened majority coalition
Estelle v. Gamble (1976)	substantive opinion revision	Rehnquist and Powell join Court majority
Coker v. Georgia (1977)	vote change on the merits	strengthened majority coalition
Lockett v. Ohio (1978)	Burger's memo in search of majority coalition	did not succeed in winning majority/plurality opinion announced
Houchins v. KQED (1978)	vote change on the merits	altered judgment of the Court
Hutto v. Davis (1982)	dissent from *per curium*	Brennan raised procedural and substantive issues
Hudson v. Palmer (1984)	memo to the Conference	Powell joins majority coalition

Rehnquist Court

Tison v. Arizona (1987)	vote change on merits/opinion assignment	*Emmund* precedent severely weakened
South Carolina v. Gathers (1989)	vote to grant certiorari to overturn *Booth* precedent	White, *Booth* dissenter, votes to uphold the precedent
Harmelin v. Michigan (1991)	vote change on the merits	6-to-3 decision becomes 5-to-4
Wilson v. Seiter (1991)	vote change on the merits	strengthened majority coalition
Callins v. Collins (1994)	dissent from denial of certiorari	Blackmun announces his opposition to death penalty

precedents were overruled in *Payne v. Tennessee* (1991), which held that victim impact statements were permitted in capital sentencing.

When the total number of cases is considered, strategic decision making was prevalent during the Warren Court period but was less common when Burger presided over the Court and even less frequent in Rehnquist Court opinions. Chief Justice Warren's strong leadership, Justice Whittaker's indecisiveness, and the activist role orientation of some of the justices may explain the incidents of strategic interaction on the Warren Court. In contrast, Chief Justice Rehnquist, who clearly has a policy agenda in prisoners' rights cases, has not shown much of an interest in using his leadership position to win the support of the other justices. With the appointment of Clarence Thomas, Rehnquist now has the votes he needs to scale back federal court intervention in prison administration, thus there is less of a need to lobby his colleagues.

As far as the other strategic relationships, external factors played less of a role in decision making. The NAACP Legal Defense Fund had some initial success in challenging state death penalty procedures in *Furman v. Georgia* (1972) and in *Coker v. Georgia* (1977), but they could not convince the Court to abolish the death penalty. As Lee Epstein and Joe Kobylka point out, by the late 1960s public opinion had moved decidedly in favor of capital punishment and the LDF was working in a political climate that was hostile to its agenda. State death penalty laws were reinstated in *Gregg v. Georgia* (1976) and the Court rejected compelling evidence of racial discrimination in capital sentencing in *McCleskey v. Kemp* (1987). The Court's relationship with other political institutions did not weigh heavily in the decision-making process. There is little evidence in any of the cases examined that the Justices were concerned with how Congress might respond to a particular decision. In fact, the relationship appears to be in the other direction. Congress followed the lead of the Rehnquist Court in passing legislation to reduce the number of prisoner lawsuits and limit federal habeas corpus review. These laws will affect how the federal courts address prisoner claims for years to come.

CONGRESS AND THE PRISON LITIGATION REFORM ACT

Congress and state legislatures have passed laws affecting prison conditions and the rights of inmates. In 1994 crime legislation, Congress expanded the federal death penalty statute to apply to over 50 crimes and enacted a federal "three strikes" law. With passage of the Anti-Terrorism and Effective Death Penalty Act in 1996, Congress codified much of the Rehnquist Court's jurisprudence in habeas corpus cases. Responding to the volume and nature of prisoner claims in the federal courts, it also enacted the Prison Litigation Reform Act (PLRA) in 1996, which limits the authority of federal courts to hear prison inmate suits. As discussed in Chapter 1, proponents of the PLRA argued that inmates have abused the constitutional protections afforded to them by flooding court dockets with frivolous claims. Critics of prisoner litigation often cite anecdotal evidence of inmates suing because they were served crumpled cake or melted ice cream for dessert in the prison cafeteria. In 1996, 53,090 lawsuits were filed by state prisoners and there were several thousand more federal cases.

The PLRA is designed to discourage inmate lawsuits in several ways. The law orders prisoners to exhaust all administrative remedies before filing a claim over conditions. It bars prisoners from suing for mental or emotional injury suffered while in custody without a prior showing of physical injury. The law also makes it more difficult for prisoners to submit pauper petitions, where the court waives the filing fees. Inmates must now supply certified copies of trust fund accounts and, when funds exist, may be required to pay an initial filing fee with additional monthly payments. Section 809 of the PLRA works to limit inmate lawsuits by giving the federal courts the power to revoke good-time credits from prisoners who are found to file frivolous or nuisance lawsuits or who present false testimony to the court. All of these provisions make it easier for the federal courts to dismiss prisoner lawsuits, and they provide sanctions for filing what are judged to be frivolous suits. Most important, the PLRA goes beyond prisoners' rights by attacking the authority of the courts to hear such cases. It limits open-ended court supervision of judgments or consent decrees by imposing a term limit of two years. Unless plaintiffs can demonstrate ongoing violations of constitutional law, the prison decree must end after two years.

In addition to these developments at the federal level, many states have passed laws making incarceration more punitive. For example, states have abolished parole, eliminated weight rooms and other recreational and educational programs for prisoners, passed mandatory minimum sentencing statutes, and enacted "three strikes" laws, which usually mandate life in prison without parole for three felony convictions.

LAW, POLITICS, AND PRISONERS' RIGHTS

Because of the current legal environment, litigators for the ACLU National Prison Project and other groups have focused their efforts on the most serious prison conditions, such as medical care and prison violence, and they are utilizing statutory rather than constitutional claims more often. For example, advocates for prisoners are employing the Americans with Disabilities Act (ADA) (1990) to file claims on behalf of disabled prisoners. In a unanimous opinion written by Justice Scalia, the Supreme

Court, in *Pennsylvania Department of Corrections v. Yeskey* (1998), held that state prisons are a "public entity" and must comply with the provisions of the ADA. Prisons must now make reasonable modifications to most facilities and services that do not impose an undue financial burden on the state. The *Yeskey* decision will take on increasing significance as the prison population ages. Until the Court overturned it in 1997, the Religious Freedom Restoration Act (RFRA) was another vehicle for protecting prisoners' religious freedom. Under the RFRA, prisoners were able to secure greater accommodations for religious practices, although lower federal courts continued to balance the free exercise rights of prisoners with the need for discipline and security. With the RFRA invalidated, federal courts have returned to the "legitimate penological interest" test established in *Turner v. Safley* (1987).

The "get tough" policies of Congress and the states with regard to prisoners, and the decisions of the Rehnquist Court, which have been more restrictive in the treatment of prisoners' religious freedom, due process protections, habeas corpus petitions, and conditions of confinement, suggest a period of diminished protection for the rights of prisoners. Despite these developments, prisoners' rights have been firmly established under the Constitution and federal law. No longer are prisoners considered "slaves of the state." The Eighth Amendment and other constitutional protections are routinely used to review state prison practices and conditions. The rights of prisoners will continue to evolve, shaped by the political divisions within the Supreme Court, the actions of Congress, interest group pressures, and the values of the American public.

Bibliography

Abraham, Henry J. *Justices and Presidents: A Political History of Appointments to the Supreme Court.* 3rd ed. New York: Oxford University Press, 1992.

Administrative Office of the U.S. Courts, Statistical Analysis and Reports Division. *Federal Judicial Workload Statistics.* Washington, D.C., Annual Publication.

Allen, Harry E. and Clifford E. Simonsen. *Corrections in America: An Introduction.* 7th ed. Englewood Cliffs, N.J.: Prentice Hall, 1995.

American Civil Liberties Union. Special Report: "Court-Stripping: Congress Undermines the Power of the Federal Judiciary." Washington, D.C., June 1996.

Barnes, Harry Elmer. "The Historical Origin of the Prison System in America." *Journal of American Criminal Law and Criminology* 11 (1921): 35–60.

Baum, Lawrence. *The Supreme Court.* 4th ed. Washington, D.C.: Congressional Quarterly, 1992.

Berger, Mark. "Withdrawal of Rights and Due Deference: The New Hands Off Policy in Correctional Litigation." *University of Missouri–Kansas City Law Review* 47 (1978): 1–30.

Berger, Raul. "The Cruel and Unusual Punishments Clause." In *The Bill of Rights: Original Meaning and Current Understanding,* Eugene W. Hickok, Jr., ed. Charlottesville: University Press of Virginia, 1991.

———. *Government by Judiciary: The Transformation of the Fourteenth Amendment.* Boston: Harvard University Press, 1977.

Berkson, Larry C. *The Concept of Cruel and Unusual Punishment.* Lexington, Mass.: D.C. Heath and Company, 1975.

Bigge, Ellen. "Prisoners' First Amendment and Marriage Rights in Conflict with Prison Regulations." *University of Missouri–Kansas City Law Review* 56 (1988): 589–602.

Biskupic, Joan. "The Rehnquist Court: Justices Want to be Known as Jurists, Not Activists." *Washington Post*, January 9, 2000, B3.

Black, Hugo. "The Bill of Rights." *New York University Law Review* 35 (1960): 865.

Blasi, Vincent, ed. *The Burger Court: The Counter-Revolution That Wasn't*. New Haven, Conn.: Yale University Press, 1983.

Bonnyman, Gordon. "Recent Federal Court Orders Spur Tennessee Toward Reforms." *National Prison Project Journal* 8 (1985): 1.

Bork, Robert H. *The Tempting of America: The Political Seduction of the Law*. New York: Simon and Schuster, 1990.

Boston, John. "Highlights of Most Important Cases." *National Prison Project Journal* 6 (1991): 6.

Brenner, Saul and Harold J. Spaeth. *Stare Indecisis: The Alteration of Precedent on the Supreme Court, 1946–1992*. New York: Cambridge University Press, 1995.

Brisbin, Richard A., Jr. "Slaying the Dragon: Segal, Spaeth, and the Function of Law in Supreme Court Decision Making." *American Journal of Political Science* 40 (1996): 1004.

Burger, Warren E. "Our Options Are Limited." *Villanova Law Review* 18 (1972): 167.

Calhoun, Emily. "The Supreme Court and the Constitutional Rights of Prisoners: A Reappraisal." *Hastings Constitutional Law Quarterly* 4 (1977): 219–247.

Canon, Bradley C. "Review of *The Supreme Court and the Attitudinal Model*." *Law and Politics Book Reviews* 3 (1993): 98–100.

———. "The Lone Ranger in a Black Robe." In *The Burger Court: Political and Judicial Profiles*, Charles M. Lamb and Stephen C. Halpern, eds. Chicago: University of Illinois Press, 1991.

Cavanaugh, Richard and Austin Sarat. "Thinking About Courts: Toward and beyond a Jurisprudence of Judicial Competence." *Law and Society Review* 14 (1980): 370.

Chayes, Abram. "Foreword: Public Law Litigation and the Burger Court, the Supreme Court 1981 Term." *Harvard Law Review* 96 (1982): 4.

———. "The Role of the Judge in Public Law Litigation." *Harvard Law Review* 89 (1976): 1281.

Chilton, Bradley S. *Prisons under the Gavel: The Federal Takeover of Georgia Prisons*. Columbus: Ohio State University Press, 1991.

Committee on the Judiciary, United States Senate. *Prison Reform: Enhancing the Effectiveness of Incarceration*. Senate Hearing 104-573. Washington, D.C.: U.S. Government Printing Office, 1996.

Cooper, Phillip J. *Battles on the Bench: Conflict inside the Supreme Court*. Lawrence: University Press of Kansas, 1995.

———. *Hard Judicial Choices: Federal District Court Judges and State and Local Officials*. New York: Oxford University Press, 1988.

Cray, Ed. *Chief Justice: A Biography of Earl Warren*. New York: Simon and Schuster, 1997.

Crouch, Ben M. and James W. Marquart. *An Appeal to Justice: Litigated Reform of Texas Prisons*. Austin: University of Texas Press, 1989.

Davis, Michael D. and Hunter R. Clark. *Thurgood Marshall: Warrior at the Bar, Rebel on the Bench*. New York: Birch Lane Press, 1992.

Davis, Sue. "Justice William H. Rehnquist: Right Wing Ideologue or Majoritarian Democrat?" In *The Burger Court: Political and Judicial Profiles*, Charles M. Lamb and Stephen C. Halpern, eds. Chicago: University of Illinois Press, 1991.

DiIulio, John J., Jr., ed. *Courts, Corrections, and the Constitution.* New York: Oxford University Press, 1990.

Diver, Colin. "The Judge as Political Power Broker: Superintending Structural Change in Public Institutions." *Virginia Law Review* 65 (1979): 43.

Elliot, Jonathan. *The Debates in the Several State Conventions on the Adoption of the Federal Constitution.* 2nd ed. Washington, D.C.: U.S. Congress, 1836.

Epstein, Lee, ed. *Contemplating Courts.* Washington, D.C.: Congressional Quarterly, 1995.

Epstein, Lee and Jack Knight. *The Choices Justices Make.* Washington, D.C.: Congressional Quarterly, 1998.

Epstein, Lee and Joseph Kobylka. *The Supreme Court and Legal Change: Abortion and the Death Penalty.* Chapel Hill: University of North Carolina Press, 1992.

Epstein, Lee and Thomas G. Walker. *Constitutional Law for a Changing America: Rights, Liberties, and Justice.* Washington, D.C.: Congressional Quarterly, 1998.

Feeley, Malcolm M. and Edward L. Rubin. *Judicial Policy Making and the Modern State: How the Courts Reformed America's Prisons.* New York: Cambridge University Press, 1998.

Fisher, William W. III, Morton J. Horowitz, and Thomas Reed, eds. *American Legal Realism.* New York: Oxford University Press, 1993.

Fliter, John A. "Justice David Souter and Criminal Law." Paper presented at the Southern Political Science Association Conference, Savannah, Ga., November 5, 1999.

———. "Another Look at the Judicial Power of the Purse: Courts, Corrections, and State Budgets in the 1980s." *Law and Society Review* 30 (1996): 399–416.

Frank, Jerome. *Courts on Trial: Myth and Reality in American Justice.* Princeton, N.J.: Princeton University Press, 1949.

Friedman, Lawrence. *Crime and Punishment in American History.* New York: Basic Books, 1993.

Fuller, Lon L. "The Forms and Limits of Adjudication." *Harvard Law Review* 92 (1978): 353.

Glazer, Nathan. "Should Judges Administer Social Services?" *The Public Interest* 50 (1978): 64.

———. "Towards an Imperial Judiciary." *The Public Interest* 40 (1975): 104.

Goldman, Sheldon and Thomas P. Jahnige. *The Federal Courts as a Political System.* New York: Harper and Row, 1985.

Granucci, Anthony F. "Nor Cruel and Unusual Punishments Inflicted: The Original Meaning." *California Law Review* 57 (1969): 839.

Greenberg, Douglas. *Crime and Law Enforcement in the Colony of New York, 1691–1776.* Ithaca, N.Y.: Cornell University Press, 1976.

Hall, Kermit L., ed. *The Oxford Companion to the Supreme Court of the United States.* New York: Oxford University Press, 1992.

Hawkins, Richard and Geoffrey P. Alpert. *American Prison Systems: Punishment and Justice*. Englewood Cliffs, N.J.: Prentice Hall, 1989.

Hensley, Thomas R., Christopher E. Smith, and Joyce A. Baugh. *The Changing Supreme Court: Constitutional Rights and Liberties*. St. Paul, Minn.: West Publishing, 1997.

Hickok, Eugene W., Jr. *The Bill of Rights: Original Meaning and Current Understanding*. Charlottesville: University Press of Virginia, 1991.

Horowitz, Donald L. "Decreeing Organizational Change: Judicial Supervision of Public Institutions." *Duke Law Journal* 83 (1983): 1265.

———. *The Courts and Social Policy*. Washington, D.C.: Brookings, 1977.

Howard, J. Woodford, Jr. *Mr. Justice Murphy: A Political Biography*. Princeton, N.J.: Princeton University Press, 1968.

Irwin, John and James Austin. *It's About Time: America's Imprisonment Binge*. Belmont, Calif.: Wadsworth, 1994.

Jost, Kenneth. *The Supreme Court Yearbook, 1996–97*. Washington, D.C.: Congressional Quarterly, 1998.

———. *The Supreme Court Yearbook, 1995–96*. Washington, D.C.: Congressional Quarterly, 1997.

Kalman, Laura. *Abe Fortas: A Biography*. New Haven, Conn.: Yale University Press, 1990.

Kurland, Philip B. *The Founders' Constitution*. Vol. 5. Chicago: University of Chicago Press, 1987.

Lamb, Charles M. "Chief Justice Warren Burger: A Conservative Chief for Conservative Times." In *The Burger Court: Political and Judicial Profiles*, Charles M. Lamb and Stephen C. Halpern, eds. Urbana: University of Illinois Press, 1991.

———. "The Making of a Chief Justice: Warren Burger on Criminal Procedures, 1956–69." *Cornell Law Review* 60 (1975): 743.

Lazarus, Edward. *Closed Chambers: The First Eyewitness Account of the Epic Struggles inside the Supreme Court*. New York: Times Books, 1998.

Levy, Leonard. *Origins of the Bill of Rights*. New Haven, Conn.: Yale University Press, 1999.

Lopez, Mark. "Decisions in *Safley* and *O'Lone* Undo Years of Progress." *National Prison Project Journal* 15 (1988): 80.

Maveety, Nancy. *Strategist on the Court: Justice Sandra Day O'Connor*. Lanham, Md.: Rowman and Littlefield, 1996.

Mays, G. Larry and William A. Taggart. "The Implementation of Court Ordered Prison Reform." In *Research in Law and Policy Studies*, Vol. 2, Stuart Nagel, ed. Greenwich, Conn.: JAI Press, 1988.

Meltsner, Michael. *Cruel and Unusual: The Supreme Court and Capital Punishment*. New York: Random House, 1973.

McWilliams, J. Michael. "Cruel and Unusual Punishments: Use and Misuse of the Eighth Amendment." *American Bar Association Journal* 53 (1967): 451.

Mosk, Stanley. "The Eighth Amendment Rediscovered." *Loyola University Law Review* 1 (1968): 4–22.

Nagel, Robert F. "Separation of Powers and the Scope of Federal Equitable Remedies." *Stanford Law Review* 30 (1978): 661.

National Prison Project. "Quarterly Report: The Courts and Prisons." Washington, D.C.: ACLU Foundation, 1992.

————. "Status Report: The Courts and Prisons." Washington, D.C.: ACLU, 1997.

Note. "Lasting Stigma: Affirmative Action and Clarence Thomas's Prisoners' Rights Jurisprudence." *Harvard Law Review* 112 (1999): 1331.

————. "Prisoners' Rights, Institutional Needs, and the Burger Court." *Virginia Law Review* 72 (1986): 161–193.

————. "Interpretation of the Eighth Amendment: *Rummel, Solem,* and the Venerable Case of *Weems v. U.S.*" *Duke Law Journal* 4 (1984): 794.

————. "The Effectiveness of the Eighth Amendment: An Appraisal of Cruel and Unusual Punishment." *New York University Law Review* 36 (1961): 846–875.

O'Brien, David M. *Constitutional Law and Politics: Civil Rights and Liberties.* New York: Norton, 1997.

————. *Storm Center: The Supreme Court and American Politics.* New York: W. W. Norton, 1996.

Orland, Leonard. *Prisons: Houses of Darkness.* New York: Free Press, 1975.

Packer, Herbert L. *The Limits of the Criminal Sanction.* Stanford, Calif.: Stanford University Press, 1968.

Palmer, John W. *Constitutional Rights of Prisoners.* 4th ed. Cincinnati, Ohio: Anderson Publishing, 1991.

Peltason, Jack W. *Understanding the Constitution.* 14th ed. Orlando, Fla.: Harcourt Brace, 1997.

Pressley, Sue Anne. "The Meanest Sheriff—and Proud of It." *Washington Post National Weekly Edition,* September 1, 1997, 31–32.

Rackove, Jack N. *Original Meanings: Politics and Ideas in the Making of the Constitution.* New York: Alfred A. Knopf, 1996.

Rudovsky, David, Alvin J. Bronstein, Edward I. Koren, and Julia Cade. *The Rights of Prisoners: An American Civil Liberties Handbook.* Carbondale: Southern Illinois University Press, 1988.

Scalia, Antonin. *A Matter of Interpretation: Federal Courts and the Law.* Princeton, N.J.: Princeton University Press, 1997.

————. "Originalism: The Lesser Evil." *Cincinnati Law Review* 57 (1989): 849.

Schwartz, Bernard. *Super Chief: Earl Warren and His Supreme Court.* New York: New York University Press, 1983.

————. "Felix Frankfurter and Earl Warren: A Study of a Deteriorating Relationship." In *The Supreme Court Review,* Philip P. Kurland and Gerhard Casper, eds. Chicago: University of Chicago Press, 1980.

Schwartz, Herman. "The Burger Court and the Prisoner." In *The Burger Years: Rights and Wrongs in the Supreme Court,* Herman Schwartz, ed. New York: Penguin Books, 1987.

Segal, Jeffrey A. and Albert D. Cover. "Ideological Values and the Votes of the U.S. Supreme Court Justices." *American Political Science Review* 83 (1989): 557.

Segal, Jeffrey A. and Harold J. Spaeth. "The Influence of *Stare Decisis* on the Votes of United States Supreme Court Justices." *American Journal of Political Science* 40 (1996): 971–1003.

————. *The Supreme Court and the Attitudinal Model.* New York: Cambridge University Press, 1993.

Simon, James F. *The Center Holds: The Power Struggle inside the Rehnquist Court*. New York: Touchstone, 1996.

Smith, Christopher E. *The Rehnquist Court and Criminal Punishment*. New York: Garland Publishing, 1997.

———. "The Constitution and Criminal Punishment: The Emerging Visions of Justices Scalia and Thomas." *Drake Law Review* 43 (1995): 593–613.

———. "Federal Judges' Role in Prisoner Litigation: What's Necessary? What's Proper?" *Judicature* 70 (1986): 144–150.

Smith, Christopher E. and Scott P. Johnson. "Newcomer on the High Court: Justice David Souter and the Supreme Court's 1990 Term." *South Dakota Law Review* 37 (1992): 901.

Spaeth, Harold J. "The Attitudinal Model." In *Contemplating Courts*, Lee Epstein, ed. Washington D.C.: Congressional Quarterly Press, 1995.

———. *The Warren Court: Cases and Commentary*. San Francisco: Chandler, 1966.

Sullivan, Larry E. *The Prison Reform Movement: Forlorn Hope*. Boston: Twayne Publishers, 1990.

Teeters, Negley L. "State of Prisons in the United States: 1870–1970." *Federal Probation* 33 (1969): 18–23.

Thomas, Jim. *Prisoner Litigation: The Paradox of the Jailhouse Lawyer*. Totowa, N.J.: Rowman and Littlefield, 1988.

United States Department of Justice. *Prisoners in 1990*. Washington, D.C.: Bureau of Justice Statistics, 1991.

———. *Prisoners in 1987–1989*. Washington, D.C: Bureau of Justice Statistics, Annual Publication.

———. *Historical Statistics on Prisoners in State and Federal Institutions, Yearend 1925–1986*. Washington, D.C.: Bureau of Justice Statistics, 1988.

Urofsky, Melvin, ed. *The Douglas Letters*. Bethesda, Md.: Adler and Adler, 1987.

Wallace, Donald H. "*Ruffin v. Virginia* and Slaves of the State: A Nonexistent Baseline of Prisoners' Rights Jurisprudence." *Journal of Criminal Justice* 20 (1992): 333–342.

Wasby, Stephen L. "Justice Harry A. Blackmun: Transition from a Minnesota Twin to an Independent Voice." In *The Burger Court: Political and Judicial Profiles*, Charles M. Lamb and Stephen C. Halpern, eds. Chicago: University of Illinois Press, 1991.

———. "Arrogation of Power or Accountability: 'Judicial Imperialism' Revisited." *Judicature* 65 (1981): 209.

Welsh, Wayne N. "History of Prisons: The Jacksonian Era." In *The Encyclopedia of American Prisons*, Marilyn D. McShane and Frank P. Williams III, eds. New York: Garland Publishing, 1996.

Wharton, Joseph. "Courts Now Out of Job as Jailers." *ABA Journal* (August 1996): 40–41.

White, G. Edward. *The American Judicial Tradition*. New York: Oxford University Press, 1988.

Whiteford, Rebekah. "Newly Minted Standard of Review for Prison Regulations Has Bittersweet Impact on Prisoners' Rights." *Washburn Law Journal* 27 (1988): 654–670.

Yarbrough, Tinsley E. "The Political World of Federal Judges as Managers." *Public Administration Review* 45 (1985): 660, 664.

Table of Cases

Index

About the Author

JOHN A. FLITER is an Associate Professor of Political Science at Kansas State University. His articles have appeared in *Law and Society Review, Southeastern Political Review, Journal of Church and State,* and *Free Speech Yearbook.* His research interests include Supreme Court decision making, civil rights and liberties, and judicial policy impact and implementation.